Roads to Consciousness

Roads to Consciousness

by
SYDNEY MENDEL

London · GEORGE ALLEN & UNWIN LTD
Ruskin House · Museum Street

First Published in Great Britain in 1974

ISBN 0 04 150043 1

Printed in Great Britain
in 11 on 12 point Plantin type
by T. & A. Constable Ltd,
Hopetoun Street, Edinburgh

To the Memory of my Father

Acknowledgements

I wish to thank the Canada Council for the award of a Leave Fellowship which enabled me to devote a year to completing this book.

I am indebted to Dalhousie University for a number of grants for the purposes of travel and research, the typing of the manuscript, and the employment of a research assistant, Mr (now Professor) Douglas Barbour, whose very competent services I am also glad to acknowledge.

Almost all of the book has been read in manuscript by Dr Alan G. Cannon of the University of Exeter, and his careful scrutiny has left its mark on nearly every page. I wish also to express my gratitude to my colleagues Malcolm Ross, Klaus D. Fricke and Devendra P. Varma, who have generously given me the benefit of their ideas, their erudition, their practical sagacity, and, perhaps above all, their unfailing kindness and interest.

Parts of the book have previously been published in *Arizona Quarterly*, *Forum: The University of Houston Quarterly*, *Dalhousie Review*, *Yale French Studies*, *Essays in Criticism*, *English Studies in Africa*, and *Wascana Review*, and I am grateful to the editors of these journals for permitting me to reprint this material.

Thanks are due to the following for permission to use copyright material from works whose titles follow in brackets:

Edward Arnold Ltd (*Howards End* by E. M. Forster); Sir Isaiah Berlin and Encounter Ltd ('A Marvellous Decade (III): *Belinsky: Moralist and Prophet*', by Sir Isaiah Berlin, published in *Encounter*, V (December 1955), 22-43); Cassell & Co. Ltd (*The Immoralist* by André Gide, translated by Dorothy Bussy); Hamish Hamilton Ltd (*Nausea* by Jean-Paul Sartre, translated by Lloyd Alexander); Alfred A. Knopf, Inc. and Hamish Hamilton Ltd (*Three Plays* by Jean-Paul Sartre, translated by Lionel Abel. Copyright 1948, 1949 by Alfred A. Knopf, Inc. Reprinted by permission of both publishers); Alfred A. Knopf, Inc. (*The Immoralist* by André Gide, translated by Dorothy Bussy. Copyright 1930 and renewed 1958 by Alfred A. Knopf, Inc. Reprinted by permission of the publisher); New Directions Publishing Corp. (*Nausea* by Jean-Paul Sartre, translated by Lloyd Alexander); Oxford University Press (*War and Peace* and *The Death of Ivan Ilych* by Leo Tolstoy, translated by Louise and Aylmer Maude); Penguin Books Ltd (*Crime and Punish-*

ment by Fyodor Dostoyevsky, translated by David Magarshack. Copyright by David Magarshack, 1966); Laurence Pollinger Ltd and the Estate of the late Mrs Frieda Lawrence and William Heinemann Ltd (*Sons and Lovers*, *The Blind Man*, and *Lady Chatterley's Lover* by D. H. Lawrence).

Finally, I must acknowledge my great indebtedness to G. Wilson Knight's books, *The Wheel of Fire* and *The Imperial Theme*.

Contents

Introduction

This study has as its point of departure the frequently observed yet rather curious circumstance that men seem to rejoice in the misfortunes of their friends. '*Dans les malheurs de nos meilleurs amis*', La Rochefoucauld says, '*il y a quelque chose qui ne nous déplaît pas.*' Now, when a man covets his neighbour's wife, he desires a real and tangible good; there may be excellent reasons why he should forego this good, but his desire for it is itself only too intelligible; but why, it may be asked, should we be pleased by the misfortunes of our friends? I do not profit from my friend's sorrows; on the contrary, his unhappiness is bound to diminish the enjoyment that I derive from him. Aquinas says that we desire all things under the appearance of good—'*omnia volumnus sub specie boni*'—and we can only explain the fact that men are pleased by the sorrows of their friends on the hypothesis that each man is filled with a mad self-love, which makes him regard all other men as his rivals, so that he welcomes any accident that damages these rivals and thus renders them less capable of competing against him.

If we ask what each man is competing for, the answer appears to be that he is competing for prestige in the eyes of other people. The man of whom La Rochefoucauld speaks, whom we shall call man at the level of Self-Consciousness, being uncertain of his own worth, seeks reassurance from other people; consequently, instead of living authentically, from within, in accordance with the law of his own being, he views himself from the outside, with the eyes of other people, and seeks to construct a self that will obtain the approval of other people. Thus Self-Conscious man is dependent on other people (since they have the power to withhold the approval he seeks), yet at the same time he is competing against other selves for approval or prestige. Hence there arises an impossible situation: if other people (including my so-called friends) are at once my competitors and my judges, it is perhaps not altogether incomprehensible that I should be pleased to see them suffer.

Since it is unreasonable to rejoice in the misfortunes of one's friends, it may be readily supposed that some men attain a degree of maturity (which we shall denote by the term, Consciousness) where they know who they are and what they are worth, so that they live in accordance with the real being, free from dependence on others and free from competitiveness. It should also be observed that some men are not sufficiently sophisticated to rejoice in the misfortunes of their friends; the man who lives authentically, in accordance with the nature of his real being, because he is *below* the level of Self-Consciousness, we shall call Unconscious man. Chapter One, accordingly, examines the concepts of the self and the real being, and in Chapter Two the difference between them is illustrated by a comparison between *Hamlet* and *Antony and Cleopatra*. In Chapter Three we shall see how the conditions of the modern period—for example, the spread of education, the improvement of morals and, above all, the ascendancy of abstract thinking—have brought it about that almost all men are now at the level of Self-Consciousness, and thus alienated from the real being and dependent on others. In Chapter Four this modern condition of dissociation is illustrated by a discussion of *Crime and Punishment*. In effect, then, the four chapters of Part One develop a modern version of the myth of the Fall of Man. Man begins his life in the paradisal innocence of the Garden of Eden of Unconsciousness. Then, with the emergence of Self-Consciousness, he falls from grace into alienation from the real being and dependence on others. Finally, if he is fortunate, he escapes from the dark wood in which fallen man stumbles, and enters a third state, which is Paradise Regained or Consciousness.

Shakespeare's Hamlet may be considered as paradigmatic of the lover of truth who seeks to follow the roads to Consciousness. In the early stages of his development, the Hamletian hero, while not unaware that he himself is 'evil', is above all conscious of the evil around him in a world where men covet their neighbours' (or their brothers') wives, and rejoice in the misfortunes of their friends. In Chapter Five, 'The Revolt Against the Father', we see the Hamletian youth denouncing the worldly father and his society from his own idealistic standpoint. However, the adolescent hero's idealism (or, to borrow an expressive phrase, his idealistic rectitudinitis) in some measure bears the taint of impurity and immaturity. For one thing, he himself is 'evil'; perhaps he sees the evil in the world with such brilliant clarity because it offers him a magnified image of the 'dram of evil' in himself. Then, too, in condemning the worldly father and his society, he appears to be saying that men ought to be better than they are, which is rather like requiring men to be taller than they actually are. Third, by his condemnation of the worldly father, the rebellious son implicitly denies his own freedom to covet his neighbour's wife or to do other forbidden acts that he may wish to do. What, after all, is the authority that says, *Thou shalt not commit adultery?* Is it the authentic voice of the real being, or the prohibitions of other people ingratiatingly or acquisitively assumed by the self?

This equivocalness of the idealistic revolt against the father is discussed in Chapter Six, 'The Ambiguity of the Rebellious Son', which paints a composite portrait of the adolescent hero, and incidentally bears witness to the representative significance of Hamlet. It is not for nothing that Coleridge says, 'I have a smack of Hamlet myself', or that writers as different as Goethe, Hazlitt, Turgenev, James Joyce, T. S. Eliot and D. H. Lawrence have wrestled with the enigma of Hamlet. Chapters Seven and Eight exhibit the hero trying to escape from the trap of a life-denying idealism by means of spurious acceptance and the crime. The discussion of spurious acceptance is, I believe, particularly opportune, since, while we hear a great deal nowadays about existential revolt, the equally important phenomenon of acceptance has passed almost unnoticed; perhaps the reason is that spurious acceptance is essentially a negative attitude of mind, while the crime is a dramatic action which lends itself admirably to literary treatment. In committing a crime, the adolescent hero is partly imitating the 'evil' father, partly defying him, and partly putting his own idealism to the proof in order to find out how far it is based on cowardice and conformity, and how far it is authentic. In Part Two, 'The Adolescent Hero', then, we find that the as yet comparatively immature Hamletian hero is still a pipe for other people's fingers to sound what stop they please, and whether he engages in moralistic condemnation, spurious acceptance or the crime, he is primarily concerned with the problem of liberating himself from dependence upon the Other.

In Part Three we follow the adventures of the mature hero of Consciousness (that is to say, the hero in the latter stages of his journey to Consciousness). Chapter Nine, 'The Descent into Solitude', and Chapter Ten, 'The Encounter with Death', can be profitably viewed in the light of a sentence from Carlyle's *Past and Present*: 'Thou must descend to the *Mothers*, to the *Manes*, and Hercules-like long suffer and labour there, wouldst thou emerge with victory into the sunlight.' In Chapter Eleven, 'The Return to Sensation', the hero does indeed emerge into the sunlight, and looks out upon the many-coloured world without fear and without envy, seeing things as in themselves they really are (as Matthew Arnold expresses it). Chapter Twelve, 'Paradise Regained', paints a composite portrait of the victorious hero, which balances the portrait of the adolescent hero in Chapter Six, and completes the history that was initiated by the departure from Eden in Chapter One. Part Three, in fine, shows the hero of Consciousness obeying the Socratic injunction, *Know thyself*, and achieving authenticity (or the recovery of real being), and hence a right relationship with his fellow-men.

To sum up, then, it may be seen that in showing how the hero arrives at a point where he no longer rejoices in the misfortunes of his best friends, we shall in fact trace a pattern of development that closely resembles the traditional account of the progress of the soul. The terms, Unconsciousness, Self-Consciousness and Consciousness, correspond to Paradise, Paradise Lost and Paradise Regained; the expulsion from the terrestrial paradise (Part One) leads inevitably to the condition of bondage in Egypt (Part Two), and the flight from Egypt precedes the sojourn in the wilderness, which paves the way for the return to the Promised Land (Part Three).

PART I

THE FALL OF MAN

CHAPTER ONE
The Loss of Eden

Nous ne nous contentons pas de la vie que nous avons en nous
et en notre propre être: nous voulons vivre dans l'idée des
autres d'une vie imaginaire, et nous nous efforçons pour cela
de paraître. Nous travaillons incessamment à embellir et
*conserver notre être imaginaire et négligeons le véritable.**

PASCAL, *Pensées*

Camus's *The Myth of Sisyphus* begins with the aphoristic statement that the only truly serious philosophical problem is that
of suicide. While one admires the bravery and *esprit* of Camus's
book, one cannot fail to ask whether this young man is really very
far removed from the sentiments of Shakespeare's Hamlet
when he asks whether it is nobler in the mind to suffer the slings
and arrows of outrageous fortune, or to make one's quietus with
a bare bodkin. If we link Hamlet and *The Myth of Sisyphus*
with Ivan Karamazov, who respectfully returns the ticket to
God because innocent children suffer, then it becomes plain
that the problem of suicide only arises because of the existence
of evil in the world. We may therefore rephrase Camus's
aphorism and say that the only serious philosophical problem is
that of evil. Now, the most successful attempt to explain the
existence of evil is that provided by the Christian doctrine of
Original Sin; in taking Original Sin as our starting-point,
therefore, we are close to the heart of the dilemma of the
Hamletian hero.

* We are not satisfied with the life that we have in ourselves and in
our own being: we wish to live an imaginary life in the opinion of other
people, and for this purpose we strive to keep up appearances. We
labour unceasingly to adorn and to preserve our imaginary being and
neglect the real one.

We may conveniently begin our discussion of Original Sin with T. E. Hulme, who is important both on his own account and because of his influence on T. S. Eliot. For Hulme, the distinguishing characteristic of post-Renaissance man is precisely his lack of belief in Original Sin. Hulme considers that a religious period such as the Middle Ages possesses a belief in absolute, transcendent values (like the idea of Perfection) that have no counterpart on the plane of human actuality:

> In the light of these absolute values, man himself is judged to be essentially limited and imperfect. He is endowed with Original Sin. While he can occasionally accomplish acts which partake of perfection, he can never himself *be* perfect. Certain secondary results in regard to ordinary human action in society follow from this. A man is essentially bad, he can only accomplish anything of value by discipline—ethical and political. Order is thus not merely negative, but creative and liberating. Institutions are necessary.[1]

(It will be noted that the whole of this passage is quoted by T. S. Eliot at the end of his essay on Baudelaire.) The humanist attitude, Hulme says, is the antithesis of the religious one:

> When a sense of the reality of these absolute values is lacking, you get a refusal to believe any longer in the radical imperfection of either Man or Nature. This develops logically into the belief that life is the source and measure of all values, and that man is fundamentally good.

Humanism, in Hulme's view, evolves ultimately into Rousseauistic romanticism, so that romantics also can be defined as 'all those who do not believe in the Fall of Man'. In general, Hulme regards the humanist and the romantic as typical products of the 'general state of mind which has lasted from the Renaissance to now' and he labels this state of mind 'trivial'.

The debate between the Augustinian and the Rousseauist (as we may call the champion of Original Sin and his opponent) is carried on in a spirit of hostility and mutual incomprehension. The Augustinian says that the Rousseauist is a superficial, undisciplined, self-indulgent person whose naïve belief in progress and human perfectibility is the product of book-learning divorced from experience. He considers that the Rousseauist is guilty of the absurdity of claiming that man is fundamentally good, but that institutions (which are the work of man) are evil. The Rousseauist replies that the Augustinian makes impossible demands upon human nature, and then falls into despair because these demands are not met. The Augustinian, he claims, shelters behind discipline and dogma because he is afraid of life and of himself, and (like the people of Argos in Sartre's play, *The Flies*) seeks to escape from his own human responsibility and freedom. The doctrine of Original Sin, the Rousseauist adds, is an absurd myth, which is refuted by the facts of geology and of evolution, and is based on a crudely anthropomorphic conception of a punitive God.

There is a good deal of force in these arguments and mutual accusations, and one is tempted to say that the Augustinian and the Rousseauist are both partly in the right. Certainly, the twentieth century, which has seen two world wars, the rise of totalitarianism and the development of nuclear warfare, con- centration camps, gas-chambers and the like, is not well able to afford any complacent belief in the rationality and perfectibility of man. On the other hand, the progress that Macaulay and other nineteenth-century writers looked forward to with such optimism has been amply achieved, and it is thanks to a stupend- ous effort of human ingenuity and co-operation that the majority of men in the Western world today live longer, healthier and happier lives than men in the past. As one writer has observed, if the Fall of Man meant that women must bring forth in pain, and men must eat bread in the sweat of their brows, then modern man has virtually eliminated the consequences of the Fall.

At bottom, however, the dispute between the Augustinian and the Rousseauist depends on something deeper than fact. In *Culture and Anarchy* Matthew Arnold calls attention to the startling contrast between the Christian (or, as he calls it, Hebraic) view of the world, and that of the Greeks:

As one passes and repasses from Hellenism to Hebraism, from Plato to St Paul, one feels inclined to rub one's eyes and ask oneself whether man is indeed a gentle and simple being, showing the traces of a noble and divine nature; or an unhappy chained captive, labouring with groanings that cannot be uttered to free himself from the body of this death.

Clearly, Hebraism and Hellenism, Augustinianism and Rousseauism, represent two fundamentally different ways of looking at the world, and the question of Original Sin is crucial to the distinction between them.

It is important to note that the quarrel between the Augustinian and the Rousseauist is not merely an academic question, but has important practical consequences. The Rousseauist, Hulme says, believes that man is fundamentally good, while the Augustinian believes that man is essentially bad, and that he 'can only accomplish anything of value by discipline—ethical and political'. The Rousseauist, then, believes in freedom and spontaneity, while the Augustinian believes in discipline and restraint. If a man is naturally good, then obviously he should be free to do exactly as he wishes, and no one can have any reason to let or hinder him. But if a man is bad or limited, then he will be tempted to seek some power outside himself to obey, and society will need to protect itself against him, and to control and proscribe his natural impulses. The two viewpoints involve characteristic attitudes to such matters as education and politics; in politics, for example, the Rousseauist is likely to be liberal and progressive, while the Augustinian will be a conservative. (One thinks of T. S. Eliot's slogan, 'Royalism, Anglo-Catholicism, and Classicism'.)

In much the same way, the Augustinian will tend to be a conformist, while the Rousseauist will be a non-conformist. If a man believes he is sinful, he will suspect his own motives and be tempted to imitate others rather than to trust himself; in so far as he deviates from traditional, established modes of behaviour he will think that he is in danger of falling into error. But if he believes with Rousseau that he is essentially good, he will assume that this good tree can only produce good fruits, and he will do what he feels prompted to do without too much regard for other people's standards. Similarly, the Augustinian will believe in self-abnegation, and the Rousseauist in self-fulfilment. Self-abnegation is one of the dominant themes of that branch of Christianity, associated with the names of St Paul and St Augustine, that laid the greatest emphasis on Original Sin. The quest for self-fulfilment, on the other hand, is the characteristic trait of Faustian man. To illustrate its spirit, one might select this quotation from Blake: 'Sooner murder an infant in its cradle than nurse unacted desires.' There we recognize the authentic note of Rousseauistic self-fulfilment, and we do indeed feel inclined to rub our eyes (as Arnold says) when we contrast Blake's aphorism with St Paul's injunction that we must die unto self nightly.

I suggested a short while ago that the Augustinian and the Rousseauist are both partly in the right, but it would perhaps be more to the point to say that both of them are partly in the wrong. The great objection to the Rousseauistic theory of natural goodness is that it simply does not square with the facts. Because it is not true that man is naturally good, those who believe in this doctrine tend to err in being uncritical towards their own faults, and intolerant of the faults of others. Rousseau's *Confessions* reveals that he himself was guilty of both these mistakes. As Blake said, 'Friendship cannot exist without Forgiveness of Sins continually. Rousseau thought men good by Nature: he found them Evil and found no friend.' Thus Rousseau himself demonstrates the unsoundness of the Rousseauistic theory! Great as is the achievement of D. H. Lawrence (whom we shall be considering at length in Chapter Eleven), it will probably be agreed that he too fell into the Rousseauistic error of being insufficiently self-distrustful.[2] Lawrence's fidelity to his deepest feelings, which was heroic, led him to suppose that his every whim and caprice was stamped with the *imprimatur* of Eternity. As a result there is a radical failure of self-criticism in Lawrence's work and in his life, also. If Lawrence often wrote very badly, as T. S. Eliot claims,* the reason was that he put too much trust in his *daimon*, and did not sufficiently practise the discipline desiderated by Hulme. When

* Dr Leavis concedes that he *sometimes* wrote badly.

Lawrence is in his ranting prophetico-dogmatic vein, we are tempted to cry out, in Cromwell's words: 'I beseech you, in the bowels of Christ, think it possible you may be mistaken.' As for the failure of self-criticism in Lawrence's life, we see this in his relationships with people such as Middleton Murry and Katherine Mansfield,[3] and in the self-delusion which prevented him from seeing that he had tuberculosis until it was too late to do anything about it.

So much for the errors of those who believe in the natural goodness of man and follow the path of self-fulfilment and non-conformity. The man who tries to avoid the consequences of his own bad or limited nature by submitting to a code of behaviour imposed by external authority runs different risks. First, any authority that a man obeys derives ultimately from imperfect, fallible human beings, so that in escaping from his personal evil he may become a victim to a worse collective evil. (This error, of course, is equal and opposite to that of the Rousseauist who thinks that man is good, but institutions are evil.) Second, wherever there is a choice between two authorities, one cannot avoid the necessity of employing one's own limited, imperfect faculties to choose between them. One sees this clearly in Cardinal Newman, who, as the arch-enemy of 'private judgement', fought a great fight against liberalism in the Church of England, only to end by himself committing a revolutionary act of private judgement in going over to Rome, because *in his opinion* the Church of England was heretical. Third and most important, the great danger for the conformist is that in obeying a code of behaviour imposed by external authority he may be doing violence to his own unique, un-created life: the wrong sort of discipline creates order in 'an unweeded garden' by rooting out all the finest flowers!

Even the man who lives the life of asceticism and self-abnegation recommended by religion is exposed to the dangers of conformity. The ascetic life offers a valid technique to those capable of arriving at the result which the technique is designed to achieve. But the problem is to discover whether you are really suited for, and desirous of following, this particular way. When this personal responsibility is faced squarely, there is no question of 'behaviour imposed by an external authority'. The position is then just as if the man who wished to become an Olympic runner were to carry out the training programme laid down by the trainer he had himself chosen. Some men, however, practise self-abnegation out of conformity and spiritual acquisitiveness.[4] They perform acts of self-sacrifice and frustrate their own real needs and desires, without possessing the love which would alone make their sacrifice meaningful and authentic. Naturally, the spiritual rewards that they have promised themselves fail to materialize, and soon the chorus of approval that greeted their self-sacrifice dies away, or else loses all relish for them. Alissa in Gide's *Strait is the Gate* illustrates this phenomenon of inauthentic self-abnegation, just as Michel in Gide's *The Immoralist* illustrates the opposite excess, the inauthentic quest for self-fulfilment.

Thus it may be seen that self-assertion and self-abnegation, spontaneity and discipline, non-conformity and conformity, all possess their dangers. It might seem, indeed, that a man has three choices before him. First, he can do what other people tell him is right; he adopts their definition of man's nature and perverts himself in order to fit that Procrustean bed. Second, he can do what he himself thinks is right, and then he runs the risk of becoming self-centred and full of *hubris*, of beginning to think that he is God. Or, finally, he can refuse to adopt any conception of man's nature or ends, in which case he remains chaotic and aimless, at the mercy of every wind, drawn hither and thither by every stray desire or sensation. And we may then apply to him an observation of St John of the Cross: 'And thus the soul whose will is divided among trifles is like water, which, having an outlet below wherein to empty itself, never rises; and such a soul has no profit.'

However, it would be naïve to suppose that these three alternatives really exhaust all the imaginable routes open to man. But what can be offered in their place? When Ruskin was three years old, he delivered a sermon which consisted of the three words, 'People, be good!' This gnomic utterance in fact epitomizes the traditional solution to the problem of living: act virtuously, we are told, obey your best self rather than your ordinary self (as Matthew Arnold puts it), and you will find peace of mind and happiness. But we have just noticed that virtuous self-sacrificing behaviour does not always bring happiness, and it is evident that 'goodness' is itself a Procrustean bed, the invention of other people. Moreover, it may be observed that if virtuous behaviour really were productive of heart's ease and tranquillity, men would have verified the experimental truth of this fact for themselves long ago, and would have gladly adopted this easy and commendable solution to the problem of living. Since millions of sermons have not achieved this happy consummation, we must conclude that experience does not support the claims of the do-gooders!

A more profitable approach to the problem of right living is suggested by the quotation from Pascal that stands at the head of this chapter:

Nous ne nous contentons pas de la vie que nous avons en nous et en notre propre être: nous voulons vivre dans l'idée des autres d'une vie imaginaire, et nous nous efforçons pour cela de paraître. Nous travaillons incessamment à embellir et conserver notre être imaginaire et négligeons le véritable.

The wealth of significance to be extracted from the ideas of the '*être veritable*' and the '*être imaginaire*' (which we shall call the 'real being' and the 'self' respectively) will become evident as we proceed. For the present, we may simply state baldly that the real being is that which is given, it is what it is, a reality independent of man's volition or consciousness. The self, on the other hand, is each man's *idea* of himself, what he seeks to persuade himself and others that he is. The aim of the self is to perpetuate itself, to protect itself, and to esteem itself; and in order for it to esteem itself, as Swedenborg has said, it is essential for it to see a favourable reflection of itself in the eyes of other people. What would be the point of painting your hair green, as Baudelaire did, if there were no one to see you? The characteristic mark of the self, then, is dependence on others, the desire to live an imaginary life in the opinion of other people.

Perhaps a brief illustration will be useful at this point.

Experiments have shown that if young children are allowed to eat as much of any and every sort of food as they like, they will, after a short period of stuffing themselves with cakes and chocolate and the like, settle down to a healthy, well-balanced diet. Children, in other words, instinctively satisfy the real needs of the real being. When the same experiment is carried out upon adults, quite different results are achieved. One man will eat too little because he is slimming, that is, because he wishes to present himself to the world with a fashionably slim appearance. Another will eat too much, because his idea of himself (as a man endowed with the inalienable right to pursue happiness) has become fixated around the pleasurable sensations of eating, so that he gratifies one part of his organism at the expense of the rest. A third will eat only rare and costly foods. A fourth will adopt some faddist dietary regimen that does not really meet the particular needs of his own body. And so forth. The desires of the self override the real needs of the organism so that its natural discrimination is destroyed. Now, if the self perverts a man's relations with his own body, how much more does it pervert his relations with others. The self-centred man either ignores the authentic needs of the social organism in favour of the imaginary needs of that part of it which is himself, or, in the hope of still greater rewards for his self (such as heaven or public approval), he sacrifices his own real needs in obedience to the commands of other people.

It is implicit in our hypothesis that all actions that derive from the real being are 'right', and those that have their roots in self are 'wrong'. The real being is 'right' because everything that has real existence, that is part of the created universe, is inherently valid and right. A tiger may be a dangerous animal, but it is part of the creation, and no one would think there was any meaning in questioning its right to exist (or the propriety of its being tigerish). Similarly, the man who is ferocious, lustful, and pitiless, though from my personal point of view he is 'evil' (since he constitutes a danger to myself), will be 'right' from the point of view of the universe in so far as he is acting in accordance with his own nature, and occupies his proper place in the scale of creation.

All actions that have their origin in the self are 'wrong' precisely because they do not possess any actuality, any real existence. The essence of the self would appear to be (metaphorically speaking) the notion that I am two inches taller than I actually am. This desire to think highly of oneself—which is, of course, the mainspring of the greater part of human activity— is, in fact, meaningless and absurd. *Which of you by taking thought can add one cubit unto his stature?* I am what I am. If I think that I am better than I am, this is simply fooling myself and can only lead to harmful results: it may cause me to attempt a task for which I am not equipped, or imitate an excellence which I do not possess (with results like those already discussed in connection with inauthentic self-sacrifice). In the same way, it is meaningless for a man to seek to be admired by other people. Since, like all creatures, I occupy a certain place in the scale of creation, it will naturally and necessarily arise that some men will admire me and other men will not admire me. If I seek to win esteem which is not properly due to me, I am merely disguising myself and creating a false situation. This is, indeed, the predicament of Shakespeare's Macbeth. If Macbeth were really by virtue of his real being a king, he would obtain his crown as naturally as water finds its level. But it is the insatiate ambition of the self that makes him overreach himself and snatch a crown that does not really belong to him:

> . . . now does he feel his title
> Hang loose about him, like a giant's robe
> Upon a dwarfish thief . . .

And this image of clothes that are ill-fitting, which as Miss Caroline Spurgeon has shown is the dominant image of the play, is an apt symbol of a universal human situation—the disproportion between the true worth of the man and the exaggerated pretensions of the self. In the order of nature there is a proper correspondence between a man's desires and his achievement, since the desire itself is the charge of energy required for encompassing the achievement. But when the self interposes between the organic nature and the task, this balance is destroyed. Thus when we acquiesce in the death of Macbeth,

we renounce, symbolically, the self, and part of the satisfaction
we experience is due to our sense of inner release from tension;
now that we confess to being shrunk to our true size, we are
released from the burden of wearing clothes that are too big
and heavy for us.

Armed with the concepts of the real being and the self, we
can perhaps now try to penetrate to the heart of the meaning of
the Fall of Man. Treated as a literal historical event (and, as
Nietzsche has said, every myth is transposed into historical
fact[5]), the story of the expulsion of Adam and Eve from the
Garden of Eden is open to numerous grave objections, quite
apart from the scientific objections already briefly alluded to.
One objection frequently made is that it is unjust that all men
have been condemned because of Adam's sin. It is said, too,
that the punishment (namely, everlasting torment in Hell for
billions of human beings) is out of all proportion to the crime.[6]
Again, it is argued that God ought not to have permitted the
unequal contest between man and Satan. This point is made in
the well-known lines of Fitzgerald:

> Oh, Thou, who Man of baser earth didst make,
> And who with Eden didst devise the Snake;
> For all the Sin wherewith the Face of Man
> Is blacken'd, Man's forgiveness give—and take!

Even Milton gives a literal and moralistic interpretation of the
Fall, and this interpretation, as Professor Waldock has con-
vincingly shown in *Paradise Lost and its Critics*, bristles with
logical difficulties. How can Adam fear a threat of death when
he does not know what death is? If the eating of the apple first
brought sin into the world, how was it possible for Adam to
commit a sin in eating the apple? Why did God have to test
Adam and Eve (and thus invite disobedience) by placing the
forbidden tree in the Garden in the first place?

All these difficulties melt away when we see that the story of
the Fall of Man is not a chronicle of an actual historical event, but
an account in mythological form of a new development in the
evolution of the human psyche: the birth of the self. Man is
born in the paradisal innocence of the Garden of Eden of

Unconsciousness. Then, with the emergence of the self, he falls from the state of grace that he had enjoyed in company with the other animals, and enters into the condition of Self-Consciousness and alienation from the real being. I suggested earlier that the essence of the self is the idea that I am two inches taller than I actually am, but this formulation represents the self as wholly given over to delusion and unreality. Suppose we say instead that my idea of myself is that I am twice as rich as I actually am, or that I am a king instead of a mere thane (to take the case of Macbeth). These models exhibit the self, not so much as deluded, but rather as alienated from the present, and absorbed in dreams of future glory that are capable of being translated into actuality. Indeed, if money is deemed to equal worth, it is comparatively easy for me to become greater than I am (at any rate, in my own eyes and in the eyes of other people). Self-Conscious man is thus involved in a conspiracy with the future against the present; man is a project, as Sartre says in *Being and Nothingness*. This character of the self as projector is the basis of man's greatness and his misery, for the emergence of a self that was able to look before and after ensured man's mastery over the creation, and also 'Brought death into the world, and all our woe', because it enabled him to foresee his own extinction,* and because it divorced him from the immediate reality of the here-and-now. Hence the Fall really is a *felix culpa*, at once the source of man's greatness and his misery, of his freedom and his alienation.

Before leaving the Garden of Eden, we should consider one further question. Why did Adam and Eve eat of the tree of the knowledge of *good* and *evil*? It must be understood that at the level of Unconsciousness, good and evil do not exist. Unconscious man acts as he does act, instinctively and spontaneously, in accordance with the parallelogram of forces in the situation (which includes himself) in which he is. Thus his actions spring from the real being, and possess the same kind of rightness and necessity as have the movements of a weathercock

---

* Cf. Pope's 'An Essay on Man':
     The lamb thy riot dooms to bleed today
     Had he thy Reason, would he skip and play?

in the wind. When the evolution to the level of Self-Consciousness takes place, the ideas of good and evil make their appearance, and, thereafter, instead of directly responding to a situation in the manner of Unconscious man, Self-Conscious man approaches the world wearing the spectacles of good and evil. Instead of merely reacting, I judge and evaluate my reaction, and try to push it towards 'good' and away from 'evil'. Instead of merely reacting, I control and discipline my behaviour for the sake of keeping up appearances and promoting the long-term interests of the self. Thus the self modifies its behaviour in order to gain approval; it adjusts itself, in other words, to the ideas, ideals and beliefs of other people. And, in its turn, it attempts to control the behaviour of other selves by the judicious distribution of praise and blame.

We can perhaps clarify this point by reverting to our observations concerning the ferocity of a tiger. Suppose you are being attacked on one occasion by a tiger and on another by a man. In the case of the tiger, you take the best evasive action that you are capable of, you go and get your wounds dressed, and then, broadly speaking, you forget about the whole matter. But when the man attacks you, you abuse him violently, you become shrill with indignation or mad with rage (like Lear), and you nurse a grudge against him for the rest of your life.

What is the reason for this difference? The reason is that you perceive the man through the spectacles of good and evil. The tiger is just a tiger, and no one can see much profit in protesting because it behaves tigerishly; but against the man we summon feelings of anger, indignation, and so on, in the effort to coerce him into adopting the desired behaviour. And the more self there is in him, the more he is dependent on other people, the more likely it is that he will be obedient to the pressure of our feelings. Hence it is that the ideas of good and evil operate chiefly as a means of mutual coercion. We can now plainly see why the advocacy of virtuous behaviour provides no solution to the problem of right living: since it is invariably in the interest of other people that I should behave well, I can best recommend myself to them by behaving as they wish. In other words, the desire to win approval, to be seen of men, gives the self a predilection in favour of hypocritical virtue, and the advocacy of virtuous behaviour tends to strengthen the self. (Of course, it sometimes happens that moral exhortation inspires in the real being an authentic love of virtue, but the point is that a practice that is just as likely to nourish the self as the real being must be of dubious value.[7])

It is evident that the concepts of the self and the real being enable us to resolve the dispute between the Augustinian and the Rousseauist. The Augustinian rivets our attention upon the evils of self, while the Rousseauist brings home to us the health and wholeness (or holiness) of the real being. If we consider the self only, we find man to be entirely evil, an inflated balloon that imagines itself to be its own creator. If, on the other hand, we confine our attention to the real being, we find only truth, rightness, and necessity. Clearly, each of these doctrines emphasized one part of the truth only, namely that part which required to be stressed under the conditions prevailing at that particular time. Thus in the eighteenth century, against a social culture that was powerful in shaping the individual to meet its demands and that was becoming increasingly divorced from the realities of human nature, Rousseau affirmed the claims of the real being, of what was deepest and most real in himself. Today, on the other hand, in an age of ruthless egoism on both the individual and national planes, it is natural that the Augustinian view should reassert itself.

The Augustinian and the Rousseauist both offer us a truth of the highest importance, but each presents only a partial, one-sided view of the truth. The undue severity of the Augustinian view of sin can be illustrated by the part of *The Confessions* in which St Augustine discusses the 'sins' of his infancy:

> Surely it was not good, even for that time of life, to scream for things that would have been thoroughly bad for me; to fly into hot rage because older persons—and free, not slaves— were not obedient to me. . . . Thus the innocence of children is in the helplessness of their bodies rather than any quality in their minds. I have myself seen a small baby jealous; it

was too young to speak, but it was livid with anger as it watched another infant at the breast.

Two pages later, St Augustine concludes:

Therefore, O God our King, when you said 'of such is the Kingdom of Heaven', it could only have been humility as symbolized by the low stature of childhood that you were commending.[8]

It is surely obvious that Augustine's figurative interpretation of Jesus's words about little children is preposterous. How can it be a sin for an infant to wish to protect its supply of food? If the infant's jealousy is a 'sin', we will presumably have to say that the primates and other higher animals share man's Original Sin. It is not self, not the desire to esteem itself or to be esteemed, but the real being that makes a child or an animal fight for food and life; rightly viewed, then, the infant's jealousy is necessary and life-enhancing, and, by the same token, the Augustinian view is life-denying. In fact, we know too well the evil results that arise from the practical applications of this Augustinian idea about the innate depravity of little children.

It may be said in partial extenuation of the passage just quoted that the holy man must be prepared to renounce food and even life itself, if need be, in order to attain his goal of union with God. The harsh Augustinian conception of sin, then, may be appropriate for those capable of making perfection their goal; but ascetic techniques which are helpful to the man who is seeking to die unto self are hardly necessary for the infant who is still in the Garden of Eden of Unconsciousness; nor, indeed, are they appropriate to the vast majority of men, who are not called to the study of perfection. Thus, to take a specific example, the command, 'Love your enemies', is a useful precept for the aspirant to sainthood, but it is not universally applicable, since for most of us it is natural and 'right' to hate your enemies—'Revenge is sweeter than honey', as Homer says. We must reject the Augustinian scheme, then, on the grounds that it seeks to apply universally and indiscriminately a theory of life and a discipline that is appropriate only to a small minority.

We must reject the Rousseauistic scheme on the grounds that it does not take sufficient account of the evil nature of the self. The case against Rousseauism can be sufficiently established with the aid of a justly famous aphorism of La Rochefoucauld, *'Dans les malheurs de nos meilleurs amis il y a quelque chose qui ne nous déplaît pas.'* The paradoxical assertion that men rejoice in the misfortunes of their *friends*, we may note, is confirmed by many observers. Thus in *Crime and Punishment* Dostoyevsky writes in connection with Marmeladov's accident:

> The lodgers, one after another, went back to the door with that strange inner feeling of self-satisfaction which can always be observed even in near relatives in the case of some sudden misfortune, and which all men without exception, however sincere their concern and sympathy, experience.[9]

Similarly, in 'The Death of Ivan Ilych' Tolstoy says:

> Besides considerations as to the possible transfers and promotions likely to result from Ivan Ilych's death, the mere fact of the death of a near acquaintance aroused, as usual, in all who heard of it the complacent feeling that, 'it is he who is dead and not I'.

The authority of these writers counts for a great deal, but am I bound to agree with them? Here, we touch upon the crux that really decides whether a man adopts the Augustinian or the Rousseauistic view of human nature. Unconscious man does not rejoice in the misfortunes of his friends, and the man at a low level of Self-Consciousness is not aware of his own malicious feelings. It is only at a fairly advanced level of Self-Consciousness that this awareness comes about. Thus the only certain proof I can have of the truth of what La Rochefoucauld says is provided by my unmediated consciousness of my own inner life. Now, I for my part know very well that, while I will do my best to help a friend who is in trouble, yet there is nevertheless something within me which is not displeased by his misfortune. Once we know our own hearts, we have a key that unlocks the hearts of others, and we can see for ourselves the truth of La Rochefoucauld's remark; I remember on one occasion telling a friend of mine about a setback that I had suffered in my professional career, and his eyes lit up with joy, though he immediately warmly and generously expressed sympathy with his lips!

Thus we know—or, rather, those of us who have reached a comparatively advanced level of Self-Consciousness know— that men secretly rejoice in the misfortunes of their friends. But why is this so? I do not appear to gain any advantage from my friend's sorrow; on the contrary, his unhappiness diminishes the pleasures that I derive from our friendship. How, then, are we to account for this pleasure in the pain of others, this apparently motiveless malignity? Surely the explanation must be that in so far as I am at the level of Self-Consciousness, and see myself through the eyes of others, and value myself according to the value they put upon me, then my success or failure depends on my position on a scale relative to other people. The misfortune of another person pushes him towards the bottom of the list of happy and enviable people, so that my own position on the list is *relatively* improved. To the extent, then, that we live an imaginary life in the opinion of others (as Pascal says), we are bound to rejoice in, and actually to desire, the misfortunes of others. This is presumably what Pascal means by that terrible sentence, '*Tous les hommes se haïssent naturellement l'un l'autre*'—All men naturally hate one another. Self-Conscious man is engaged in a mad competition against the whole of the rest of the human race, so that his heart makes holiday when his competitors come to grief.

If Dostoyevsky, La Rochefoucauld, Tolstoy and Pascal are right (as they are), then the Rousseauistic theory of natural goodness is utterly demolished and annihilated: if it is true that '*Tous les hommes se haïssent NATURELLEMENT l'un l'autre*', we must adopt a theory of natural badness rather than of natural goodness! It would seem, then, that on the whole the Rousseauist is farther from the truth than the Augustinian. The Augustinian may err in putting his faith in institutions, infallible churches, and the like, and he may underestimate the amount of authentic goodwill that is to be met with among men, but he does recognize the grand fact of the Fall of Man, or (to

B

employ a convenient periphrasis) he sees that men are pleased by the misfortunes of their friends. The virtue of the Rousseauist is that he reminds us of what man should be (and sometimes is), but the Rousseauist errs lamentably in so far as he does not take due account of the nature of the self. Even if he perceives the malice in the world around him (and how could he fail?) he fails to recognize the manifestations of self in himself, and thus is alienated from his fellow-men by his denial of the common bond of guilt. But, then again, the Augustinian is apt to think that by admitting the fact of the Fall, he too somehow escapes the consequences of the Fall, and deserves to be numbered among the elect. It is only through strenuous thought, deep experience and the growth of our self-knowledge and humility that we can combine the appropriate elements from Augustinianism and Rousseauism so as to form a right view of the human condition.

Finally, it may be said that these observations about the self and the real being set the stage for our discussion of the roads to Consciousness. The Hamletian hero is typically a Rousseauist who follows the way of freedom, spontaneity and self-fulfilment, but falters when the true nature of the self is revealed to him.* If we imagine an idealistic young man who at last makes the discovery that other men are pleased by his misfortunes, and who recognizes in himself, too, the guilty malevolence of man at the level of Self-Consciousness, we can understand something of the evil of existence as it appears to a Hamlet or an Ivan Karamazov. Clearly, the only escape from this predicament (short of committing suicide) is for the hero to found himself upon the rock of the real being, and liberate himself from the self with its concomitant dependence on others, so that he can succeed in loving his friends with a love untainted by envy and competitiveness. (It is for the saint to love his enemies; the rest of us are hard put to it to love our friends!) The distinction

---

* Cf. Wordsworth's 'Ode to Duty':

> I, loving freedom, and untried,
> No sport of every random gust,
> Yet being to myself a guide,
> Too blindly have reposed my trust.

between the real being and the self is thus a valuable conceptual tool, but its practical utility is greatly diminished by the fact that, once man is expelled from the Garden of Eden and alienated from the real being, he is often unable to distinguish between that in him which is of the self and that which is of the real being. Only by completing the journey to Consciousness can the hero regain the paradise of the real being, and become who he is, and know who he is. In tracing the history of the Hamletian hero, therefore, we are committed to the task of exploring the roads to Consciousness.

CHAPTER TWO

Hamletian Man

Ac that moste moeued me · and my mode chaunged,
That Resoun rewarded · and reuled alle bestes,
Saue man and his make . . .

Piers Plowman

At the beginning of the *Bhagavad-Gita*, the warrior Arjuna is
preparing to go out to do battle against his evil kinsmen, the
children of Dhritarashtra. He is troubled at the thought of the
slaughter that is about to take place, and he cannot decide
whether he ought to fight or not. 'Is this real compassion that I
feel', he asks, 'or only a delusion? My mind gropes about in
darkness. I cannot see where my duty lies.'[1] The answer to his
question is a treatise on the path to enlightenment.

Shakespeare's *Hamlet* is also concerned with the hero as
seeker of enlightenment and his encounter with the evil nature
of fallen man. When Adam and Eve are expelled from the
Garden of Eden, they learn three things: first, that they must
die; second, that they are naked (that is, that their sexuality is
shameful); third, that they are sinners, and that they are to be
breeders of sinners. These are precisely the topics with which
Hamlet is concerned. The play is occasioned by the death of the
elder Hamlet, and its plot revolves around Hamlet's efforts to
avenge the murder of his father by killing Claudius. The
appearances of the Ghost, the burial of Ophelia, the reflections
of the grave-diggers, Hamlet's meditations upon suicide or his
remarks about worms and kings going a progress through the
guts of a beggar, the stabbing of Polonius and the deaths of
Gertrude, Laertes, Claudius and Hamlet at the end of the play,
all these matters provide variations upon the theme of death.

If 'the noble dust of Alexander' may be used to stop a bunghole, man is no more than a quintessence of dust. Thus, as Wilson Knight says in *The Wheel of Fire*, 'Death is over the whole play.'[2]

Second, *Hamlet* is profoundly concerned with the evil nature of sexual desire. Hamlet is seen in his first soliloquy to be more distressed by his mother's 'o'erhasty marriage' than by his father's death. His disgust with sex is revealed in his treatment of Ophelia ('Get thee to a nunnery'), and in his violent onslaughts upon his mother:

> Nay, but to live
> In the rank sweat of an enseamed bed,
> Stew'd in corruption, honeying and making love
> Over the nasty sty.

For Hamlet, the procreative mystery of life is appropriately represented by the figure of the sun breeding maggots out of a dead dog. This negative attitude towards sexuality is expressed most forcibly by Hamlet himself, but it pervades the entire play, which abounds with references to bawds, brothels, whores, strumpets and the like. Laertes urges Ophelia not to open her chaste treasure to Hamlet's 'unmaster'd importunity', and she in turns warns him not to tread the primrose path of dalliance like a 'puff'd and reckless libertine'. Ophelia in her madness sings bawdy songs, and the Ghost makes a Hamlet-like comment upon the adultery of Gertrude and Claudius:

> So lust, though to a radiant angel link'd,
> Will sate itself in a celestial bed,
> And prey on garbage.

Third, *Hamlet* is concerned with the sinful nature of fallen man. Again, Hamlet carries the chief burden of this theme. When Polonius says that he will use the players according to their deserts, Hamlet rounds on him: 'God's bodkin, man, much better! Use every man after his desert, and who shall 'scape whipping?' When Ophelia says that she believed his protestations of love, Hamlet exclaims: 'You should not have believed me, for virtue cannot so inoculate our old stock but we shall relish of it.' All men, being of Adam's stock, bear the taint of Original Sin, so that to beget children is necessarily to be 'a breeder of sinners'. The world that Shakespeare offers us in this play bears witness to the justice of Hamlet's dark view of human nature: something is rotten in the state of Denmark. Claudius, like Macbeth a murderer who has obtained his crown by an act of treachery against his kinsman and his Lord, acknowledges his guilt:

> O my offence is rank, it smells to heaven!
> It hath the primal eldest curse upon't:
> A brother's murder.

(It is to be noted that this reference to the crime of Cain, which is taken up later in Hamlet's remark about 'Cain's jaw-bone, that did the first murther', explicitly connects the play with the biblical account of the Fall.) Gertrude has committed incest and adultery, and she too knows that she is guilty:

> To my sick soul, as sin's true nature is,
> Each toy seems prologue to some great amiss.
> So full of artless jealousy is guilt,
> It spills itself in fearing to be spilt.

Hamlet's father reports that he is condemned to 'fast in fires, / Till the foul crimes done in my days of nature / Are burnt and purg'd away'. If even the best of men are guilty of foul crimes, we may conclude that all men are criminals.

While dramatic crimes of murder and lust are certainly among the most notable consequences of the Fall, the fallen condition of mankind most characteristically manifests itself in the ordinary affairs of everyday life which reveal the baseness and egotism of human-beings. What could be more cynical, for example, than Polonius's advice to Laertes:

> Neither a borrower, nor a lender be;
> For loan oft loseth both itself and friend,
> And borrowing dulls the edge of husbandry.

If I dare not help a friend for fear that he will steal my money

and betray our friendship, there can be no such thing as friendship. As the Player King says:

> The great man down, you mark his favourite flies;
> The poor advanc'd makes friends of enemies.
> And hitherto doth love on fortune tend,
> For who not needs shall never lack a friend;

Rosencrantz and Guildenstern, those faceless twins, illustrate
the truth of the Player King's words; Hamlet welcomes them
warmly with the greeting, 'My excellent good friends', but they
prove to be, not friends, but mere tools of the new king. Osric
illustrates another aspect of the *vil razza damnata* of courtiers.
He appears to be a harmless little creature—he is a 'water-fly',
a 'chough' or a 'lapwing' who has 'got the tune of the time and
outward habit of encounter'—but if we reflect that man is made
in the image of God, we perceive that a conformistic nincom-
poop like Osric is as typical a symptom of the Fall as a murderer is.

It is not necessary here to examine all the evidence (such as
the disease-imagery, for example) that shows that the Court of
Elsinore is a symbol of the ordinary fallen world, but we may
usefully consider one consequence of this fact. If every man's
hand is secretly against his neighbour, then, in order to survive
in this harsh world, every man will be obliged to wear a disguise
himself, and will seek to penetrate the disguises of others.
Hamlet is full of disguise and deception. Words like 'cozenage',
'tricks' 'practice' and 'treachery' occur frequently. After telling
Ophelia to read a pious book to provide some 'colour' for her
loneliness, Polonius observes that 'with devotion's visage / And
pious action we do sugar o'er / The devil himself'. This
reflection causes Claudius to exclaim:

> O 'tis too true!
> How smart a lash that speech doth give my conscience!
> The harlot's cheek, beautied with plastering art,
> Is not more ugly to the thing that helps it
> Than is my deed to my most painted word.

Painting, then, can be a means of disguise. Claudius asks Laertes
if he is merely 'like the painting of a sorrow / A face without a

heart'. He proposes putting a 'double varnish' on Laertes's reputation as a swordsman, and speaks of 'offence's gilded hand'. Rosencrantz and Guildenstern 'have not craft enough to colour' the true reasons for their visit to Hamlet. Women paint their faces ('God hath given you one face, and you make yourselves another', Hamlet says). Again, a man's outward behaviour can disguise his real thoughts and purposes. One may smile and smile and yet be a villain. Hamlet puts on an 'antic disposition'. The grief shown by the Court upon the death of the elder Hamlet is mere counterfeit, 'actions that a man might play'. In plotting with Laertes to kill Hamlet, Claudius is afraid lest 'our drift look through our bad performance'. Words also can serve as a disguise, and the Court of Elsinore is by no means ignorant of 'that faculty of lying, so perfectly well understood and so universally practised among human creatures', as Swift justly observes. Claudius, as we saw a moment ago, contrasts his ugly deed and his 'most painted word'; he invents a 'forged process' to account for the death of the elder Hamlet. Religion can be a mere 'rhapsody of words'. Polonius instructs his servant to tell lies about Laertes ('Your bait of falsehood takes this carp of truth'). Hamlet says that 'to be honest, as this world goes, is to be one man picked out of ten thousand', and he tells Guildenstern that playing a recorder is 'as easy as lying'. So prevalent is false flattery that Hamlet feels the need to insist that his praise of Horatio is sincere ('Nay, do not think I flatter'). Polonius tells Ophelia not to believe Hamlet's vows, because they are 'like sanctified and pious bawds', that seek to beguile her. Life is an affair of warring interests, and each man employs language to deceive his brother.

If appearances, actions and words are all deceptive, each man will be defensively suspicious of his neighbour, and will seek to ferret out his secret purposes. Claudius wishes to discover the hidden meaning of Hamlet's 'distemper', and he sends Rosencrantz and Guildenstern to try to pluck out the heart of his mystery. Claudius and Polonius, as 'lawful espials', observe unseen the encounter between Ophelia and Hamlet. Polonius hides behind the arras to overhear Hamlet's interview with his mother. Reynaldo spies on Laertes. Hamlet devises the play-within-the-play in order to make Claudius's 'occulted guilt' disclose itself. Doubt and suspicion are everywhere. The very opening of the play, at night, with the sentry's challenge (delivered by the wrong man) ringing out into the darkness, creates an atmosphere of suspicion, tension and uncertainty:

> Who's there?
> Nay, answer me; stand, and unfold yourself.

Even the Ghost is not to be trusted, since the devil may be tricking Hamlet by assuming his father's shape. The Player King doubts the Player Queen's assurances that she will not marry again after his death. The naïve love-poem that Hamlet sends to Ophelia has the word, 'doubt', in every line:

> Doubt that the stars are fire;
>> Doubt that the sun doth move;
> Doubt truth to be a liar;
>> But never doubt I love.

Yet in the nunnery scene Hamlet says to Ophelia, 'I loved you not', and she replies sadly, 'I was the more deceived'. Only a 'green girl' believes a lover's vows; 'We are arrant knaves all; believe none of us', Hamlet says. To avoid deception one must be, not 'credent' but distrustful. Laertes warns Ophelia, 'Be wary then; best safety lies in fear', and Hamlet calls Rosencrantz and Guildenstern, 'My two school-fellows, / Whom I will trust as I will adders fang'd'. We are in the fallen world of treacherous snakes and universal distrust and suspicion.

It may be seen, then, that the Court of Elsinore presents us with an image of fallen man. Now, the myth of the Fall of Man requires an observer or a narrator who is conscious of the Fall. Hamlet, like Arjuna in the *Bhagavad Gita*, is a reflective observer, a noble but inexperienced young man, who encounters the evil that is in the world. This evil is above all terrible because it is incurable and unalterable. One can perhaps punish a murderer like Claudius, but one cannot eradicate lust and ambition, or hatred and fear, the soil out of which murder grows. Evil is then a permanent aspect of the human condition:

> For who would bear the whips and scorns of time,
> Th'oppressor's wrong, the proud man's contumely,
> The pangs of dispriz'd love, the law's delay,
> The insolence of office, and the spurns
> That patient merit of th'unworthy takes,
> When he himself might his quietus make
> With a bare bodkin?

As many critics have pointed out, Hamlet is not here speaking of the particular evils that he is faced with, but of universal evils that afflict all mankind. Only death can bring release from these evils, so that by a curious paradox, death, which is itself the greatest of evils, becomes desirable as a means of escape from evil.

There is another reason why the reflective hero longs for death: he is himself infected by the fallen condition of mankind. If all men are evil, then Hamlet, being a man, is evil too. If the premises are correct, then the conclusion is inescapable. On the other hand, the opposite might be said with equal truth: because Hamlet knows himself to be evil, he is peculiarly sensitive to the presence of evil in others. The 'vicious mole of nature' in other men leads him naturally to the contemplation of his own faults, and an equally natural transition carries him from the thought of his own 'offences' to those of other men. He says to Ophelia:

> I am myself indifferent honest, but yet I could accuse me of such things that it were better my mother had not borne me. I am very proud, revengeful, ambitious, with more offences at my beck than I have thoughts to put them in, imagination to give them shape, or time to act them in. What should such fellows as I do crawling between earth and heaven? We are arrant knaves all; believe none of us.

What is the meaning of this catalogue of faults? The man who has achieved some degree of insight into the condition of Self-Consciousness perceives that all the works of men are perverted by self. As Pascal says, '*La nature de l'amour-propre et de ce* moi *humain est de n'aimer que soi et de ne considérer que* *soi.*'* Hamletian man (or man at an advanced level of Self-Consciousness) knowing that all his actions and desires are tainted by self, distrusts himself as much as he distrusts other people. Arjuna doubts his own feelings of compassion ('Is this real compassion that I feel or only a delusion?') and Hamlet asks, 'Am I a coward?' The interrogative form, which occurs so frequently in *Hamlet*, is naturally adapted to the expression of this profound self-doubt. Consider this speech of Hamlet's:

> Does it not, think thee, stand me now upon?
> He that hath kill'd my king and whor'd my mother,
> Popp'd in between th'election and my hopes,
> Thrown out his angle for my proper life,
> And with such cozenage—is't not perfect conscience
> To quit him with this arm?

Here, in the last scene of the play, after he has enumerated the crimes of Claudius, Hamlet does not positively declare that his own cause is just, but merely asks the question: 'Is't not perfect conscience / To quit him with this arm?' If all men are evil (or, rather, since all men are evil), no man can know for certain that he is acting justly. The Ghost may be the devil taking advantage of Hamlet's 'weakness and (his) melancholy' to deceive him and lead him to damnation. Hamlet says to Horatio:

> If [the king's] occulted guilt
> Do not itself unkennel in one speech,
> It is a damned ghost that we have seen,
> And my imaginations are as foul
> As Vulcan's stithy.

The Ghost as a source of information, and Hamlet's own mind and imagination as instruments for receiving and interpreting information, are both untrustworthy. A man who is a prey to weakness and melancholy, who suspects that his 'imaginations are as foul / As Vulcan's stithy', is hardly qualified to act, in the manner of Othello, as both judge and executioner in his own

---

* 'It is the nature of self-esteem and of the human *ego* to love self alone, and to have regard for self alone.'

cause.* In the fallen condition, justice is inevitably unattainable. 'In the corrupted currents of this world / Offence's gilded hand may shove by justice', Claudius says, but the point is not so much that the judge is corruptible as that he is corrupted; as King Lear says:

> Thou rascal beadle, hold thy blood hand!
> Why dost thou lash that whore? Strip thy own back.
> Thou hotly lusts to use here in that kind
> For which thou whipp'st her.

Not only is evil ineradicable, it is also ubiquitous, and there is no vantage ground of purity from which to set about the task of combating it: one cannot sweep a floor clean with a dirty broom.

Hamlet's introspective soliloquies exhibit a concern with the self and a struggle towards the ideal of the kind that we associate with Protestantism, and especially with that predominantly Protestant tradition of self-examination of conscience which re-enacts the Fall by dividing each man inwardly into judge and accused. In the second soliloquy, for example, Hamlet begins by accusing himself of being 'a rogue and peasant slave' and 'a dull and muddy-mettled rascal'. Then he asks:

> Am I a coward?
> Who calls me villain? breaks my pate across?
> Plucks off my beard and blows it in my face?
> Tweaks me by the nose? gives me the lie i' th' throat,
> As deep as to the lungs? Who does me this, ha?
> 'Swounds, I should take it, for it cannot be
> But I am pigeon-liver'd, and lack gall
> To make oppression bitter . . .

Next, he cries out for vengeance, and then, catching himself striking this new attitude, turns on himself and accuses himself of unpacking his heart with words like a whore. Throughout the soliloquy Hamlet both speaks and watches himself speak;

---

* We may note, incidentally, that the play-within-the-play is a crude and unreliable means of arriving at 'objective' truth. Why should Hamlet trust his own judgement of Horatio, or their combined estimates of Claudius's reaction to the play?

he stands apart from himself and passes judgement on his own being from an external point of view. Thus he asks if he is a coward and argues deductively that he must be pigeon-livered: he does not look into his own heart to see whether he is afraid or not. The same externality is evident in the third soliloquy:

> To be, or not to be,—that is the question:
> Whether 'tis nobler in the mind to suffer
> The slings and arrows of outrageous fortune,
> Or to take arms against a sea of troubles
> And by opposing end them?

Instead of asking himself what he really wants to do, Hamlet tries to discover and conform to some ideal notion of what is 'nobler in the mind'. This struggle towards the ideal, as we saw in Chapter One, is profoundly ambiguous, because the idealism of Self-Conscious man, however sincere it may be, always contains a tincture of acquisitiveness, of the desire to convince himself and others that he is better than he really is. Thus Hamlet's adverse judgement of himself may be said to arise partly out of a genuine insight into the nature of the self, and partly out of the excessive demands that he makes of himself in the imaginary interests of the self. In Self-Conscious man even the desire for perfection is tainted by imperfection. Once again, then, we see that there is no vantage ground of purity from which one might set about the task of eradicating evil in oneself or in others: how shall the corrupt tree bring forth good fruit, or how shall fallen man raise himself by his own boot-straps?

The disparity between the ideal of human perfection and the reality of human imperfection poses the question, 'What is a man?'

> What is a man,
> If his chief good and market of his time
> Be but to sleep and feed? A beast, no more.

Man is endowed with 'godlike reason', 'noble and most sovereign reason', infinite faculties and angelic apprehension; yet on the other hand man (that 'paragon of animals') is a beast and worse than a beast. Hamlet declares that 'a beast that wants discourse of reason, / Would have mourn'd longer' than his mother. He accuses himself of 'bestial oblivion', and he compares Claudius to a satyr, a creature that is half-man, half-beast. He observes in connection with Osric, 'Let a beast be lord of beasts, and his crib shall stand at the king's mess'. Thus the enigma of the nature of man—'What a piece of work is a man!'—presents itself again and again.

Hamlet says of his father, 'He was a man! take him for all in all, / I shall not look upon his like again.' If the Court of Elsinore exhibits the beastly characteristics of fallen man, the elder Hamlet is possessed of the godlike qualities of unfallen man:

> See what a grace was seated on this brow:
> Hyperion's curls, the front of Jove himself,
> An eye like Mars, to threaten and command,
> A station like the herald Mercury
> New-lighted on a heaven-kissing hill,
> A combination and a form indeed,
> Where every god did seem to set his seal,
> To give the world assurance of a man.

The objection to this highly idealized portrait (which may be profitably compared with the description of Adam in Book IV of *Paradise Lost*) is that it seems to give the world assurance of a god, rather than of a man; certainly, in the world of the play we are made to feel that Claudius (who is 'like a mildew'd ear / Blasting his wholesome brother') is a much more typical representative of humankind than the former king.

Hamlet says to Horatio, 'Horatio, thou art e'en as just a man / As e'er my conversation cop'd withal', and he explains the grounds of his admiration as follows:

> . . . for thou hast been
> As one, in suffering all, that suffers nothing,
> A man that fortune's buffets and rewards
> Hast ta'en with equal thanks; . . .

The Horatio of Hamlet's imagination represents a not impossible ideal of manhood.* Nevertheless, in the play itself Horatio remains as shadowy and ineffectual a figure as Hamlet's father, and he provides only the merest hint of a satisfactory answer to the question, 'What is a man?' This hint, however, suffices. In a play about the Fall of Man—indeed, to conceive the very idea of the Fall—one requires at least a fragmentary notion of that original dignity and high estate from which man has fallen. The ideal qualities of Hamlet's father and Horatio, then, serve the purposes of a touchstone, and throw into darker relief the actual world of *Hamlet*, which is the fallen world of death, lust, deception, treachery, madness and murder.

I propose now to undertake a comparison between *Hamlet* and *Antony and Cleopatra*, for *Antony and Cleopatra* is written from the standpoint of Consciousness and communicates a vision of life in which the problems of Hamletian man are successfully resolved.

We may begin by contrasting the attitudes to death in the two plays. One of the distinguishing characteristics of Conscious man is that in him thought and feeling are not consecrated to the service of the self. From the point of view of Consciousness, the Hamletian, time-bound attitude towards death, which feeds upon the worm and decay and thinks that the certainty of death makes a mockery of life, is seen to be rooted in self-love and self-pity. Death is terrible because it signifies the destruction of the self, and evil is a term applied to that which is a source of danger to the self. To this attitude, Consciousness replies: If life was not good, what could death destroy? If life is good, enjoy it! Conscious man is happy to be a man (that is to say, the noblest manifestation of created life); being free from anxiety and self-protectiveness, he enjoys the creation, and affirms himself so completely in this life that death cannot cheat him of his joy.

We noted earlier the paradox that in Hamlet's eyes death is

* It is the ideal that is set before Arjuna in the *Bhagavad-Gita*. The illumined seer, Krishna says, is not disturbed by misfortune or elated by good fortune. 'A serene spirit accepts pleasure and pain with an even mind, and is unmoved by either.'

loathsome, and yet he is ready to welcome death as a means of escaping from the slings and arrows of outrageous fortune. It is to be observed that Hamlet is young and unfledged, so that his longing to die, to sleep, appears as a mark of weakness. Antony and Cleopatra, on the other hand, have earned their immortal repose ('Unarm me, Eros. The long day's task is done / And we must sleep'), and have won the right to liberate themselves from the thousand natural shocks that flesh is heir to:

> And it is great
> To do that thing that ends all other deeds,
> Which shackles accidents and bolts up change,
> Which sleeps, and never palates more the dung,
> The beggar's nurse and Caesar's.

Hamlet dies young, but Antony and Cleopatra die at the culminating point of their lives, in the perfect ripeness of their humanity. From the point of view of the unfulfilled life of Hamlet, death means annihilation; the perfectly fulfilled lives of Antony and Cleopatra, on the other hand, are like a splendid jewel for which death provides an immaculate setting.

In *Hamlet*, death represents a shameful, ignominious defeat brought about by poisoning, treachery or (in the case of Polonius) mere accident. In *Antony and Cleopatra*, on the contrary, not only Antony and Cleopatra, but also Enobarbus, Eros, Iras and Charmian, die by their own choice; each of them could say 'I am conqueror of myself', so that their deaths bear witness to the freedom and greatness of the human spirit. For Hamlet death means a decaying corpse rotting in or above the ground. He upbraids himself for not fattening 'all the region kites / With [Claudius's] offal', and says: 'we fat all creatures else to fat us, and we fat ourselves for maggots'. The graveyard scene is full of references to the indignities suffered by the 'whoreson dead body'; we hear of the stench of rotting corpses, chapless skulls, fine pates full of fine dirt, my Lady Worm, and the like. *Antony and Cleopatra* is profoundly different. Antony means to be:

> A bridegroom in my death, and run into't
> As to a lover's bed.

The extraordinary positive sexual image is partly to be accounted for by the fact that in *Antony and Cleopatra* death is not associated with physical decay but rather with physical immortality. Thus Antony, believing that Cleopatra is dead, hastens to join her:

> I come, my queen. . . . Stay for me.
> Where souls do couch on flowers, we'll hand in hand
> And with our sprightly port make the ghosts gaze.

Similarly, when Iras dies, Cleopatra is anxious to hurry after her, because

> If she first meet the curled Antony,
> He'll make demand of her, and spend that kiss
> Which is my heaven to have.

While it is not easy to enter into the idea of an after-life in which lovers walk hand in hand and kiss, one can at least see that here again the difference between *Antony and Cleopatra* and *Hamlet* is determined by the question of fulfilment or lack of fulfilment. Hamlet knows neither love nor empire, wisdom nor joy; he dies before he has begun to live, so that his uncreated life is aborted for ever. The perfectly consummated love of *Antony and Cleopatra*, however, has achieved a species of immortality in so far as it has entered into the fabric of existence, and can never be expunged.*

We have just seen how in *Antony and Cleopatra* the Hamletian attitude towards death is reversed, and it will not be difficult to show that the other values of *Hamlet* are also rejected in the later play. In *Hamlet* sexual desire is evil, in *Antony and Cleopatra* it is good. Antony, like Claudius, commits adultery, but he is not seen as an incestuous, adulterate beast, but rather as 'the greatest prince o' th' world' and the 'noblest of men'. Cleopatra is, like Gertrude, a middle-aged woman and an

---

* From this point of view we may note that Hamlet's disgust at the thought of the noble dust of Alexander stopping a bunghole, itself bears witness to the enduring greatness of Alexander, and disproves Hamlet's own view that the memory of a great man will barely outlive his life by half a year.

adulteress; in addition to bearing children by Julius Caesar and Mark Antony, she has been the wife of Ptolemy and the mistress of Pompey, not to speak of the 'hotter hours, / Unregist'red in vulgar fame' that she has lustfully enjoyed. Yet instead of Hamlet's morbid denunciation of his mother for honeying and making love over the nasty sty, we have in *Antony and Cleopatra* Enobarbus's splendid description of Cleopatra, whose sexuality becomes a symbol of fertility:

> Other women cloy
> The appetites they feed, but she makes hungry
> Where most she satisfies; for vilest things
> Become themselves in her, that the holy priests
> Bless her when she is riggish.

In *Antony and Cleopatra* sexual desire is a manifestation of life itself, so that if life is holy, sexual desire is holy, too.

In discussing *Hamlet* I suggested that evil is ineradicable because lust and ambition, which are incurable features of human nature, will always sow the seeds of murder and other crimes. *Antony and Cleopatra* is largely concerned with lust and ambition, and it too introduces us to a world in which murders are apt to occur. Pompey is murdered by one of Antony's officers, and it will be remembered that at the feast on board Pompey's galley, Menas offers to cut the throats of Antony, Caesar and Lepidus. Betrayal and treachery are important ingredients in the later play. (The word, 'betrayed', in fact occurs more frequently in *Antony and Cleopatra* than in any of Shakespeare's other plays.) Seleucus, a 'slave of no more trust / Than love that's hir'd', betrays Cleopatra to Caesar. Mardian deceives Antony with a false report of Cleopatra's death. Antony tells Cleopatra, 'None about Caesar trust but Proculeius', yet Proculeius proves to be untrustworthy. When Antony's fortunes begin to decline, his followers go over to Caesar in large numbers; even Enobarbus deserts his master and becomes a 'master-leaver and a fugitive'. The relationship between Antony and Cleopatra itself is not immune. At the start of the play before his departure for Rome, Antony assures Cleopatra of his devotion, but inwardly resolves to break 'these strong Egyptian fetters'. Cleopatra perceives the falsity of his 'mouth-made vows', and accuses him of treachery:

> O, never was there queen
> So mightily betray'd! Yet at the first
> I saw the treasons planted.

(In so far as Cleopatra's words are not altogether sincere, we may say that she deceives even in proclaiming that she is deceived.) When Antony is defeated, Cleopatra has no scruples about negotiating with Caesar, who is willing to treat her generously if she will drive Antony out of Egypt or take his life. After his last battle, Antony blames his defeat upon Cleopatra, calling her 'triple-turn'd whore' and 'foul Egyptian':

> Betray'd I am.
> O this false soul of Egypt! this grave charm
> . . .
> Like a right gipsy hath at fast and loose
> Beguil'd me to the very heart of loss!

Thus on a superficial view even the love-relationship between Antony and Cleopatra (particularly in the absence of the two lines that I omitted from the last speech) seems to demonstrate that each man loves himself alone and is without love for others.

Antony and Cleopatra, then, acknowledges the existence of lust, ambition, treachery, deception and other consequences of the Fall, but it does not view them in the same misanthropic light as *Hamlet*. Hamlet thinks that men ought to be truthful and faithful, and he is embittered by his encounter with lying and treachery; in *Antony and Cleopatra* the emphasis is not on what men ought to be, but on what they actually are. It is, for example, his firm grasp of reality that enables Enobarbus to foresee correctly the consequences of the marriage between Antony and Octavia. 'Antony will use his affection where it is. He married but his occasion here', he says, and the blunt phrase, *use his affection where it is*, bespeaks a mind that is accustomed to look facts in the face. Antony also acknowledges realities: 'I will to Egypt; And though I make this marriage for my peace, / I' th' East my pleasure lies'. Ventidius, again, declines to pursue the advantage that he has won by his victory in Parthia, because he sees that by achieving too much he will offend Antony:

> Who does i' th' wars more than his captain can
> Becomes his captain's captain; and ambition,
> The soldier's virtue, rather makes choice of loss
> Than gain which darkens him.

Silius's unequivocal commendation of this speech indicates that Ventidius is not a cynic (as some critics suppose) but rather a man who possesses a mature, soldierly capacity to recognize facts and to shape his actions in accordance with them. A proper respect for *that which is* is apparent even in Antony's humorous description of the crocodile: 'It is shap'd, sir, like itself, and it is as broad as it hath breadth. It is just so high as it is, and moves with its own organs', etc. The Clown who brings Cleopatra the asp, says: 'You must think this, look you, that the worm will do his kind'. So we may say that each creature behaves according to its kind, each man obeys the law of his own being, and each receives his appropriate reward—for Caesar, Empire, and for Antony, death in Cleopatra's arms. This result is inevitable and right; the Soothsayer had in fact predicted that Caesar's fortunes would rise higher than Antony's, and the Soothsayer's insight into the real nature of things—'In nature's infinite book of secrecy / A little I can read', he says—is further evidence of that strong hold upon reality that we find in the play.

In *Antony and Cleopatra*, then, the world is seen as it really is, and the protagonists meet its challenge with zest. The mature man understands that men's interests sometimes conflict, so that it inevitably happens that they occcasionally find it to their advantage to tell each other lies. What of that? In a market where it is customary to haggle, no one is deceived by the outrageous price that a merchant asks for his goods. So we may say that deception usually occurs in circumstances where one is not surprised to meet it. Thus when Caesar tries to lull Cleopatra's suspicions by assuring her that he is her 'friend', she replies submissively, 'My master and my lord', but as soon as he goes away, she says: 'He words me, girls, he words me, that I should not / Be noble to myself!' On the other hand, if one is sometimes taken in by a deception, that too is part of the natural course of things.* It is fear that makes deception and conflict hateful to Self-Conscious man—does not Nietzsche say that fear is the mother of morality?—but the man who faces up to reality is ready to meet danger gaily. Thus Antony looks forward to the next day's battle, which 'promises royal peril' (that is, peril worthy of a royal spirit), and on his return from the field Cleopatra says:

> Lord of lords!
> O infinite virtue, com'st thou *smiling* from
> The world's great snare uncaught?
> (My italics)

The blithe, carefree spirit of the play, which is especially apparent in those who are attached to Antony's cause, is well brought out in a brief passage between Enobarbus and Lepidus:

Eno.　　　　　　　　By Jupiter,
　　　Were I the wearer of Antonius' beard,
　　　I would not shave't to-day!

Lep.　　　　　　　　'Tis not a time
　　　For private stomaching.

Eno.　　　　　　　　Every time
　　　Serves for the matter that is then born in't.

Just as heresies are necessary in order that the righteous may be made manifest, so war and danger and difficulty and defeat are necessary in order that the heroic, magnanimous heart may manifest itself. Antony defies fortune, saying 'Fortune knows / We scorn her most when most she offers blows', and Cleopatra tells Seleucus, 'I shall show the cinders of my spirits / Through

---

* Carlyle says in *On Heroes and Hero Worship*: 'Dupes indeed are many: but, of all *dupes*, there is none so fatally situated as he who lives in undue terror of being duped.'

th'ashes of my chance'. Pompey, who exhibits on a smaller scale the generous warrior-values of Antony, says:

> I know not
> What counts harsh fortune casts upon my face
> But in my bosom shall she never come
> To make my heart her vassal.

Time and misfortune can wear out the flesh, but they cannot subdue the noble heart.

When Antony says, 'Bid that welcome / Which comes to punish us, and we punish it, / Seeming to bear it lightly', he perhaps seems to acquiesce in the same stoical philosophy as Hamlet. What distinguishes the two, however, is the fact that the stoicism of Hamlet—'Since no man has aught of what he leaves, what is't to leave betimes?'—is akin to despair,* while Antony's stoicism is compatible with a lusty enjoyment of life. We noted earlier that Conscious man enjoys the creation, and this observation very clearly applies to Antony; he may scorn fortune when she offers blows, but he thoroughly appreciates her favours. In the first scene of the play he says: 'There's not a minute of our lives should stretch / Without some pleasure now'. 'Our courteous Antony, / Whom ne'er the word of "no" woman heard speak' enjoys women; he enjoys that 'royal occupation' war, and the imperial glory it brings him; he enjoys laughter, friendship, feasting and sport. Where Hamlet priggishly condemns the carousing at the court of Denmark, the rich vitality of Antony finds natural expression in his love of drinking and feasting. With all his faults, Antony possesses an abundant energy, a joyous wealth of life and a magnanimity of spirit that recall no one in literature so much as King David in the Old Testament (who also had faults). After Antony's death Cleopatra says of him:

> His delights
> Were dolphin-like; they showed his back above
> The element they liv'd in.

---

* Cf. Swift's remark that the Stoic cuts off his feet to escape the misfortune of having no shoes.

The youthful stoic (like Camus's Sisyphus) shows his mettle by enduring the vicissitudes of this absurd world; Antony resists when resistance is necessary (Octavius Caesar reports that he endured famine 'with patience more / Than savages could suffer'), but his delights, too, provide an opportunity for his spirit to pour forth its abundance.

Our discussion up to this point goes some way towards explaining why *Antony and Cleopatra* is free from misanthropy, but we still have the crux of the problem to deal with. The heart of unbelief in Hamletian man lies in his conviction that each man loves himself alone, and serves his own interests to the exclusion of everything else. *'La nature de l'amour propre et de ce* moi *humain est de n'aimer que soi et de ne considérer que soi.'* Courtiers are notoriously sycophantic, vain and above all self-seeking, and the Court of Elsinore appears to provide grounds for the Player King's belief that 'love on fortune tend[s]', (that is, that love is not a reality). 'You cannot call it love', Hamlet says of his mother's sentiment for Claudius, and he tells Ophelia, 'I loved you not'. Claudius says of Hamlet, 'Love! his affections do not that way tend', and the observation is of fairly general application in the play. One incident will suffice to illustrate the point. In the last scene of the play, Claudius tells Gertrude not to drink from the poisoned cup; when she pays no attention to his warning, instead of wresting the cup from her, he callously allows her to die rather than run the risk of inculpating himself. As Julien Sorel says in *Scarlet and Black* 'Each man for himself in this desert of egoism men call life.'[3]

In *Antony and Cleopatra* we are primarily concerned with soldiers, with men in whom self-consciousness is not highly developed, men who combine a zest for life with a professional readiness to quit it at any moment. The strong realism of the play recognizes that love and loyalty are as 'natural' as treachery and self-seeking. Those who are loving and faithful will behave according to their kind, and those who are selfish and disloyal will behave according to their kind also. Eros belongs to the first category: when Antony asks him to kill him, Eros says: 'Turn from me then that noble countenance / Wherein the worship of the whole world lies', and he kills himself to escape the sorrow of killing Antony. Mardian, Seleucus and Canidius, on the other hand, have no compunction about deserting Antony and Cleopatra when fortune deserts them. Enobarbus represents an intermediate case. He decides that his best interests require him to go over to the winning side, but after he has adopted this prudent course, he realizes that he has 'done ill'. When Antony sends Enobarbus's treasure after him (thereby showing that his motives at any rate are not coldly selfish and prudential), Enobarbus repents of his treachery:

> I am alone the villain of the earth,
> And feel I am so most. O Antony,
> Thou mine of bounty, how wouldst thou have paid
> My better service, when my turpitude
> Thou dost so crown with gold!

Like Simon Peter's betrayal of Christ, Enobarbus's betrayal of his master and his subsequent repentance reveal how things really stand with men; they show us that while it is natural to want to preserve one's own life, it is also natural for men (or, at any rate, for some men) to love and keep faith with those who are lovely and worthy of devotion.

Antony and Cleopatra, like Enobarbus, possess a love of life which disposes them to prefer their own interests to those of another. Antony betrays Octavia without hesitation, and he toys with the idea of deserting Cleopatra: 'I must from this enchanting queen break off'. That he is finally faithful to Cleopatra indicates that the force that connects him with her is stronger than the force that draws him away from her. Paradoxically enough, his very readiness to desert Cleopatra, because it shows that his devotion to her is not determined by conscientious considerations (or the struggle towards the ideal), is the basis of our confidence in the freedom and authenticity of his love. If a man is faithful to his wife because he considers that adultery is 'wrong', he affirms his own moral worth. If he is faithful to his wife because she is so lovely that he is under no temptation to commit adultery, he affirms her worth. In the first case, everything hinges upon the man's subjective determination to behave morally; in the second place, the very nature of things sustains the relationship. We see, then, that the love that draws Antony and Cleopatra together—'I come, my queen', 'Husband, I come!'—rests upon the secure foundation of reality, and thus demonstrates that men are not isolated in a desert of egoism, but related and connected.

As far as doubt, indecision and self-doubt are concerned, the contrast between the two plays is very marked. The scene of *Hamlet* is set in the northern, Protestant part of Europe, a region of darkness, shadows, ghosts and gloom. The love of Antony and Cleopatra is born in the bright Mediterranean sunlight of Egypt, where doubt and uncertainty are out of place. In *Hamlet* men are busy deceiving one another all the time, so that doubt and suspicion are ever-present. The world of *Antony and Cleopatra* is less opaque; each man may be seen to behave according to his kind, in obedience to the law of his own being; even deception possesses a satisfying intelligibility and meaning, like a code message that one must patiently decipher. As for Antony, he is free from self-doubt because he is not involved in the struggle towards the ideal. Instead of asking whether this or that conduct is 'nobler in the mind', Antony simply does what he wants to do; in other words, he reacts authentically, in accordance with the nature of his real being, and, as we saw a moment ago, the fact that he deserts Octavia and is faithful to Cleopatra tells us more about them than about him. Because he does not make excessive demands upon himself or other people, Antony is capable of compassionate understanding. Thus where Hamlet attacks his mother with smug superiority ('Forgive me this my virtue, / For in the fatness of these pursy times / Virtue itself of vice must pardon beg.') Antony comments quietly on the desertion of Enobarbus: 'O, my fortunes have / Corrupted honest men!' He does not ask himself doubtfully whether he was perhaps mistaken in Enobarbus or denounce the treachery of man; he is sufficiently detached to see that there is a difference between honest men and dishonest men, even though in certain circumstances an honest man may be 'corrupted' or deflected from his natural bent. Antony's judgements upon himself, similarly, are free from doubt, self-justification and self-abasement. After his flight from the sea-battle, for example, he says:

> I have fled myself, and have instructed cowards
> To run and show their shoulders.

And, again:

> I have offended reputation—
> A most unnoble swerving.

If we compare Antony's self-condemnation with Hamlet's, we find that Antony is passing a valid judgement on a single action from the standpoint of his own values, where Hamlet, when he says 'O what a rogue and peasant slave am I!' is passing an invalid judgement on his own being from an external standpoint. Hamlet's constant self-interrogation shows that he is self-divided, but Antony's code of honour sits easily upon him, for it is as much a part of his nature as his love of feasting and war. He is most authentically himself when he accuses himself of being 'unnoble', that is, of failing to behave in accordance with his own kind. Thus, paradoxically, we may say that essentially Antony's self-condemnation is not a manifestation of self-doubt, but rather a form of self-affirmation.

In conclusion we may observe that if *Hamlet* asks the question, 'What is a man?' *Antony and Cleopatra* supplies an answer in the person of Antony. But what is Antony? He is a 'strumpet's fool', an 'amorous surfeiter', and a 'libertine'. Caesar calls him 'the abstract of all faults / That all men follow', and he even refers to him as 'the old ruffian'. 'Th' adulterous Antony' (as Maecenas calls him) invites defeat by his error in fighting at sea, and then compounds that error by fleeing from the battle like a 'doting mallard'. On the other hand, we hear about Antony's 'absolute soldiership'; he is 'the greatest soldier of the world' and his eyes glow 'like plated Mars'. 'Your emperor / Continues still a Jove' says the soldier who brings Enobarbus's treasure to him.* Cleopatra calls Antony 'My

---

* It is worth recalling that Hamlet mentions both Mars and Jove in the idealized portrait of his father quoted earlier in this chapter.

man of men', 'the arm / And burgonet of men', and 'noblest of men'.

> Noblest of men, woo't die?
> Hast thou no care of me? Shall I abide
> In this dull world, which in thy absence is
> No better than a sty?

One valuable clue to the nature of Antony lies in the fact that in the play the word 'Antony' (which occurs with remarkable frequency) seems to possess an independent life of its own, distinct from the man who bears the name. In the opening scene, Demetrius says:

> Sir, sometimes when he is not Antony
> He comes too short of that great property
> Which still should go with Antony.

When Antony's spirits recover after the first defeat, Cleopatra says: 'It is my birthday. / I had thought t'have held it poor; but since my lord / Is Antony again, I will be Cleopatra.' Discovering the ambassador kissing Cleopatra's hand, Antony cries out, 'Have you no ears? I am / Antony yet.' In all these quotations it is as if the word *Antony* denotes something like 'the most generous-hearted and noblest of men', and the man Antony is not at all times equal to himself ('Where hast thou been, my heart?' Antony asks himself at one point).

Two important passages throw some light on this matter. After the last battle, when his life stands on the threshold of his death, Antony experiences a moment of doubt; he describes a cloud that seems to take the shape of a dragon, then of a bear or a lion, changing form continually until it vanishes altogether, and he says to Eros:

> My good knave Eros, now thy captain is
> Even such a body. Here I am Antony;
> Yet cannot hold this visible shape, my knave.

In this passage, as elsewhere, Shakespeare uses the cloud as a symbol of the ephemerality and insubstantiality of man; even an Antony is mortal and fallible, 'a poor, bare, forked animal'.

However, a very different facet of Antony is revealed by Cleopatra's great dream of Antony:

> *Cleo.* I dreamt there was an Emperor Antony—
> O, such another sleep, that I might see
> But such another man!
> *Dol.*   If it might please ye—
> *Cleo.* His face was as the heav'ns, and therein stuck
> A sun and moon, which kept their course and lighted
> The little O, the earth.

Clearly, what we are offered here is not the description of a mortal man, but rather an archetypal form or Platonic Idea of a man. Cleopatra's dream reveals a hitherto invisible dimension of the Antony we have seen, so that we may now say that the difference between the man Antony and the word 'Antony' is to be explained by the fact that, magnificent as Antony is, he is but an imperfect copy of the essential idea of Antony. When Cleopatra asks Dolabella if there could be such a man as the Antony she has dreamed of, the unimaginative Roman answers, No, and Cleopatra says:

> You lie, up to the hearing of the gods!
> But, if there be or ever were one such,
> It's past the size of dreaming. Nature wants stuff
> To vie strange forms with fancy; yet, t'imagine
> An Antony were nature's piece 'gainst fancy,
> Condemning shadows quite.

In this passage, which almost seems to anticipate Coleridge's distinction between fancy and imagination, Shakespeare is saying that fancy can contrive strange forms, but imagination (or visionary dream) reveals a reality which transcends the natural world and its contents. Together, the image of the cloud and the image of the dream unite in Antony's quintessential manhood to provide an answer to the question, 'What is a man?' To deny the dream is to see man as a beast; to deny the cloud is to entertain the delusion that man is a god; and to pursue the ideal acquisitively is to conscript the dream in the interests of the self. Only when imperfection is acknowledged as the human condition, and the dream is received as a gift from the gods,* can there be man. Man is not even a thinking reed (as Pascal says), but a reed that sometimes receives miraculous visitations of thought.

This comparison between *Hamlet* and *Antony and Cleopatra* has, I trust, helped to give flesh and substance to the concepts of Self-Consciousness and Consciousness, and thus served to establish the point of departure and the destination of the Hamletian hero. In the next two chapters it will be necessary to consider some modern instances of the phenomenon of Self-Consciousness, in order to complete our discussion of the Fall of Man.

* Cf. ' 'Tis the god Hercules, whom Antony lov'd, / Now leaves him.'

CHAPTER THREE

The Problem of Dissociation

The rational instinct, therefore, taken abstractedly and unbalanced, did in itself, and in its consequences, form the original temptation, through which man fell.

COLERIDGE, *The Statesman's Manual*[1]

In his essay of 1921 on 'The Metaphysical Poets' T. S. Eliot argued that the poets of the eighteenth and nineteenth centuries had suffered from a 'dissociation of sensibility' which made their feeling more crude, and their thinking reflective or ruminative. 'Tennyson and Browning', Eliot wrote, 'are poets, and they think; but they do not feel their thought as immediately as the odour of a rose. A thought to Donne was an experience: it modified his sensibility.' The phrase 'dissociation of sensibility' rapidly achieved popularity; it provided a formula for expressing the revolt of the contemporary mind against the poetry of the neo-classical period and of the romantics, and it also reflected, vaguely, the pessimism and disillusionment with regard to modern man that characterized the post-war period. In the course of time, however, Eliot's phrase came in for a good deal of criticism,[2] and in 1947 Eliot himself in his address on Milton before the British Academy withdrew his earlier assertion that it was Milton and Dryden, as the most influential poets of the seventeenth century, who were to a considerable extent responsible for the dissociation of sensibility. He suggested that the phenomenon was not purely a literary matter, but that it had profound historical causes. It is dissociation in this broader sense that we shall be concerned with in this chapter.

A convenient starting-point is provided by Eliot's distinction between the thinking of Tennyson and Browning and that of Donne, between 'ruminative thinking' on the one hand, and the kind of thinking that modifies the sensibility on the other. One way of formulating the distinction is to say that Tennyson and Browning are engaged in abstract thinking, the thinking of the mind alone, while Donne practises concrete thinking, or the thinking of the body.[3] 'He who sings a lasting song, / Thinks in a marrow-bone', as Yeats says. The difference between the two kinds of thinking can be illustrated by means of an analogy from the field of psychoanalysis. The psychoanalyst recognizes two stages in the growth of his patient's understanding. First, the patient acknowledges that the interpretation of his symptoms offered by the analyst constitutes a hypothesis theoretically adequate to the facts. Then, in the second stage, which may occur some time later, the patient experiences a direct, unmediated encounter with the unavowed feelings that are buried within him. It is this achievement of insight, when the patients knows the truth with intuitive certainty, with his whole body, that corresponds to concrete thinking. What was before merely known verbally, abstractly, he now experiences as concrete knowledge that modifies his sensibility.

From what has just been said it will be clear that thinking of the body cannot really be communicated; all that can be done is to set up the conditions most favourable for allowing another person to experience the thought that the thinker has experienced. Here one might draw an analogy with poetry, for the words on the printed page are designed to make it possible for the experience that is the poem to be re-created in the mind of the reader; no one supposes that by merely memorizing a poem one possesses it. Abstract knowledge, on the other hand, can be readily communicated: a boy of twelve can acquire a knowledge of the scientific discoveries made by Newton, though he cannot possess himself of the wisdom of Plato.[4] (Unfortunately, he can be made to *seem* to comprehend Plato; as T. S. Eliot observes in *The Use of Poetry and the Use of Criticism* it is easy to substitute a 'sham acquisition of taste' for the genuine development of it.[5]) Because abstract thinking can be communicated (and concrete thinking can be 'abstracted' and then communicated), a man can accumulate abstract knowledge with great rapidity. His swift progress in acquiring abstract knowledge is of course only possible because he travels light, leaving his body behind him; the train moves off at tremendous speed because the carriages remain behind in the railway station. This is precisely the situation of modern man: the desire for quick and easy gains has led him to cultivate abstract thinking at the price of a loss of contact between head and heart, and body and spirit, or, more precisely, at the price of dissociation of the senses, dissociation of the feelings, and dissociation of the identity.

The nature of dissociation of the senses can best be illustrated by a kind of parable. A shepherd who has a dozen sheep knows each of them by name, by a hundred details of its appearance, almost by its smell. If one sheep dies, the shepherd experiences in its concrete, sensuous reality the death of that sheep. When the flock becomes larger, it is more difficult for him to preserve his personal relationship with all his sheep. Then, we may suppose, someone teaches him a little elementary arithmetic, and the problem of keeping a grasp on what is going on is simplified. Now he will say, not 'Fitch is lost', but 'I have only got in forty-nine sheep; one of them must be lost.' Armed with this knowledge, he will perhaps see his affairs prosper, until the time comes when he has a huge flock, but hardly knows what a sheep looks like, because he spends all his time in an office working out complicated calculations concerning costs, production, profits, and the like. Finally, of course, such a high level of abstraction is reached that his work can be performed more satisfactorily by a machine than by the man himself.

This, in simplified form, is the story of modern industry. Our shepherd turned accountant (or organization man) deals with ciphers, abstractions, symbols, signs or words, rather than with things, and this is precisely the situation of the modern businessman. The worker in the factory, too, though not so completely cut off from the senses as the executive, is also alienated from the products of his work. It is important also to note that the scientist, who is responsible for the technical progress on which modern industry is based, uses an approach which in certain respects resembles that of our shepherd. The shepherd turned accountant gained an ability to organize complex material, but at the price of a loss of direct sensory contact with the object. He withdrew himself as a person out of the experience, for any man—or machine—could reach the same results from the same figures. The scientist, too, carries out an experiment with the idea of excluding his own individual tastes, opinions, and so on, so that the results he obtains will have universal application, and can be tested and verified by other scientists—or machines—in other parts of the world. Like the shepherd, again, the scientist ignores the concrete, sensuous reality of the object, for the sake of understanding and mastering it. In order for Newton to relate the falling of the apple to the movement of the planet, it was necessary for him to ignore something of the unique, concrete particularity of that individual apple.

It may seem at first sight strange to offer the scientist as an example of the man who is dissociated from the senses, for it is usually assumed that the scientist owes his allegiance to the senses, to what is demonstrable, tangible, and measurable. There is a basis of truth behind this assumption, of course, but the important point is that the scientist only considers the particular, as it were grudgingly, for the sake of abstracting from it a generalization that should ideally be capable of expression in mathematical terms, that is, with the maximum degree of abstraction.[6] The scientist, in fact, like the medieval schoolman, turns away from the senses to a more unified, satisfactory, and tractable world governed by universal laws. This truth, which philosophers of science have been stressing recently, was noted by Gerard Manley Hopkins eighty years ago. In a letter of 1886, he writes:

The study of physical science has, unless corrected in some way, an effect the very opposite of what one might suppose. One would think it might materialize people (no doubt it does make them or, rather I shd. say, they become materialists; but that is not the same thing: they do not believe in Matter more but in God less); but in fact they seem to end

c

in conceiving only of a world of formulas, with its being properly speaking in thought, towards which the outer world acts as a sort of feeder, supplying examples for literary purposes.[7]

And, as Whitehead pointed out in *Science and the Modern World*, the 'formulas' with which the scientist works, for example the idea of a straight line without breadth or thickness, are highly abstract, and in fact unreal, though of course extremely useful. But then the abstractions of the shepherd who builds up a big business are likewise extremely useful.

It is essential to note that a heavy price has to be paid for the gains achieved by the process of abstraction. Our conquest of nature encourages us to seek solutions to our problems outside ourselves, and we fail to realize that the growth of our wealth or our power cannot keep pace with the growth of our desires when they are dissociated from the senses. In his book *The Image*, an excellent study of the phenomenon of dissociation in the twentieth-century American, Daniel Boorstin observes: 'Never have people been more the masters of their environment. Yet never has a people felt more deceived and disappointed. For never has a people expected so much more than the world could offer.'[8] This criticism has, indeed, been a commonplace of romantic thought for 150 years. As Shelley writes in his *Defence of Poetry* (1821): 'The cultivation of those sciences which have enlarged the empire of man over the external world, has, for want of the poetical faculty, proportionally circumscribed those of the internal world; and man, having enslaved the elements, remains himself a slave.'[9]

Second, even our ability to cope with life at the physical level is threatened by the success of abstract thinking in subjugating the natural world. The intractability of things-in-themselves constitutes a challenge (in Toynbee's sense) that calls forth man's energy and courage. Too complete a mastery over the external world creates a cosy, air-conditioned nightmare in which the powers of sensation atrophy, and man finds himself in the situation prophetically foreshadowed in H. G. Wells's story *The Time Machine* where the Eloi, those 'graceful children of the upperworld', cling together pathetically in a vain effort to escape the consequences of their dependence on the horrible, subterranean, cannibalistic Morlocks, who alone are tough enough to encounter brute reality. *The Time Machine* can be read as a parable of the class struggle precisely because it is the middle classes who have been most successful in overcoming the difficulties of life, and thus in cutting themselves off from reality. We shall see in the chapters that follow that dissociation of the senses has hitherto manifested itself principally among people in the middle classes: it is only when the shepherd is converted into an accountant that he forgets what sheep look like! Now, however, the machine has begun to take over the duties of a working class, so that most men are exposed to what Professor Boorstin in the opening paragraph of *The Image* describes as 'the thicket of unreality which stands between us and the facts of life'.

Third, once we have lost contact with reality, we are forced to rely on other people to tell us what the object (e.g. the sheep) is really like. We come to resemble blind men (except that we do not develop our other senses) in that we do not look at the world, but depend on others to describe it for us: thus we find ourselves at the mercy of *other people*, and above all, of course, at the mercy of the symbol-manipulators. (In *Nineteen Eighty-Four* Orwell showed how easily the Ministry of Truth could manipulate public attitudes in Oceania, making the people transfer their alliance from Eastasia to Eurasia with incredible rapidity.) The man who is rooted in the senses has some chance of resisting the infection of public opinion, because, like the child in the tale, he simply *sees* that the emperor has no clothes on; but where there is dissociation, where the organism is receiving no direct information about the nature of things, it is obliged to accept on trust whatever information it gets at second-hand from other people. Dissociation of the senses, then, like all the forms of dissociation, increases our dependence on other people, and the 'other-directed man' described by Riesman in *The Lonely Crowd*, who does not attend to things-in-themselves, or even to things in relation to himself, but instead has his antennae delicately adjusted to other people, is essentially a product of an age of dissociation.

It will be evident from what has been said so far that dissociation of the senses inevitably leads to dissociation of the feelings. Remoteness from the object destroys the bond of love that naturally links a man with the things he touches. Our shepherd can love his sheep, but he cannot love his money (except in a slightly insane and dissociated fashion). Once the loving bond with the created world is broken, the attitude towards things changes to one of fear. The feelings we have about something (such as a sheep, a person, or an institution) are in the natural course of things rooted in our physical relationship with that thing, and acquire substance and reality from a multitude of contacts with it in the course of the rough-and-tumble of everyday living. But when we have no physical relationship with the object—whether it be the goods we sell or the enemy we hate—then our feelings, liberated from the restrictions that reality normally imposes, are free to run riot in fantasy, swelling to monstrous proportions, or oscillating from one extreme to another. In the passage from *Nineteen Eighty-Four* referred to a moment ago, Orwell stresses the point that the feelings of the people of Oceania could be manipulated so easily only because they existed in a vacuum:

> If he [the average citizen of Oceania] were allowed contact with foreigners he would discover that they are creatures similar to himself and that most of what he has been told about them is lies. The sealed world in which he lives would be broken, and the fear, hatred, and self-righteousness on which his morale depends might evaporate.[10]

It is arguable that Orwell is here uncharacteristically optimistic, for the evidence seems to suggest that stereotypes about foreigners are not much modified by experience of them; in certain areas almost all men are dissociated from the senses so effectively that they become permanently trapped in a sealed world into which no direct information can penetrate. In any case, owing to the effect of modern communications, we are all today in a situation where our feelings are to a considerable extent concerned with objects—like TV stars or astronauts or national political figures—that we never see or touch. And even in the case of those objects that we do touch and see—for example, our wives, our neighbours, and our colleagues—we can avoid the labour of adjusting our feelings to their complex reality, because the mobility of modern society makes it easy to switch to another wife, another neighbourhood, or another job. Thus the conditions of modern life, which are the fruit of technological progress due to abstract thinking, create first dissociation of the senses, and thence dissociation of the feelings.

We must next consider the way in which abstract thinking has led directly to dissociation of the feelings. We can begin by glancing at a speech in *Hamlet* in which Claudius, echoing the arguments previously used by Gertrude, urges Hamlet to cease mourning for his father:

> But, you must know, your father lost a father;
> That father lost, lost his; and the survivor bound
> In filial obligation for some term
> To do obsequious sorrow; but to persever
> In obstinate condolement is a course
> Of impious stubbornness; 'tis unmanly grief:
> . . .
>   Fie! 'tis a fault to heaven,
> A fault against the dead, a fault to nature,
> To reason most absurd, whose common theme
> Is death of fathers.

This speech offers the interesting spectacle of one man telling another that he 'ought' not to have the feelings that he in fact does have. In this situation three things can happen. One man will ignore the advice that is offered to him (as Hamlet in fact does); another will perhaps find that the offered advice strikes a chord in his mind, awakening in him an authentic desire to master his grief; and a third man will be persuaded to 'accept' the advice at a verbal level, altering his behaviour or his ideas accordingly, although no genuine change has taken place in his feelings. Clearly, the difference between the second man and the third man corresponds to the difference between unified sensibility and dissociated sensibility, or between genuine development of taste and the sham acquisition of it. And just as the man whose taste is an artificial acquisition does not know what he *really* feels about a work of art, so the man who disguises or suppresses his real feelings, loses contact with himself, and becomes dissociated from his feelings.

Abstract thinking encourages the kind of response seen in the third man, because it fosters the tendency to stand apart from oneself and look at a situation from a detached point of view. Consider, for example, the famous passage of *Political Justice* in which Godwin argues that if a man were able to save one of two people from a fire, in circumstances where the other would have to be left to perish, he ought to elect to save Fénelon rather than his own valet, or even his own father or mother. Godwin formulates as follows the moral that his anecdote is meant to illustrate:

> . . . the soundest criterion of virtue is, to put ourselves in the place of an impartial spectator, of an angelic nature, suppose, beholding us from an elevated station, and un-influenced by our prejudices, conceiving what would be his estimate of the intrinsic circumstances of our neighbour, and acting accordingly.*

And again:

> What magic is there in the pronoun 'my' to overturn the decisions of everlasting truth? My wife or my mother may be a fool, or a prostitute, malicious, lying or deceitful. If they be, of what consequence is it that they are mine?

Political Justice exercises a powerful attraction, as Wordsworth admitted even after repudiating Godwinism,[11] because it combines the authority and prestige of science and Holy Scripture with the meretricious appeal of abstract thinking. (Note that Godwin conveys the impression that virtue can be achieved easily and rapidly.) It is, of course, true that the scientist adopts

---

* Cf. John Stuart Mill's *Utilitarianism*: 'As between his own happiness and that of others, utilitarianism requires him to be as strictly impartial as a disinterested and benevolent spectator.'

towards physical problems an attitude of angelic disinterested-
ness, and puts himself 'in the place of an impartial spectator'
when he carries out an experiment. The religious man, too,
in imitation of Christ, seeks to free himself from the bonds of
merely personal feeling and natural affection.[12] But, we must
note, the scientist, quite apart from any selfless enthusiasm for
his subject that he may feel, knows that only scientific impartiality produces results, so that he has good and sufficient *selfish*
reasons for desiring to be impartial. As for the religious man,
after long exercise in spiritual endeavour and self-discipline, he
experiences more joy in the love of God and in the love of truth
than in the love of father and mother, so that he too has a kind
of selfish reason (or, at any rate, a valid inner motivation) for
practising holy dispassion. It is clear, then, that the scientist
and the saint are special cases that offer little guidance for
ordinary mortals.

Faced with Godwin's suggestion that he ought to prefer
Fénelon to his father, the ordinary man, it would seem, can
react in any one of the three ways I discussed a moment ago.
He can reject Godwin's advice, saying, in effect: 'But this
particular person happens to be *my* father, and, from my own
limited, subjective point of view, I place a higher value upon
him than upon any other man in the world, Fénelon included.'
Or, he can make a deliberate effort of will to train himself in
obedience to Godwin's rule, perhaps seeking to cultivate the
Stoic virtue of *apatheia* that we find, for example, in Swift's
Houyhnhnms, who feels no grief on the death of a parent or
friend. Or, finally, he may conduct himself in outward conformity to Godwin's recommendations, without being authentically inspired by the Godwinian ideal. In this last category, we
may for our present purposes distinguish three sub-divisions:
first, the conscious hypocrite who pretends to have motives that
will meet with the approval of others; next, the man who is self-
deceived, who flatters his vanity by pretending to himself and
to others that he is better than he really is, and, as Hazlitt says
in his essay on Godwin in *The Spirit of the Age*, mistakes a
'heartless indifference for a superiority to more natural and
generous feelings';[13] third, the man who is self-ignorant, who

does not know what he feels, and meekly allows other people to tell him what he must feel and what he must do. Both the man who is self-deceived and the man who is self-ignorant are alienated from their own feelings. Abstract thinking, then, invites a man to adopt a universal point of view, to look down on himself with angelic impartiality from an 'elevated station', with the result that, like the shepherd we spoke of before who forgot what sheep look like, he loses contact with himself and forgets what he really feels; in other words, he becomes dissociated from his feelings.

It is evident, I think, that dissociation of the feelings constitutes a more advanced stage of dissociation than dissociation of the senses. It is strange, but not incredible, that a man should pay no attention to the outside world, and should fail to make proper use of his powers of sensory discrimination. But how is it possible for him to deceive himself?[14] And how is it possible for him to be ignorant of what he actually feels? In the case of dissociation of the senses, the organism is, as it were, asleep, so that it fails to respond to stimuli from outside. With dissociation of the feelings, the man receives the 'message', but does not even know that he has received it; he is ignorant of what is going on inside him. It may be possible to throw some light on this curious phenomenon when we have looked at the closely related problem of dissociation of the identity.

All the forms of dissociation are mutually related, and it can be said that dissociation of the identity is both a result and a cause of the other forms of dissociation. Our identities are to a considerable extent shaped by objects in the world, by the feelings that we have about these objects, and by the sentiments and aspirations that we form in relation to them; inevitably, then, lack of sensation and spurious feeling tend to produce a spurious identity. On the other hand, one of the main reasons why we falsify feelings is to tailor them to fit the false identity that we have chosen. Thus, if we identify ourselves with holy or saintly men, we dissociate ourselves from the unregenerate feelings of anger, hatred, and so on, that arise in our breasts; if we model ourselves upon the Napoleonic or Nietzschean *Übermensch*, then we disown our feeling of compassion or weakness; and if we follow the path of conformity, then, like Riesman's other-directed man, we keep our antennae delicately attuned to other people, taking care to rebroadcast the same tune that they are playing, and fleeing from the feelings that would brand us as outsiders. Clearly, whether we copy Christ or Napoleon or the Joneses next door, whether we aspire to be a lotus flower or a violet in the middle of a bunch of violets, we are perverting ourselves and blighting our true flowering if we imitate the outward forms of an excellence (or a mediocrity) prescribed for us by other people. And it cannot be too often repeated that this is really the heart of the matter: the essence of dissociation of the identity, as of all the forms of dissociation, is that we do not obey the inner law of our own being but rather the voice of other people.

At this point it is desirable to establish a connection between dissociation and the concepts of the self and the real being discussed in Chapter One. Since the essence of dissociation is that we do not obey the inner law of our own being, it is clear that dissociation is a modern, severe and chronic form of alienation from the real being. Abstract thinking teaches us to adopt a detached standpoint, to see with the eyes of other people, and we are now in a position to say that the self is, in essence, the life seen from the outside, from the viewpoint of other people. With the Fall of Man, the unique, interior self-knowledge that is the mark of the concrete thinking of the body is replaced by the exterior abstract knowledge that is common to all men: we see ourselves as others see us. This is, indeed, D. H. Lawrence's view of the Fall. 'At a certain point in his evolution', Lawrence says, 'man became cognitively conscious: he bit the apple: he began to know.' And he adds: 'But the moment man became aware of himself he made a picture of himself, and began to live from the picture: that is, from without inwards.'[15] On this view, dissociation of the feelings is less incomprehensible: just as we often do not know what other people feel, so, when we see ourselves from without, with the eyes of other people, we are strangers to our own feelings. On this view, again, we can understand the paradox that the growth of individualistic self-seeking since the Renaissance has in fact resulted in greater

dependence on the Other (to give the word the capital importance that Jean-Paul Sartre attaches to it). The chief value of
Sartre's work, it may be observed, lies in his brilliant analyses
of the nature of *being-for-others*. Here, for example, is his
famous description of the café-waiter:

> Let us consider this waiter in the café. His movement is
> quick and forward, a little too precise, a little too rapid. He
> comes toward the patrons with a step a little too quick. He
> bends forward a little too eagerly: his voice, his eyes express
> an interest a little too solicitous for the order of the customer.
> . . . All his behavior seems to us a game. He applies himself
> to chaining his movements as if they were mechanisms, the
> one regulating the other: his gestures and even his voice seem
> to be mechanisms: he gives himself the quickness and pitiless
> rapidity of things. He is playing, he is amusing himself. But
> what is he playing? We need not watch long before we can
> explain it: he is playing *at being* a waiter in a café.[16]

Since play suggests an idea of freedom and spontaneity which
is the reverse of the mechanical constraint of the waiter,
perhaps we can venture to say that Sartre's waiter is not so
much playing as disguising himself in the protective anonymity
of waiterdom, and assuming a role that will give him an identity
in the eyes of other people.

In *St Mawr* D. H. Lawrence gives an account of the Texan
cowboy that nicely complements Sartre's description of the
waiter:

> Cowboys just as self-conscious as Rico, far more sentimental,
> inwardly vague and unreal. Cowboys that went after their
> cows in black Ford motor-cars: and who self-consciously
> saw Lady Carrington falling to them, as elegant young ladies
> from the East fall to the noble cowboy of the films, or in
> Zane Grey. It was all film-psychology.
>
> And at the same time, these boys led a hard, hard life,
> often dangerous and gruesome. Nevertheless, inwardly they
> were self-conscious film-heroes. The boss himself, a man
> over forty, long and lean and with a great deal of stringy

energy, showed off before her in a strong silent manner, existing for the time being purely in his imagination of the sort of picture he made to her, the sort of impression he made on her.

So they all were, coloured up like a Zane Grey book-jacket, all of them living in the mirror. The kind of picture they made to somebody else.[17]

One might ask, since a man is actually inside his own skin, how does he manage to see himself from the outside, from the point of view of the other? Lawrence here indicates one of the answers to this question: the book or the film holds a (magnifying and distorting) mirror up to nature, and the man at the level of Self-Consciousness spends his life looking in this mirror, and contorting himself to fit the image that he finds there.

If the Parisian waiter and the Texan cowboy, who belong to rich, technologically advanced societies, caricature themselves for the sake of acquiring the security or illusory glamour of an identity, the man who belongs to a more stable, technically backward society does the same thing for the sake of the *money* that his richer neighbour possesses. This point is well made in Professor Boorstin's *The Image* in the chapter on 'The Lost Art of Travel':

> Not only in Mexico City and Montreal, but also in the remote Guatemalan Tourist Mecca of Chichecastenango and in far-off villages of Japan, earnest honest natives embellish their ancient rites, change, enlarge, and spectacularize their festivals, so that tourists will not be disappointed. In order to satisfy the exaggerated expectations of tour agents and tourists, people everywhere become dishonest mimics of themselves. To provide a full schedule of events at the best seasons and at convenient hours, they travesty their most solemn rituals, holidays, and folk celebrations—all for the benefit of tourists.[18]

The desire for money is so important a factor in dissociation that it really deserves a chapter to itself. For the present, however, I will merely note that money, like abstract thinking, enables a man to overcome the restrictions imposed by his environment, or to escape from his environment altogether. Abstract, neutral, and quantitative itself, it is nevertheless the *equivalent* (that is, the equal in value) of any concrete, material object in the universe. If Newton withdraws from the individual falling apple and translates it into a gravitational force, so the man who lives in a money-dominated economy 'withdraws' from his house, his garden and his books, and translates them into an abstract force of money.* I desire money in order to put myself beyond the power of the Other; yet the quest for money puts me within the power of the Other. In money, then, we see reflected in little the paradoxicalness that character-izes all the manifestations of dissociation.

I suggested a short while ago that Napoleon, Christ, or the Joneses next door, are commonly adopted as models by those who imitate the external forms of behaviour prescribed by the Other. We shall henceforth be concerned with the Hamletian figure who sets himself to imitate a heroic model, but it is worth while to pause for a moment to glance at the numerically far superior group of those who imitate the man next door. There seems to be general agreement that conformity has increased, is increasing, and ought to be diminished. Abstract thinking, in itself and in its consequences (rapidity of change and social mobility, the growth of individualism and the strengthening of consciousness, the improvement of moral standards and the diffusion of education, the growth of the commercial spirit and the worship of money, the shift of population from the country to the city), has inevitably created a condition of uprootedness in which men have become more remote from one another at the deeper levels, and yet more closely related at the verbal level. In this situation, an outward, fearful, and, as it were, reluctant conformity (which is really a kind of self-mutilation) is bound to flourish. The classical statement on this subject has been made by John Stuart Mill in *On Liberty*:

* George Eliot says in *Middlemarch*: 'But as Warren Hastings looked at gold and thought of buying Daylesford, so Joshua Rigg looked at Stone Court and thought of buying gold.'

In our times [he says], from the highest class of society down to the lowest, everyone lives as under the eye of a hostile and dreaded censorship . . . even in what people do for pleasure, conformity is the first thing thought of; they like crowds; they exercise choice only among things commonly done; peculiarity of taste, eccentricity of conduct, are shunned equally with crimes: until by dint of not following their own nature they have no nature to follow: their human capacities are withered and starved: they become incapable of any strong wishes or native pleasures, and are generally without either opinions or feelings of home growth, or properly their own.

Clearly, Mill's description of those who conform 'until by dint of not following their own nature they have no nature to follow' approximates fairly closely to the concept of dissociation of the identity developed in this chapter. It is true, as Mill says, that the individuality which is starved and denied can wither away for lack of nourishment. On the other hand, perhaps Mill does not sufficiently recognize (what, indeed, we can see very clearly from his own *Autobiography*) that feelings that are repressed by a rigid, life-denying conscious philosophy, tend to go underground, maintaining a secret life in opposition to consciousness, and thus perpetuating the condition of dissociation.

The Hamletian young man who imitates Christ or Napoleon is more interesting than the ordinary conformist, because of the greater complexity of his mind and his capacity for growth. At some level he is, as Dostoyevsky says of Raskolnikov in *Crime and Punishment*, 'dimly aware of the great lie in himself and his convictions'.[19] His plunge into dissociation, then, is in part an attempt to escape from dissociation. In Chapter Four, accordingly, we shall consider Raskolnikov as a modern Hamletian hero, who exhibits the phenomenon of dissociation in its most acute, and, as it were, classical form, and at the same time provides us with a glimpse of the beginnings of the hero's arduous journey to Consciousness.

CHAPTER FOUR

Crime and Punishment: A Study of Dissociation

The ego is a wall that limits the view, rising higher in
proportion as the man is greater.

REMY DE GOURMONT, *A Virgin Heart*[1]

Wordsworth's play *The Borderers*, as Basil Willey has said, is
essentially an anti-Godwinian document that seeks to demonstrate that the 'attempt to live by the naked reason, though it
might be a noble aspiration, is apt to produce monsters rather
than supermen'.[2] What Wordsworth attempted but by common
consent failed to achieve in *The Borderers*, Dostoyevsky perfectly
succeeded in doing in *Crime and Punishment*. In this chapter,
therefore, we shall consider *Crime and Punishment* as a study of
dissociation.

If Hamlet is the embodiment of the Renaissance hero trapped
in the condition of Self-Consciousness, Raskolnikov surely
performs the same representative function for the modern
period. The resemblances between the two are numerous and
significant, though Raskolnikov is of course much more profoundly dissociated. Both Hamlet and Raskolnikov are highly
intelligent, introspective, self-divided young men. Raskolnikov
dominates the novel just as Hamlet dominates the play. In
Horatio and Razumikhin each has the support of a friend who is
a decent, honourable man and a university student like himself.
Apart from this, both of them are already cut off from their
fellow-men when we first make their acquaintance, and are then
still further alienated by the wish to kill in the one case, and
by the fact of having killed in the other. Both have profoundly

divided minds: one fails to kill, but wishes to, while the other succeeds in killing, but only by violating his own nature. It may fairly be said, I think, that both are at war with society, and both are engaged in a life and death struggle with 'mighty opposites', in the persons of Claudius and Porfiry, who may be regarded as the champions of society. The fathers of both the young men are dead, and they both seem to feel a strange blend of love and hatred towards their mothers. Both seek to protect women from the lecherousness of other men. Hamlet tells his mother not to sleep with Claudius, and advises Ophelia to go to a nunnery. (Nunnery has the cant meaning of brothel, and it is worth recalling that Sonia actually is a prostitute, and Raskolnikov's fiancée, his landlady's invalid daughter, had wanted to enter a nunnery.) Raskolnikov calls a policeman to keep a watch on the stout gentleman who is following the drunken girl in the park; he forbids his sister to prostitute herself by marrying Luzhin, and he tries to protect her from Svidrigailov. Both young men appear to be chaste themselves. Ernest Jones's interpretation of *Hamlet* in terms of the Oedipus complex is well known, and *Crime and Punishment* obviously lends itself to similar kinds of interpretation.[3] Both Hamlet and Raskolnikov are driven near to madness. It is suggested that before the events that take place in the play and the novel, both of them were estimable and virtuous young men. We get glimpses of the old Hamlet in his relationship with Horatio, as well as in the words of Ophelia: 'O what a noble mind is here o'erthrown / The courtier's, soldier's, scholar's eye, tongue, sword'. The former worth of Raskolnikov is implied by the devotion he has inspired in his mother and his sister. It is also established at his trial, when it is mentioned in his defence that he had been seriously burned while rescuing two young children from a fire, and also that he had supported a tubercular fellow-student and his ailing father. It would be possible to extend the comparison between Hamlet and Raskolnikov considerably, but, assuming that I have established my point, I will add only one further observation: Hamlet and Raskolnikov are alike in that each kills unintentionally an innocent person, as well as the person that he actually intended to kill.

To discuss the question of dissociation of the senses in *Crime and Punishment*, we can profitably borrow some of the concepts employed in Chapter Two to contrast *Hamlet* and *Antony and Cleopatra*. *Antony and Cleopatra*, as we saw, was characterized by the positive values associated with feasting, drinking, sunlight, spaciousness, action, social and sexual intercourse. It is apparent that the world of Raskolnikov, like that of Hamlet, is almost entirely deficient in these values. Raskolnikov is cut off from life completely, solitarily spawning the fantasies of a 'mono-maniac' in his tiny room. The little room itself, as we learn on the first page of the novel, is 'more like a cupboard than a living-room'.[4] Raskolnikov's confinement in this 'coffin' (as it is twice called) is partly the cause of the unnatural growth of his fantasies—'it was there, in that awful cubby-hole of his, in that terrible cupboard, all *that* had taken shape in his head for the past month!' And, in the scene where he confesses the murder to Sonia, Raskolnikov himself explains the effect his physical environment had on him:

> I sat skulking in my room like a spider. You've seen my hovel, haven't you? And do you realize, Sonia, that low ceilings and small, poky little rooms warp both mind and soul? Oh, how I loathed that hovel of mine! And yet I wouldn't leave it. Wouldn't leave it on purpose. Didn't go out for days. Just lay about. If Nastasya happened to bring me something, I'd eat; if not, a whole day would pass without my tasting anything. I wouldn't ask for anything deliberately, out of spite. At night I had no light, so I would lie in the dark.

The image of the spider is an apt one for the lonely young man spinning a subtle web of self-deceiving illusion in dark and sordid surroundings. The same image, we may note in passing, had previously occurred in connection with Svidrigailov's description of eternity, and we meet it again two pages after the passage just cited, when Raskolnikov tells Sonia, 'I did not care a damn whether I would become the benefactor of someone, or would spend the rest of my life like a spider catching them all in my web and sucking the living juices out of them'.

It would be easy to go on citing evidence of the dissociation of the senses in Raskolnikov, but the point hardly needs to be pressed. Raskolnikov neglects to eat ('for two days now he had hardly anything to eat') and he does not work; and eating and working are the chief means by which we are brought into contact with things and with people. He is cut off from family, from friends, and from society generally—Razumikhin says he is 'a man who's been confined to his room for months without speaking to a single soul'—and he has no woman. His acute state of dissociation, then, can be summed up appropriately by means of an apt simile used by Dostoyevsky: 'He had withdrawn from the world completely, like a tortoise into its shell.'

It would be wrong, however, to put too much stress on the fact of dissociation. Part of the aim of *Crime and Punishment*, as indeed the title suggests, is to demonstrate that it is impossible to live dissociatedly, without eating, without relationship with others, and as the novel proceeds we are gradually prepared for the conclusion in which Raskolnikov is brought 'back to life'. So brilliant is Dostoyevsky's art that the prevailing atmosphere of Raskolnikov's life is firmly established in the marvellous opening pages, and then Dostoyevsky is able to show us his hero in an entirely different context, going into a public-house, drinking beer and eating a rusk, making the acquaintance of Marmeladov, and throwing aside for a moment his diseased thoughts. Paradoxically, even the murder, a crime against society, helps to root Raskolnikov in life. It brings him into relationship with Porfiry and others, and it brings about his illness, which exacts the help of Razumikhin and the doctor, Zossimov. While he is ill, Razumikhin feeds him as if he were a baby—'he put his left arm round Raskolnikov's head, raised him up, and began giving him tea in spoonfuls'—and also puts fresh clothes upon him. When his mother and sister come to Petersburg, we find that his room, though still sometimes the abode of the solitary spider, is occasionally so thronged with people as to resemble rather a railway-station. Finally, of course, the love of Sonia restores Raskolnikov to relationship of touch and feeling. And though we are told that during his first months in prison Raskolnikov 'always took her hand as though with loathing', still he did take her hand, and the flow of relationship continues, as it were, until the moment of their final union at the end of the novel.

We saw in the last chapter that Godwin asked us 'to put ourselves in the place of an impartial spectator, of an angelic nature, suppose, beholding us from an elevated station'. But once we have learned to stifle or ignore our own natural impulses, what is to prevent us from doing this in the interests of evil rather than of good? When our feelings are no longer rooted in our own unique organism, we have a 'freedom' whose fruits will vary according to the theory or principle that guides it. And the theoretical position that Raskolnikov has adopted is that great men are superior to ordinary morality. In deference to this theory, he repudiates his own emotions, and murders the old woman ('I wanted to become a Napoleon—that's why I killed the old woman'), even though the crime fills him with revulsion and abhorrence. The extent of this repugnance towards the sordid and beastly murder is made clear in the first chapter:

> 'Good Lord, how disgusting it all is! And will I—will I really. . . . No! It's impossible! It's absurd!' he added firmly. 'And how could such a horrible idea have occurred to me? What a foul thing my heart is capable of, though! Yes, the chief thing is it's so foul, so horrible, so disgusting, disgusting!'

However, Raskolnikov's conscious standpoint obliges him to stifle or disown his instinctive reactions. The conflict between heart and head is repeatedly emphasized: for example, 'his casuistry was as sharp as a razor, and he could no longer find any *conscious* objections to his plans in his *mind*. But at *heart* he never really took himself seriously' (my italics). In so far as he is conscious of his feelings, then, he refuses to be governed by them, but follows the dictates of his will and reason. But in any case, because he identifies himself with his intellect, his conscious self, he is in fact to a great extent ignorant of, and dissociated from, his true feelings. His breakdown after the murder, his dreams (for example, the dream about the old mare that is beaten to death), and his delirium sufficiently demonstrate the degree of his ignorance of self, and the extent to which he has underestimated the real force and character of his feelings.

The fact is that he has adopted a personality role, a Napoleonic mask, and the feelings that are inappropriate to this role he conveniently ignores or represses. For example, after he has drawn the policeman's attention to the man who has designs on the drunken girl in the park, he suddenly repents of his humaneness, and tells the policeman to leave them alone and let the man 'have his fun'. Similarly, after he has made determined efforts to stop Dunya from marrying Luzhin, even telling her that she must choose between Luzhin and himself, he suddenly reverses his attitude, and says to her, 'What am I making such a fuss about? Why all this clamour? Marry whom you like, for all I care!'

Again, quite early in the novel, he impulsively gives the Marmeladov family almost all the money he has just received from his mother; immediately afterwards, he regrets his fall from Olympian detachment. 'What the hell did I do that for?' he asks himself, reflecting sardonically that no doubt the money will be needed to buy make-up for Sonia so that she can carry on her trade as a prostitute. Then again, to cite one last example, Raskolnikov's reaction to the letter from his mother reveals strikingly the contrast between his true feelings and the attitudes he chooses to adopt:

> Almost all the time he was reading the letter, from the very beginning, Raskolnikov's face was wet with tears; but when he had finished it, his face was pale and contorted, and a bitter, spiteful, evil smile played on his lips. He put his head on his old pillow and thought a long, long time.

In short, in every instance the same mechanism is at work: Raskolnikov's feelings spontaneously manifest themselves in a particular situation, and are then rejected or ignored because the hero dissociates himself from feelings that link him with common humanity and its weaknesses.

As was the case with dissociation of the senses, it is important to stress that dissociation of the feelings is most acute at the start of the novel, and that during the course of the action

Raskolnikov is brought into closer contact with his feelings. Actually, the conflict between heart and head continues throughout the novel, but whereas at the beginning he obeyed his head (notably, in carrying out the murder), by the end he is obeying his heart. Thus, in Part Six, his mind still tells him that it was not a crime to kill an evil old woman, and he can see no logical reason for confessing. Nevertheless, in obedience to his feelings and the directions of Sonia, he kisses the earth that he has sinned against, and makes his confession. The conflict within him is revealed by the manner in which he informs Sonia of his decision to give himself up. 'I've come for your crosses', he announces with a malicious grin, and then adds, 'I've come to the conclusion that this way will perhaps be more to my advantage.' Sonia is profoundly shocked by his frivolity at this moment, but then she becomes aware that 'his tone and his words were not genuine'. In short, the gulf between his feelings and his conscious attitudes is so great that it is impossible for him to speak or act without being divided against himself.

Even in prison, Raskolnikov's mind continues to assert that the murder was not a crime, and we are told that the other prisoners are instinctively aware of his Satanic pride, and attack him as an atheist. Finally, however, as we have already seen, in the very last pages of the novel Raskolnikov, through the love of Sonia, is brought back to life and relationship with his fellow-men, and Dostoyevsky intimates that the conflict between thinking and feeling is now finally resolved:

> Besides, now he would hardly have been able to solve any of his problems consciously; he could only feel. Life had taken the place of dialectics, and something quite different had to work itself out in his mind.

I observed in the last chapter that dissociation of the feelings is closely connected with dissociation of the identity, because one of the main reasons why we falsify feelings is to tailor them to fit the false identity that we have chosen. This proposition clearly applies to Raskolnikov, who, as we have seen, imagines himself as a person of Napoleonic stature, and tries to act and feel accordingly. As he says to Sonia, 'I wanted to become a

Napoleon—that's why I killed the old woman.' His reasoning runs as follows: a great man like Napoleon will commit crimes because he is superior to ordinary morality. I am (or wish to be) a great man. Therefore I will commit crimes that violate ordinary morality. There seems to be a trace of the fallacy of undistributed middle in this reasoning: even if it is true that great men commit crimes, it does not follow that all criminals are great men. What is more important for our purposes, however, is that Raskolnikov's reasoning betrays the imitativeness that is characteristic of dissociation of the identity; he accepts from *other people* an idea of what greatness is, and then tries to act in such a way as to qualify himself for the title of great man. Raskolnikov admits to Sonia not only that he murdered the old woman in order to become a Napoleon, but also that in murdering her he tried to model himself upon Napoleon:

> And if he [Napoleon] had had no other alternative, he would have strangled her without the slightest hesitation, and done it thoroughly, too. Well, so I, too, hesitated no longer and—and murdered her—following *the example of my authority*.
>
> (My italics)

The truly great man, we may presume, does not copy the merely outward forms of so-called greatness, but spontaneously acts as he has to act, in accordance with his own nature, and so fulfils himself. The *idea* of being a great man is a concept acquired from outside; and, as we have seen, to adopt false or inappropriate ideas of conduct from other people is to be betrayed into dissociation of the identity.

The evidence of dissociation of the identity in Raskolnikov is really supplied by the split between conscious attitudes and real feelings that we have already examined; I shall therefore add only one or two further remarks on this subject. According to Raskolnikov's theory, the ordinary people have to lead a life of strict obedience, and it is only the extraordinary who are, under certain circumstances, entitled to transgress the law. In the long discussion of the theory that occurs in Part Three, Profiry broaches the question of the problem that could arise if 'a member of one category imagines that he really belongs to the other and begins "to eliminate all obstacles".' The remark bears directly on the problem under discussion, of course, for to 'imagine' (that is to say, to delude yourself) that you are this or that kind of person, and to shape your behaviour accordingly, is to display precisely what I have called dissociation of the identity. A few pages later Porfiry slyly insinuates that Raskolnikov perhaps regards himself as a 'wee bit' extraordinary, and when Raskolnikov denies that he considers himself a Mahomet or a Napoleon, Porfiry interjects: 'But, good heavens! who does not consider himself a Napoleon in Russia to-day?' The remark obviously carries two implications: first, that Raskolnikov does delusively 'imagine' himself to be a Napoleon, and, second, that his case is a typical one, that is to say, that this particular form of dissociation of the identity is common among their contemporaries.

One further illustration will suffice. Razumikhin paints a portrait of Raskolnikov for the benefit of Mrs Raskolnikov and Dunya that shows a full awareness of Raskolnikov's dualistic or dissociative character:

> I've known Roddy for a year and a half: he's morose, gloomy, proud, stuck up. More recently (and perhaps for a long time) he's been rather suspicious and moody. He dislikes showing his feelings, and he'd rather be cruel than put his real feelings into words. There are times, however when he is not moody, but simply cold and inhumanly callous, *just as if there were two people of diametrically opposed characters living in him, each taking charge of him in turn.*
>
> (My italics)

It is worth noting in passing that Razumikhin serves as an admirable, partly humorous, foil for Raskolnikov. Where Raskolnikov is morose, gloomy, and proud, Rasumikhin is 'warm-hearted, frank, simple-minded, honest, strong as a giant'. That he is rooted in the senses is attested by his exuberant energy, his drinking bouts, his fights and his escapades (for instance, felling a six-foot policeman at one blow). The spontaneity and truth of his feelings is evident all the time, especially in his relationship with Raskolnikov and in his love of Dunya. And his humility ('Who was he compared to such a girl—he, a drunken ruffian and an unconscionable braggart?' he reflects on the morning after his first meeting with Dunya) makes him proof against Napoleonic delusions. On a number of occasions, Razumikhin acts as a mouthpiece for Dostoyevsky's own attacks on the progressives. For example, he says of them:

> What they're after is the absolute renunciation of one's own personality. They find that so fascinating. Only not to be yourself—to be as unlike yourself as possible. That in their opinion is the highest achievement of progress.

And he continues a few lines later:

> Talk rot by all means, but do it in your own way, and I'll be ready to kiss you for it. For to talk nonsense in your own way is a damn sight better than talking sense in someone else's; in the first case, you're a man; in the second, you're nothing but a magpie!

One could hardly wish for a more vigorous refutation of the Godwinian idea that we ought to 'put ourselves in the place of an impartial spectator', and the 'renunciation of one's own personality' (or the dissociation of the identity) that it encourages.

Razumikhin's various outbursts against the progressives form one important part of Dostoyevsky's attack on abstract thinking, or what Ernest J. Simmons has called 'the unholy intellectualism of the West'.[5] Another device Dostoyevsky employs is to put absurd or detestable ideas into the mouths of the progressives. Lebezyatnikov, for example, applauds Sonia for becoming a prostitute, on the grounds that her action is a forceful protest against the organization of society! The contemptible Luzhin, on the other hand, expresses false and noxious ideas, which are all the more repellent because he does not really believe what he is saying, but is merely trying to create a favourable impression by mouthing the platitudes fashionable among the progressives. Thus when he visits Raskolnikov's room, he declares that 'many harmful prejudices have been eradicated. . . . In a word, we have cut ourselves off irrevocably from the past, which, in my opinion, is already something. . . .' A few lines later he observes that progress has rendered obsolete the command to love your neighbour as yourself: 'But science tells us, "Love yourself before everyone else, for everything in the world is based on self-interest." '

I argued in the last chapter that science and abstract thinking are intimately linked, and it is important to note that Dostoyevsky, as in the passage just quoted, frequently includes science in his attacks on abstract thinking. For example, when Raskolnikov decides that the plump gentleman should be allowed to 'have his fun' with the young girl in the park, he reasons that it is a simple matter of statistics—science shows that it is essential that a certain percentage of the young girls should be raped or become prostitutes each year.* Early in the novel, the point that science renders us inhuman is made very explicitly through Marmeladov:

> But Mr Lebezyatnikov, who keeps abreast of modern ideas, explained the other day that in our age even pity has been outlawed by science, and that in England, where they seem to be very keen on political economy, people are already acting accordingly.†

The student whom Raskolnikov overhears talking to an officer offers the following justification for killing the old woman: 'One death in exchange for a hundred lives—why, it's a simple sum in arithmetic! And, when you think of it, what does the life of a sickly, wicked old hag amount to when weighed in the scales of the general good of mankind?' The 'simple sum in

---

* Cf. the reply Tom Gradgrind makes to his father in *Hard Times:* 'So many people are employed in situations of trust; so many people, out of so many, will be dishonest. I have heard you talk, a hundred times, of its being a law. How can *I* help laws? You have comforted others with such things, father. Comfort yourself!'

† Again there is a parallel in *Hard Times*, where Sissy Jupe confesses she is stupid because she cannot understand political economy '. . . she had only yesterday been set right by a prattler three feet high, for returning to the question, "What is the first principle of this science?" the absurd answer, "To do unto others as I would that they should do unto me." '

arithmetic', the scales which purport to measure accurately, and the Benthamite concept of the general good of mankind, these all reflect the typical language employed by those who would introduce scientific accuracy and objectivity—the felicific calculus—into the realm of ethics.[6] Raskolnikov himself employs language similar to that used by the student. 'No, I couldn't do it! I just couldn't do it! Even if there were no mistake whatever in all my calculations, even if anything I had decided during the past months were as clear as daylight and as true as arithmetic.' In addition to the argument from arithmetic, there is perhaps here also an oblique reference to the 'clear and distinct' ideas of the rationalist, Descartes.

It is, of course, Raskolnikov himself and the murder he commits that provide the most effective demonstration of the evils of abstract thinking. We have already seen that Raskolnikov identifies himself with his thinking and dissociates himself from his feelings; 'he was young, fond of abstract reasoning, and, therefore, cruel', Dostoyevsky says of him. He is a reflective young man, who writes articles, pursuing his ideas through to their logical conclusion; as Porfiry observes, he is a young man 'in the first flush of youth, as it were, and that is why you prize the human intellect so highly, as all young men do. You can't help admiring the playful keenness of wit and the abstract deductions of reason'. It is this fondness for the abstract deductions of reason which makes Raskolnikov receptive to the abstract and pseudo-scientific arguments justifying the murder. In a letter to Katkov of September, 1865, Dostoyevsky briefly outlines his plot, and describes his murderer-hero as a young man 'obsessed with the "half-baked" ideas that are in the air just now'.[7] Porfiry develops the same idea more fully in his final talk with Raskolnikov:

We're dealing with quite a fantastic affair here, a sombre affair, a modern one, a case characteristic of our time, when men's hearts have grown rank and foul. . . . We're dealing with bookish dreams here, with a heart exacerbated by theories. . . . Forgot to close the front door, but murdered, murdered two people for the sake of a theory.

The thoroughly abstract and dissociated character of Raskolnikov's theorizing is beautifully illustrated a short while later
in the same conversation, when Porfiry says to him: 'I suppose,
it's a good thing you only murdered an old woman. If you'd
thought out another theory, you'd probably have done something
a thousand times worse!'

The history of Raskolnikov, then, demonstrates that abstract
thinking is divorced from life, is opposed to life, and that, since
it is divorced from feeling and tradition, it is capable of bringing
forth any and all kinds of unnatural, monstrous, and hideous
acts. The solution, according to Porfiry, is to 'give yourself up
to life without thinking', and in the Epilogue, as we have already
seen, Dostoyevsky indicates that this is the correct solution,
and that Raskolnikov through Sonia discovers it: 'Besides, now
he would hardly have been able to solve any of his problems
consciously; he could only feel. Life had taken the place of
dialectics, and something quite different had to work itself out
in his mind.'

There is one final chain in the argument that remains to be
forged. I pointed out in the last chapter that at the heart of
abstract thinking there lies an abstraction, the idea of the self,
and I said that the original Fall of Man consists in the emergence
of this idea. Dostoyevsky in *Crime and Punishment*, similarly,
makes it clear that if Raskolnikov 'murdered two people for
the sake of a theory', the ultimate responsibility for the crime
must be attributed, not to abstract thinking, but to the cardinal
theological sin of pride. *Initium omnis peccati superbia*. In his
notebook Dostoyevsky writes of Raskolnikov: 'In his person will
be expressed in the novel the idea of immeasurable pride,
arrogance, and scorn towards society.'[8] This conception is
clearly, though unobtrusively, enforced throughout the novel.
It is pride that sets Raskolnikov apart from his fellow students,
and pride that makes him think he is one of the extraordinary
men who are able to 'step over'. The physician, Zossimov,
describes him as 'A man possessed by exceptional, quite insane
vanity.' And when Dunya asks what motives Raskolnikov could
have had for committing murder, Svidrigailov mentions
poverty, lack of food, sordid surroundings, and the theory about

the great man, but insists that above all Raskolnikov was moved by pride and vanity. This pride asserts itself fantastically at Raskolnikov's final meeting with his sister before he goes to prison. 'One day perhaps you'll hear about me', the murderer tells her. 'I won't disgrace you, you'll see. I'll show them yet!' And in prison, Dostoyevsky tells us in the Epilogue, Raskolnikov falls ill through wounded pride. We may conclude, then, that while it is perhaps true, as Porfiry claims, that Raskolnikov murdered two people for the sake of his theory, in a deeper sense he murdered them for the sake of his pride.

There are other references to pride in *Crime and Punishment*, but it is perhaps only necessary to remind ourselves of one further point; namely, that Dostoyevsky approaches the theme of pride from a specifically Christian point of view. We are told of Luzhin, for example, that 'The black serpent of injured pride had been gnawing at his heart all night.' And the overtly Christian humility of Sonia is the antithesis of Raskolnikov's pride. Thus when Raskolnikov takes up Sonia's cross of cypress wood (the sort that the common people wear), and bows down to the people, and kisses the earth that he has sinned against, he is performing a symbolical abasement of his pride in typically Christian form.

To sum up the argument of this chapter, then, I would say that *Crime and Punishment* admirably illustrates the thesis I have been trying to put forward so far. Pride or self-love represents the Original Sin that lies at the basis of the dissociation of man. Abstract thinking offers itself as a suitable instrument by means of which the aims of self-love can be accomplished. And abstract thinking in its turn aggravates the original condition of dissociation, creating dissociation of the senses, dissociation of the feelings, and dissociation of the identity.

PART II

THE ADOLESCENT HERO

CHAPTER FIVE

The Revolt Against the Father

'Who of us does not desire his father's death?'
    IVAN KARAMAZOV in *The Brothers Karamazov*

For the adolescent the central fact of existence is the domination of the father. This domination of the father can be interpreted, in the manner of medieval allegory, at several different levels. At the literal level, for example, it simply refers to the flesh-and-blood father who enjoys wealth, authority, prestige, and, if you like, undisputed possession of the women. At the allegorical level, the father corresponds to God, conceived as a huge old man with a beard, the introjected father-figure of the Freudians. At the moral level, the father represents the conscience which says *Thou shalt not*, and has its prohibitions enforced by all the awful might of God the Father. At the political level we may say that the father is the representative of society, and that through him the commands of society, the pressures towards conformity, are transmitted to the son. At the anagogical level, finally, the father stands for any absolute system of values which *commands* our allegiance.

The chief task of the adolescent hero is to throw off the yoke of the father, and become his own master. But, we may ask ourselves, how is this puny David to do battle against a Goliath that has the advantages of wealth, experience, and the collaboration of the powers that be? Very often, the adolescent hero employs the time-honoured revolutionary device of justifying his rebellion against the authority of the father by an appeal to more ancient authority; in effect, he uses the name of God the Father to attack the real father, judging and condemning the father and society generally by the severe standards of the puritanical conscience. My purpose now is to apply these generalizations to *Hamlet* and *The Wild Duck*.

The Court of Elsinore and the society depicted in *The Wild Duck* are both symbols of the ordinary world, that is, of imperfect but humanly viable social groups. They are presented to us essentially in terms of social activities—dinner-parties, wedding-feasts, court ceremony, and the like—and these social activities revolve around the father-figures, Claudius and Werle. In their respective environments, Hamlet and Gregers are lonely, alien figures, denouncing the world because it does not satisfy the 'claims of the ideal'. Both are young men, bachelors, possessed of few friends, and given to solitary brooding. The soliloquizing Hamlet is the type of the melancholy man, and Gregers bears the same stamp; when Hialmar asks him how he has been getting on at the works, he replies: 'I have had a delightfully lonely time of it—plenty of time to think and think about things.' Both are tortured by feelings of guilt: Gregers tells his father, 'I am continually haunted and harassed by a guilty conscience', and Hamlet says, 'I could accuse me of such things that it were better my mother had not borne me'—and, no doubt as a consequence, both harbour thoughts of suicide and are full of self-hatred. Hamlet calls himself a rogue and a peasant slave, and asks: 'What should such fellows as I do crawling between heaven and earth?' A very similar note is struck in a conversation between Gregers and Hialmar:

> *Gregers*: But when one has the misfortune to be called Gregers—! 'Gregers' and then 'Werle' after it; did you ever hear anything so hideous?
> *Hialmar*: Oh, I don't think so at all.
> *Gregers*: Ugh! Bah! I feel that I should like to spit upon the fellow that answers to such a name.

Much as the adolescent hero despises himself, he despises other people more. In the bedroom scene, for example, Hamlet attacks his mother with smug superiority:

> Forgive me this my virtue;
> For in the fatness of these pursy times
> Virtue itself of vice must pardon beg.

And Gregers, who values his purity so highly that he refuses to accept his lawful share of his father's tainted wealth, feels a profound contempt for his father:

> *Werle*: Gregers—I believe there is no one in the world you detest as you do me.
> *Gregers*: (softly): I have seen you at too close quarters.
> *Werle*: You have seen me with your mother's eyes.

In effect, the adolescent hero is in the same situation as Gulliver when he returns from the land of the Houyhnhnms: he despises himself because he is incapable of living in accordance with the exalted Houyhnhnm ideals, but he feels infinitely more contempt for the other European Yahoos who are so base that they do not even recognize or pay homage to these ideals.

Most important of all, both Hamlet and Gregers give their allegiance to a dead parent, representing the ideal (or the parent magnified and ennobled by the child's imagination), and are at odds with the living parent, representing flesh-and-blood and its frailties. (There is an interesting parallel here to the traditional folk-tale about the little child with one good parent and a wicked step-parent.) In both cases, the living parent has been guilty of adultery, and it is from the injured party that the son learns of the crime. Hamlet's father returns from the grave to accuse his murderer and to denounce his 'seeming-virtuous queen', and Gregers learns of Werle's love-affair with Gina almost from his mother's dying lips:

> *Gregers:* My poor unhappy mother told me; and that the very last time I saw her.
> *Werle*: Your mother! I might have known as much! You and she—you always held together. It was she who turned you against me, from the first.
> *Gregers*: No, it was all she had to suffer and submit to, until she broke down and came to such a pitiful end.

D

Both young men, then, feel that they have a 'mission' to set to rights a world that is out of joint as a result of the evil deeds of the father-figure.

Devoted to a dead parent and an exalted ideal, filled with self-contempt and contempt for others, the adolescent hero understandably seeks something outside himself in the living world that he can admire. Both Hamlet and Gregers in their loneliness and isolation lean on a friend, who, they believe, shares their ideals, and yet is without their defects. Hialmar is the wholly inappropriate object of Gregers's admiration. Relling paints an amusing and unflattering portrait of Hialmar ('I am simply giving you an inside view of the idol you are grovelling before'), and he points out that it is in the nature of Gregers's disease for him to prostrate himself before idols with feet of clay:

> *Relling*: Yours is a complicated case. First of all there is that plaguy integrity-fever; and then—what's worse—you are always in a delirium of hero-worship; you must always have something to adore, outside yourself.
> *Gregers*. Yes, I must certainly seek it outside myself.
> *Relling*: But you make such shocking mistakes about every new phoenix you think you have discovered.

Horatio, similarly, though a shadowy figure as far as the audience is concerned, is seen by Hamlet as the embodiment of those virtues which Hamlet himself lacks:

> Since my dear soul was mistress of her choice,
> And could of men distinguish her election,
> Sh'hath sealed thee for herself, for thou hast been
> As one in suff'ring all that suffers nothing,
> A man that Fortune's buffets and rewards
> Hast ta'en with equal thanks . . .

The father-figures (one of course is a real father, the other a step-father) with whom Hamlet and Gregers have to contend are strikingly similar. Both are rich, worldly, and powerful—Claudius rules a kingdom and Werle is a captain of industry—and both obtain their power by dishonest means, which involve the destruction of another man (in the one case Hamlet *père*, and in the other Old Ekdal, 'a broken-down being, past all help', who haunts the play rather like the ghost in *Hamlet*). Both Claudius and Werle are adulterers. They are both surrounded by servile people who find it profitable to turn a blind eye to their wrongdoings. (It is interesting that Mrs Sörby tells the Chamberlains that they are dependent on the sunshine of court favour, while Hamlet complains that he is 'too much i' th' sun': since the sun, both from the standpoint of the medieval system of correspondences and of modern psychology, is the symbol of the king and the father, the two passages aptly illustrate the contrast between the obsequious majority and the rebellious son.) Both father-figures are middle-aged men who seek to consolidate their positions by marriage, and summon the young men, their heirs, to lend countenance to the weddings by their presences. As Gregers says to Werle: 'No doubt it will have an excellent effect when it is reported that the son has hastened home, on the wings of filial piety, to the grey-haired father's wedding-feast.' The young men, for their parts, are far from thoughts of marriage. Gregers says, 'So you are a married man, Hialmar! That is further than I shall ever get', and Hamlet declares, 'We will have no more marriages.' Whether or not we accept Ernest Jones's interpretation of Hamlet in terms of the Oedipus complex (and those who do accept it will not find it hard to apply a similar interpretation to Gregers), we must surely agree that the hatred that Hamlet and Gregers feel towards the father-figure is partly inspired by jealousy, of a sexual nature. The fathers, meanwhile, have little understanding of their sons, and are perplexed and troubled by what they regard as their over-scrupulosity and neuroticism.

The similarities between the women are less remarkable but still interesting. Gina and Gertrude are both representative specimens of ordinary womanhood, of *la femme moyenne sensuelle*. They possess common sense and an earthy feminine practicality, but they are unimaginative. When Gregers says that Hialmar's family is oppressed by darkness and gloom, Gina takes the lampshade off. Gertrude thinks that Hamlet needs to have his mind taken off things: 'Did you assay him / To any pastime?' she asks Rosencrantz and Guildenstern. They are affectionate parents and loyal wives—at least that is how they are represented before us on the stage*—and one feels that it was human frailty rather than criminal lust that led them to yield to the importunities of their lovers. As Gina rather charmingly puts it: 'He [Werle] gave me no peace until he'd had his way.' Lastly, in the final analysis, both women turn against the father-figure who enjoys the kingdom of this world, and espouse the cause of those who are in the opposite camp. (One would like to be able to say that they join forces with the son against the father; this is indeed true of *Hamlet*, but Hialmar is of course not Werle's son, though Werle plays the role of father to him to the extent of providing him with a wife, a profession, and considerable financial support.)

I will not press the analogies between Ophelia and Hedvig further than to note that they both commit suicide (or, at the least, they both die by their own hands), and that they may both be regarded as the innocent victims of the destructive daimon of the adolescent hero. The adolescent hero, as we have already observed, identifies himself with the attitude of God the Father; he is thus never so happy as when he is issuing commands—especially commands of a restrictive or prohibitive character—to other people. Hamlet, for instance, exhorts his mother, 'go not to my uncle's bed', and tells Ophelia, 'Get thee to a nunnery', and Gregers persuades Hedvig to sacrifice the wild duck as a 'free-will offering' for her father's sake. In short, the conscience-driven young man constitutes a life-denying force both for himself and for other people.

What makes *Hamlet* and *The Wild Duck* so strikingly different, in spite of the many resemblances I have noted, is that the attitudes of the authors towards the adolescent hero are diametrically opposed. Shakespeare identifies himself with Hamlet, and he uses Horatio, the disinterested onlooker, to

---

* The crimes of murder, adultery, and so on, were committed before the plays begin, so that the audience tends to view them almost exclusively through the eyes of the adolescent hero—an important circumstance that we shall touch upon again later.

enlist our sympathy for him: 'Now cracks a noble heart. Good night, sweet prince. / And flights of angels sing thee to thy rest!' Ibsen, on the other hand, is *against* Gregers, and he asks us to accept the view of Relling that Gregers is a sick person, whose mind is poisoned by a malady to which the whole nation is periodically subject: 'He is suffering from an acute attack of rectitudinitis.' In addition to using Relling as his mouthpiece to attack Gregers, Ibsen shapes our attitude towards Gregers by presenting him entirely from the outside. Imagine Hamlet presented without the soliloquies, and perhaps also without the intimate conversations with Horatio, and you see revealed that aspect of Hamlet to which Professor G. Wilson Knight has directed our attention; namely, Hamlet as a dangerous man who is bringing chaos and disaster to a reasonably harmonious society; and this is precisely how Gregers strikes us.

Because Shakespeare shares the misanthropic vision of the adolescent hero, he presents, as an objective correlative, a darker world than Ibsen, a world in which the destructiveness of the hero seems more justifiable. Thus Claudius, an incestuous murderer, is much more evil than Werle, and it is typical of the contrast between them that Claudius seeks to have Hamlet killed, where Werle merely uses persuasion in an effort to silence Gregers. Then, too, the crimes of Werle were committed several years ago, and it seems that Gregers is alone in his obsession with past events that other people have more or less forgotten about or adjusted themselves to. The murder in *Hamlet*, on the other hand, was committed only a few months before the play begins, and since the king of Denmark is the murderer, the whole of society is inevitably involved. The appearances of the Ghost, the confession of Claudius in the prayer-scene, the admission of guilt by Gertrude, and the play-within-the-play, all provide supporting evidence for the view that Hamlet is objectively in the right. Because the royal bed of Denmark is 'A couch for luxury and damned incest' it can be plausibly argued, as for instance Francis Fergusson argues, that it was Hamlet's duty to find and destroy the 'hidden imposthume'. With respect to *The Wild Duck*, however, despite all the wrongs done by Werle, it can hardly be maintained that

Gregers did well to interfere with the happy and thriving (though deluded) family of Hialmar Ekdal. Note, too, that Hamlet does achieve a tragic purgation by killing the murderer and by dying himself. Gregers, on the other hand, only succeeds in destroying the innocent child, Hedvig, and he goes off at the end of the play to pursue his destiny as the 'thirteenth at table', that is, as a troublemaker. In sum, then, each author creates an action which reflects his vision of the world: Shakespeare feels that there is evil in the world and that the adolescent hero has got to fight it, while Ibsen takes the view that if the world is imperfect and less than ideal (if you like, evil), it is because it is its nature to be so, and the young man who would reform it is himself sick in soul.

It is generally agreed that in *The Wild Duck* Ibsen is attacking his old self in the person of Gregers Werle, and is dissociating himself from his past errors. He is therefore, perhaps, unduly severe in his delineation of Gregers. In a way, by allowing Hialmar and his family to supply the main interest of his play, Ibsen wrote *The Wild Duck* just as if the centre of the stage in *Hamlet* were occupied by Polonius, Ophelia and Laertes. If you focus your attention on Polonius, then what you are most strongly aware of in Hamlet is his destructiveness. But if you look within Hamlet, perhaps you scarcely see the destructiveness; at any rate, you certainly also see much that is of value. The fact is, surely, that there is an ambiguity about these young men (an ambiguity which I have tried to reflect by my choice of the term 'adolescent hero') that lends itself to widely differing interpretations. To prepare the way for an exploration of this ambiguity, we must turn aside for the moment from *Hamlet* and *The Wild Duck*, and look at Hamlet from a fresh angle, as it were, by means of a comparison with another play, Sartre's *Dirty Hands*. We shall then be ready in the following chapter to attempt to analyse the nature of the fundamental ambiguity that lies at the heart of Hamletian man.

It is probably true that in the twentieth century the flesh-and-blood father has to some extent abdicated, so that the revolt against the father has shifted onto society (or some official

representative of society, such as the schoolmaster or the judge)
as the focus of authority and inhibition. Nevertheless, the flesh-
and-blood father is the *natural* symbol of authority, and the
struggle against him is still profoundly significant; it is easy to
enter into the feelings of the unsophisticated Irish peasants in
Synge's *The Playboy of the Western World*, who shower gifts
and praise on 'the young man who killed his da'. In Sartre's
work, perhaps because his father died when he was two and he
was brought up by a Victorian grandfather, the theme of
rebellion against a dominant father is of the greatest importance.
In both *The Flies* and *The Condemned of Altona* the hero kills
the literal father; in *Dirty Hands*, where it is the adopted father
who is killed, Sartre perhaps achieves his most mature and
compassionate insight into the ambiguous nature of the rebellious son.

Hugo Barine, the adolescent hero (or, if you like, unhero)
of *Dirty Hands*, is a young middle-class intellectual, who rebels
against his class and joins the Proletarian Party (that is, the
communist party) in his native Illyria, an imaginary country
in Eastern Europe. Hugo is given the job of editing an underground newspaper, but he is not satisfied with his useful but
comparatively secure and humdrum work, because he wishes to
undertake a dangerous mission, and to prove himself a real
man of action. In the situation that occurs at the start of the
play he gets his chance. Hoederer, the leader of the Proletarian
Party, has decided that it is necessary, on grounds of expediency, to form a temporary alliance with the bourgeois and the
reactionaries. He succeeds in persuading a majority of the
Proletarian Party that his policy is right, but an opposition
group within the party believes that he has turned traitor, and
they decide that he must be assassinated. Hoederer had recently
asked for a secretary to be found for him, so the opposition
group details Hugo to take the job, and to seize an opportunity
to kill Hoederer. Hugo, accordingly, moves with his wife,
Jessica, into the country house from which Hoederer operates.
Once they begin living in close contact with each other, Hugo
finds that he is greatly attracted to Hoederer, who treats him
with kindness and respect, and he begins to waver in his deter-

mination to kill him. Finally, one day when he catches Hoederer kissing his wife, he does kill him. He goes to prison, and while he is there, the party receives new orders from Moscow to adopt the very line that Hoederer had recommended. When Hugo comes out of prison, the party-line has been changed accordingly, and Hugo is told that he must forget his previous identity, and the fact that he shot Hoederer, otherwise he will be killed. He refuses to accept the conditions laid down by the party, and thus in effect chooses to die. And the play ends as he goes out of the door to meet his death.

Hugo is clearly something of a Hamletian character, even though he is built on a very much smaller scale. Hamlet is a university student; Hugo, we are told, has his doctorate. Hamlet hates his step-father, and Hugo hates his father. Hamlet meditates upon the idea of committing suicide, and Hugo, who hopes to get himself killed on a dangerous mission on behalf of the Proletarian Party, wants to put a bullet in his head when he finds that he is unable to carry out his assignment. Both Hamlet and Hugo have been given orders by *other people* to carry out a sort of judicial murder and both fail to act decisively and effectively in carrying out their tasks, but finally kill their man on the spur of the moment, in connection with a situation that really arises over a woman. The indecision of both Hamlet and Hugo is partly due to the typical inability of the intellectual to act. Hamlet makes this accusation against himself:

> Thus conscience does make cowards of us all,
> And thus the native hue of resolution
> Is sicklied o'er with the pale cast of thought.

(The two 'thus's' are infallible signs of the analytical approach of the thinking type.) And Hoederer tells Hugo that he has the same failing: 'One has to be born a killer, Take you, you think too much; you couldn't do it [i.e. assassinate someone].'[1] Instead of acting, Hugo and Hamlet talk. Louis describes Hugo as 'that damned chatterbox', and Hugo admits several times that he has too many ideas in his head and that he talks too much. Hamlet, in a famous passage, condemns himself for the same fault:

> This is most brave
> That I, the son of a dear father murder'd,
> Prompted to my revenge by heaven and hell,
> Must, like a whore, unpack my heart, with words,
> And fall a-cursing, like a very drab,
> A scullion!

The talkativeness of Hugo arouses an instinctive dislike in Hoederer's bodyguards, who are genuine proletarians:

> *Slick*: He uses words he finds in his head; he thinks with his head.
> *Hugo*: What do you want me to think with?
> *Slick*: When your belly's growling, pal, it's not with your head that you think.*

Sartre here, through Slick, seems to be groping towards the kind of distinction that T. S. Eliot makes between the thought of Donne, which was an experience that modified his sensibility, and the ruminative kind of thinking practised by Tennyson and Browning. Both Hugo and Hamlet as university students have been educated in the Western academic and intellectual tradition, which trains young men to achieve a high degree of development of their powers of verbalization and of rationalization. In Hugo, as in a great many young men in recent times, this intellectual development has been obtained at the expense of his other capacities. Sartre is at pains to point out that the growth of Hugo's powers as an abstract thinker has been accompanied by a stunting of his powers of sensation. He cannot use his hands; he does not notice what sort of clothes people are wearing or what they look like; and, we are given to understand, he would not even know the colour of his wife's eyes if she had not told him in so many *words*. We may say, then, that dissociation of the sensibility is much more advanced in Hugo than it is in Hamlet. It is, for example, wholly appropriate that in the underground movement Hugo has taken the name 'Raskolnikov'. The name, indeed, is significant in several ways. It provides

---

* In D. H. Lawrence's *Women in Love* Ursula says to Birkin, 'How can you have knowledge not in your head?'

evidence, if further evidence is needed, that Hugo's mind and imagination inhabit the world of books rather than the world of men.* Above all, it demonstrates that Hugo takes as his ideal the man who wishes to 'become a Napoleon', that is to say, the man who wishes to destroy the father and his society, and take power himself.

The most important clue to Hugo's character, in fact, lies in his desire to revolt against the father, and, since he is even less capable than Raskolnikov of actually becoming the father himself, in his need to find a 'good' father to submit to. Again we note the affinity with Hamlet, who defies the 'remorseless, treacherous, lecherous, kindless villain', his step-father, Claudius, but only in obedience to the commands of Hamlet *père*, the good father, with 'a station like the herald Mercury / New-lighted on a heaven-kissing hill'. Just as Hamlet is obsessed by Claudius, so Hugo is evidently obsessed by his father, who looms over him when he looks in a mirror:

> *Hugo*: I want to see if I look like my father. [a pause] With a moustache the resemblance would be striking.
> *Olga*: [shrugging her shoulders] What of it?
> *Hugo*: I don't like my father.
> *Olga*: We all know that.

It is of course primarily as a means of striking at his father and his father's class that Hugo joins the Proletarian Party. Since Communism is a revolutionary, rationalistic, and—on its theoretical side—idealistic system, it is very natural that it should appeal to the son who is rebelling against the father. It is agreed among psychologists that it is a characteristic of the rebellious son to attach himself to a left-wing political party, which is dedicated to the destruction of the society in which the father flourishes. J. C. Flügel, for example, in *Man, Morals and Society* distinguishes between

---

* Hugo interprets his experience in literary terms, as a sort of play-within-the play. 'I watched them search the place, and I told myself: "We're in a play." ' And he suggests at different times that the play is a comedy, a tragedy, and finally a farce.

. . . the 'right' or conservative attitude resulting from a predominance of obedience to, admiration of, and identification with the parental figure or its substitutes in the external world or as introjected in the super-ego; the 'left' or radical attitude resulting from a rebellion against this figure.[2]

Once Hugo has joined the Proletarian Party, the leaders with whom he is in contact become the new father—'To me, you are the party', he says to Louis and Olga—and it is in a spirit of blind obedience to them that he undertakes the assignment to kill Hoederer. At one point he tells his wife that Louis cannot be wrong, and when she asks him why not, he replies: 'Because. Because he's Louis.' (Both the style and the content of this reply reflect the unreasoning faith of the child in the infallibility of the father.) But since Hoederer is an exceptionally fine and strong man, who respects the dignity of Hugo as well as that of every other human-being, he too begins to be an image of the 'good' father for Hugo, and Hugo begins to have doubts about the rightness of killing him. (This doubt is the typical fate of the Hamletian figure who refuses to see that there is no way of evading one's own ultimate, existential responsibility. Hamlet himself also vacillates because he doubts the authority of the father that he has chosen to obey. 'The spirit that I have seen / May be the devil', Hamlet says to himself, thus acknowledging that no 'authority' can command unconditional, uncritical obedience.) But Hugo shirks his own solitary, adult responsibility, and tries to shift the burden onto his wife by asking her to advise him what to do. Finally, when he catches Hoederer kissing his wife and shoots him at last, it is really the old pattern of rebellion against the father who has let you down that determines his behaviour.

The ambiguous nature of Hugo's decision at the end of the play to die rather than forget the past and renounce his action in killing Hoederer has been noted by several critics—for example, by Philip Thody, who in his book, *Jean-Paul Sartre: A Literary and Political Study*, gives his chapter on *Dirty Hands* the title 'Tension and Ambiguity'—and, from the point of view of this study, one can agree that the play's ending finely expresses the essential ambiguity of the adolescent hero in rebellion against the father. Is Hugo dying nobly to assert the principle that the ends do not justify the means (that is, that expediency can never justify an alliance with the bourgeois and Fascist parties)? Or is he punishing himself for killing the father? Is he trying, in the fashion of one whose outlook on the world has been shaped by books, to give a conventional tragic form to events that are really without meaning? (Hoederer's last words had been 'What a goddamn waste!'; yet Hugo, just before he dies, declares romantically: 'A man like Hoederer doesn't die by accident.'[3]) Is this, finally, the free, responsible act of a man who has at last learnt to make his own decisions, to assume his own acts? It is certainly true that Hugo makes his decision entirely on his own responsibility, but it is also true that the decision to die is in some ways an easy and an irresponsible one, especially for the man who has no love of life. There is, I think, something of the same ambiguity in Hamlet's decision to ignore the intuition that tells him that his duel with Laertes will cost him his life. 'If it be now, 'tis not to come; if it be not to come, it will be now; if it be not now, yet it will come: the readiness is all.'

Here we touch upon a point that is of crucial importance. Hugo, who tells Olga 'I have no wish to live', is like Hamlet in his longing for death as an escape from the slings and arrows of outrageous fortune. In both of them, moreover, the impulse towards self-destruction is accompanied by a very pronounced aggressiveness directed towards others. This aspect of Hamlet's nature is sometimes glossed over, but it is manifestly and importantly there: 'Now could I drink hot blood, / And do such bitter business as the day / Would quake to look on.' The orthodox Freudian explanation of this aggressiveness would be that the over-repressed, Oedipal child imposes on others the unduly severe demands of the life-denying super-ego, and thus punishes other people because 'somebody' is causing it to punish itself. Sartre, it would seem, agrees with this view. When Hugo's wife Jessica sees some photographs of him as a child in starched collar and velvet jacket, she comments:

What a beautiful little man, what a well-behaved child! It's the well-behaved children, madame, that make the most formidable revolutionaries. They don't say a word, they don't hide under the table, they eat only one piece of chocolate at a time. But later on they make society pay dearly. Watch out for good boys.

In Hugo, aggression chiefly takes the form of a wish to kill himself and a lot of other people at the same time. At the beginning of the play, for example, after confessing to Louis that he cannot do anything with his hands, Hugo goes on to describe the kind of action that he can imagine himself performing:

> In Russia at the end of the last century there were characters who would place themselves in the path of a grand duke with bombs in their pockets. The bombs would go off, the grand duke would get blown up, and the guys too. That's the sort of thing I can do.

Then, in the scene where Hugo gets drunk, the same fantasy reappears in a much more explicit form:

> The whole point is to light the fuse. . . . The fuse, that's what it comes down to. Light the fuse. Then everybody is blown up and I along with them: no need for an alibi. Silence. Night. Unless the dead too play comedies.

The phrase 'no need for an alibi' is revealing: it suggests the resentment of the little boy who is constantly being required to justify his actions to a strict or over-solicitous parent. The last sentence, 'Unless the dead too play comedies', possesses the same ambivalence that we find in the famous soliloquy in which Hamlet longs to die (Hugo actually quotes the words 'To be or not to be' a few lines later), but then is put off by the thought of the dreams which may come to trouble the sleep of death; it reminds us that if the adolescent is fascinated by death, he is also afraid of it.

Hoederer has some illuminating things to say about Hugo. He points out that Hugo does not love men, but only his principles (that is, part of himself), and he perceives that Hugo's fidelity to his principles is essentially infantile:

> How you cling to your purity, young man! How afraid you are to soil your hands! All right, stay pure! What good will it do you? Why did you join us? Purity is an idea for a yogi or a monk. You intellectuals and bourgeois anarchists use it as a pretext for doing nothing. To do nothing, to remain motionless, wearing kid gloves. Well, I have dirty hands. Right up to the elbows. I've plunged them in filth and blood. But what do you hope? Do you think you can govern innocently?

Here, especially in the phrase 'Do you think you can govern innocently?' we have the authentic reply of the father to the rebellious son, who, from the vantage-point of his own innocence and inexperience, presumes to judge him. And words like *purity*, *soil*, *filth*, *dirty* (and perhaps *motionless*) seem to hint at the idea that Hugo's idealism and purity have the compulsive character that is to be met with in those whose toilet training has been too severe.

A few lines later in the conversation I have just quoted, the image of blowing up the world occurs in connection with Hugo for the third time. Hoederer says to him:

> You, I know you now, you are a destroyer. You detest men because you detest yourself. Your purity resembles death. The revolution that you dream of is not ours. You don't want to change the world, you want to blow it up.

Here we have a truth that is not restricted to Hugo or Hamlet or Raskolnikov. In his revolt against the father, who enjoys wealth, authority, prestige, the love of women, and the collaboration of the powers that be, the rebellious son is essentially a destructive force. His weakness and his impotent frustration make him seek to thwart others as he himself has been thwarted. Since he gets no pleasure out of life, and since there appears to be no solution for his problems except death, it is natural that the rebellious son should be preoccupied with death, and even that he should be willing to blow himself up, provided he destroys a number of other people at the same time. (Hamlet, of course, although without design, achieves precisely what Hugo dreams of doing.)

Up to this point I have concentrated my attention on the task of analysing the defects of Hugo, but it is important to bear in mind that the final truth about the rebellious son has to take account of his essential ambiguity. The nature of this ambiguity of the rebellious son I shall consider at length in the next chapter; in the meantime, it is worth noting that one of the most interesting points of resemblance between Hamlet and Hugo is that each evokes such diverse feelings. Nineteenth-century critics such as Coleridge and Hazlitt were inclined to identify themselves with Hamlet, and to love and pity him as a 'sweet prince' righteously condemning a wicked world; modern writers, for example Wilson Knight and L. C. Knights, how-ever, have laid more stress on Hamlet's immaturity, neuroticism and destructiveness. In the same way, audiences have tended to sympathize with Hugo, looking upon him as the hero of *Dirty Hands*, as the one person with principles in a world of Machiavel-lian schemers. On the other hand, as I have tried to suggest, it is perfectly possible to regard Hugo as an immature, narcissistic, destructive figure. Sartre himself, as a matter of fact, has protested against the romantic, sentimental interpretation of the play, and has stated that he himself did not like Hugo, and certainly did not intend him as his hero.[4] It seems, then, that one's verdict upon Hamlet or Hugo will largely depend on whether one's sympathies lie with the rebellious son or with the father.

Sartre, even though he does not like Hugo, is careful to maintain the dramatic tension and to avoid weighing the scales against him. It is, after all, proof of Hugo's generosity of spirit that, like Sartre himself, he identifies himself with the cause of those who are oppressed: 'I abandoned my family and my class the day I understood what oppression was.' (Sartre himself, needless to say, is a middle-class intellectual like Hugo; and that he dislikes Hugo is by no means a reason for thinking he is not *like* him!) Then, too, it is a redeeming point in Hugo that he did love Hoederer, even if he protests about it too much. 'But I loved him more than you could ever love him', he tells Olga. (One is inevitably, though perhaps irrelevantly, reminded of Hamlet in the graveyard-scene: 'I lov'd Ophelia: forty thousand brothers / Could not, with all their quantity of love, / Make up my sum.') Moreover, if Hugo chooses at the end of the play to follow the path of Raskolnikov and bring on himself condign punishment for his crime in killing the good father, can we view his quixotic and futile action entirely without compassion?

Hoederer, who tells Hugo 'I have contempt for no one', perhaps comes as close at one can hope to come to pronouncing the final judgement on Hugo, when he says to him, 'You're a kid for whom the passage to maturity is not easy, but you'll make a fair enough man if somebody helps you over the hump. If I escape their bombs, I'll keep you with me and help you.' What Hoederer says about Hugo could very well be applied to Hamlet or Raskolnikov. For some people the passage to maturity is easy: Hoederer, for example, tells Hugo, 'I went directly from childhood to maturity', and Hugo replies that youth is a 'bourgeois malady', adding laughingly, 'And many people die of it.' The rebellious son is often more than usually gifted, but his very gifts render him all the more liable to suffer from the bourgeois malady of youth; in the remaining chapters of Part Two (after a brief pause in Chapter Six to summarize and reflect upon our conclusions about the adolescent hero) we shall study some of the ways in which the adolescent hero tries to help himself over the hump of immaturity.

CHAPTER SIX

The Ambiguity of the Rebellious Son

> . . . what said the little boy that rode behind his father on
> horseback? . . . 'When you are dead, father', said he, 'I hope
> that I shall ride in the saddle.'
>
> JOHN WEBSTER, *The White Devil*

We have now considered four representative examples of the
adolescent hero, the young man in revolt against the father, and
the time has come to summarize our results and try to paint
a sort of composite portrait of the rebellious son. It would be
foolish to pretend that Hamlet, Raskolnikov, Gregers and Hugo
all possess all the characteristic traits of the adolescent hero, and
equally foolish to ignore or underestimate the enormous
differences between them, differences that are hardly to be
wondered at in works of literature produced by four different
nations over a period of four centuries. But, after all, there
are enormous differences between a tiger and the ordinary
Felis domestica, yet it is still profitable to define the characteristics of members of the cat family. In order to keep
repetition to a minimum, and at the same time bring into
view some of the wider implications of the concept of the
adolescent hero, I shall occasionally make use of fresh material
to illustrate the argument of this chapter; in particular, I
shall refer to Carlyle, whose spiritual autobiography *Sartor
Resartus* is one of the great classic studies of the adolescent
hero.

The adolescent hero is young; he is likely to be a university

student or a university graduate;* he talks too much. Raskolnikov, at the beginning of *Crime and Punishment*, says to himself:
'I'm talking too much. It's because I talk too much that I do
nothing.' And, later, explaining to Sonia how he came to do
the murder, he observes: 'And good Lord, how sick I was of
all that silly chatter. . . . I wanted to stop chattering.' We saw
in the last chapter that Hugo and Hamlet are both chatterboxes
who unpack their hearts with words. As Olga says to Hugo:
'You talk too much, Hugo. Always have. You have to talk to
make sure you're alive'. I suggested earlier that Sartre perhaps
resembles Hugo more than he does Hoederer, and it is noteworthy that the first volume of Sartre's autobiography, which
has the significant title *Les Mots*, shows him to have been
remarkable as a youth for 'feverish and incessant verbalizing',
as one reviewer puts it.[1]

The father, on the other hand, is not young; he is a man of
the world; he is silent or he talks only when necessary. 'Why
should the oak tree prove logically that it ought to grow, and
will grow?' Carlyle asks in his chapter on 'The English' in
Past and Present. This chapter is so relevant to our present
discussion that I will venture to quote an entire paragraph from
it:

> How one loves to see the burly figure of him, this thick-
> skinned, seemingly opaque, perhaps sulky, almost stupid
> Man of Practice, pitted against some light adroit Man of
> Theory, all equipt with clear logic, and able anywhere to
> give you Why for Wherefore! The adroit Man of Theory, so
> light of movement, clear of utterance, with his bow full-bent
> and quiver full of arrow-arguments,—surely he will strike
> down the game, transfix everywhere the heart of the matter;
> triumph everywhere, as he proves that he shall and must do?
> To your astonishment, it turns out oftenest No. The cloudy-
> browed, thick-soled, opaque Practicality, with no logic
> utterance, in silence mainly, with here and there a low grunt

* Carlyle's Teufelsdröckh, also a university man, reports that 'out
of England and Spain, ours was the worst of all hitherto discovered
Universities'.

or growl, has in him what transcends all logic-utterance: a Congruity with the Unuttered. The Speakable, which lies atop, as a superficial film, or outer skin, is his or is not his: but the Doable, which reaches down to the World's centre, you find him there!

The strong, silent Man of Practice, with his cloudy brows (suggestive of Jupiter and his thunder on Mt Olympus?), and the light, arrow-argumentative Man of Theory, with his bow bent waiting for an opportunity to strike, are surely archetypal forms —to some extent, even caricatures—of the father and the rebellious son.[2] They belong with David and Goliath, with Jack and the Giant up the Beanstalk! What is significant is that Carlyle's sympathies lie with the father, and since I shall be mainly concerned in this chapter with *Sartor Resartus*, it is as well to note at this point that Carlyle's admiration for the father (whom he himself perhaps resembles as little as Sartre does) becomes more intemperate as he grows older. In *Sartor Resartus*, published in 1833 when Carlyle was thirty-eight (that is approximately midway in point of age between the father and the son), there is a fruitful tension between the standpoint of the father and that of the son, but by the time of *Past and Present*, written when Carlyle was forty-eight, the balance has begun to incline strongly towards the father, and there is a certain loss of polarity, a less felicitous balance or reconciliation between the opposite views.*

The contrast in the paragraph just quoted between the thick-skinned, burly, opaque figure and the light, clear Man of Theory brings into view another interesting characteristic of the adolescent hero. As a man of letters and of words, he feels himself to be insubstantial and unreal. André Gide says of himself: '*Ce à quoi je parviens le plus difficilement à croire c'est à ma propre réalité.*'[3] Sartre's distinction between *Being* and

---

* For the sake of the record, we may note that Shakespeare was approximately thirty-six at the time of *Hamlet*, Sartre forty-three when *Dirty Hands* appeared, Dostoyevsky forty-four when he wrote *Crime and Punishment*, and Ibsen fifty-six when *The Wild Duck* first saw the light.

Nothingness can perhaps be considered, from our present point of view, as a philosophical rendering of the contrast between the substantial father and the insubstantial son.* 'Good God', Hugo cries in *Dirty Hands*, 'When you're going to kill a man, you should be able to feel as heavy as stone. There should be silence in my head. Silence!'⁴ A little while before that, he confesses, 'Nothing seems to me to be entirely real.' This, of course, has reference to himself and his own experience, for the father-figure has for the adolescent hero a character of rocklike reality. Thus Hugo says of Hoederer: 'Everything he touches seems real. He pours the coffee in the cups. I drink. I watch him drinking and I feel that the taste of the coffee in his mouth is real. [A pause] That it's the real flavour of coffee, real warmth, the real essence that is going to vanish.' Associated with the adolescent hero's sense of his own insubstantiality is his ineptitude when he quits the world of words where he is at home and moves into the 'real' world of the senses. I have already spoken at length of Hugo and Raskolnikov in connection with the dissociation of the senses in the last chapter and in Chapter Four. Although the theme of dissociation of the senses is not prominent in *The Wild Duck*, Ibsen does appear to suggest that Gregers is ill-at-ease in the physical world. After he moves into the room that is to let at the Ekdal's house, Gregers is determined to do everything for himself; however, when he tries to light the stove, he screws down the damper, thus filling the room with smoke; then he tries to set things right by emptying the water-jug into the stove, which makes 'the whole floor one filthy puddle', as Gina declares indignantly. It seems reasonable to suppose that part of the function of this incident is to hint that if Gregers had been more handy, more at home in the world, he might have felt less of a mission for reforming it. Hamlet, of course, besides being a student, is a Renaissance courtier and the son of a king, possessing 'The courtier's, soldier's, scholar's, eye, tongue, sword', so that what I am saying about the lack of physical dexterity of the adolescent hero does

---

* Sartre himself suggests in *Les Mots* that he perhaps wrote all his books to impress, retrospectively, the grandfather in whose charge he was brought up.

not apply to him. While it is true that another Renaissance figure, Don Quixote, was adversely affected by the reading of books, it was probably not until the eighteenth century that books really began to carry the day against experience. Rousseau reports in the *Confessions* that he was unfitted for life by the reading of novels. More relevant to our present discussion, perhaps, is the case of John Stuart Mill, who in the first chapter of his *Autobiography* writes as follows about his education:

> I could do no feats of skill or physical strength, and knew none of the ordinary bodily exercises . . . my amusements, which were mostly solitary, were in general, of a quiet, if not a bookish turn. . . . I consequently remained long, and in a less degree have always remained, inexpert in anything requiring manual dexterity . . .

A few lines later, Mill draws a contrast with his father that accords perfectly with the son-father pattern that I am discussing: 'My father was the extreme opposite in these particulars: his senses and mental faculties were always on the alert; he carried decision and energy of character in his whole manner and into every action of his life.'[5]

The man who is incompetent and imperceptive in handling things is likely to be equally imperceptive in relation to people, who are also objects of sensation. We saw earlier that Hugo did not know what colour his wife's eyes were, and we may assume that he had never looked attentively into those windows of the soul. However, if you do not look at people, you cannot learn much about them. The 'idealism' of the young man, then, sometimes merely reveals a want of realism, that is, an inability to perceive other people as they really are. Gregers, for example, unlike his father, totally misjudges Hialmar, and repudiates the accurate but unflattering portrait of him painted by Relling:

> *Gregers* [indignantly]: Is it Hialmar Ekdal you are talking about in this strain?
> *Relling*: Yes, with your permission; I am simply giving you an inside view of the idol you are grovelling before.

Gregers: I should hardly have thought I was quite stone blind.
Relling: Yes, you are—or not far from it.

The father, on the other hand, in order to cope with his enemies successfully and retain his power, needs to be shrewd, practical, alert and observant. Since it is evident that Claudius, Werle, Porfiry, and Hoederer answer to this description, I will not take up space establishing the point.

The adolescent hero's sense of his own unreality and his lack of ease in the physical world appear to be intimately connected with the fact that he is cut off from deep relationship with women. Hamlet and Gregers, we have seen, condemn the adulterous parent, and are both denied the enjoyment of woman. Hamlet loses his mother and then Ophelia to the enemy. Gregers I have already quoted as saying, 'So you are a married man, Hialmar! That is further than I shall ever get.' Teufelsdröckh, who loses his beloved Blumine to his best friend, is a bachelor who appears to have a puritanical attitude towards love.[6] Raskolnikov, who condemns the lechery of Svidrigailov and the plump gentleman in the park, is, during the crucial period prior to the murder, completely isolated from women as well as from men. Hugo, of course, is married, but even he cannot be said to have any genuine relationship with a woman, for it is made perfectly plain that his marriage to Jessica is unreal. Jessica, for example, tells Hoederer: 'I'm not a girl, but I'm not a woman either. I've lived in a dream, and when I was kissed I always wanted to laugh.' And Hugo says to Jessica: 'Your body is cold and you have no warmth to give me ... when I took you in my arms and asked you to be my wife, you weren't up to it.' And a few lines later, he says: 'Don't you know that our love was just a game?'

In marked contrast to the adolescent hero, the father-figure includes as part of his mastery over, and delight in, the created world, a lusty enjoyment of women. We see the sexual power of Claudius through the eyes of the Ghost and Hamlet. The Ghost describes feelingly the 'witchcraft' by which Claudius 'won to his shameful lust' the queen. Hamlet compares his uncle to a satyr, the satyr being of course a symbol of lasciviousness. Then, in the closet-scene, with a kind of fascinated revulsion, Hamlet imagines Claudius making love to his mother: 'Let the bloat king tempt you again to bed; Pinch wanton on your cheek; call you his mouse' and so on. As for Werle, we are given to understand that he had had affairs with a number of women before he seduced Gina, and, in fact, the play opens with a discussion of his sexual life, with one servant confiding to another: 'I've heard tell as he's been a lively customer in his day.' In *Dirty Hands* there is a brief but sufficiently convincing display of Hoederer's power and virility. 'Jessica, I'm not in the habit of refusing what is offered me', Hoederer says, 'and it's six months since I've touched a woman. You still have time to go, but in five minutes it will be too late.' Then while he is kissing Jessica (who, needless to say, does not laugh this time), Hugo enters the room and shoots him. In each case, then, the virginal son condemns the lecherous father.

The next point that I would like to make about the adolescent hero is that he is afraid, or at the least he is afraid of being afraid. No doubt, the rebellious son's ignorance, inexperience and weakness provide him with potent reasons for being, or suspecting himself of being, afraid of the puissant father. Hamlet, for example, more than once suggests that his delay in avenging his father's murder is due to cowardice:

> Am I a coward?
> Who calls me villain? breaks my pate across?
> Tweaks off my beard and blows it in my face?
>
> . . .
>
> Swounds, I should take it, for it cannot be
> But I am pigeon-liver'd, and lack gall
> To make oppression bitter . . .

Gregers in *The Wild Duck* admits to his father that he ought to have taken a stand against him fourteen or fifteen years earlier at the time of the trial and imprisonment of Old Ekdal, but he confesses: 'I did not dare to, I was so cowed and spiritless. I was mortally afraid of you—not only then, but long afterwards.' The subject of fear is not given any prominence in *Dirty*

Hands, though it does crop up in one brief conversational exchange:

Jessica: You're not a coward, my love.
Hugo: I'm not cowardly, but I'm not courageous either. Too many nerves.

Better evidence of Sartre's awareness of the problem of fear in relation to the adolescent hero can be found in *The Flies* or in *Nausea*. In *Nausea*, for example, the entire entry for one day in the diary of Antoine Roquentin consists solely of the following words: 'I must not be afraid.' In *Sartor Resartus* we learn that Teufelsdröckh lived in a constant state of causeless anxiety, very similar to the existentialist *Angst*: 'Having no hope, neither had I any definite fear, were it of Man or of Devil. . . . And yet, strangely enough, I lived in a continual, indefinite, pining fear; tremulous, pusillanimous, apprehensive of I knew not what.' The crisis of the book, which occurs in the chapter 'The Everlasting No', where Carlyle ascribes to Teufelsdröckh as he walks down the Rue Saint-Thomas de l'Enfer the experience that he himself had in Leith Walk, Edinburgh, consists essentially of an encounter with, and victory over, this fear:

'What *art* thou afraid of? Wherefore, like a coward, dost thou forever pip and whimper, and go cowering and trembling? Despicable biped! What is the sum-total of the worst that lies before thee? Death? Well, Death; and say the pangs of Tophet too, and all that the Devil and Man may, will or can do against thee! Hast thou not a heart; canst thou not suffer whatsoever it be; and as a Child of Freedom, though outcast, trample Tophet itself under thy feet, while it consumes thee? Let it come, then; I will meet it and defy it!' And as I so thought, there rushed like a stream of fire over my whole soul; and I shook base fear away from me forever.

And Teufelsdröckh, who describes this Protest, this Everlasting No, as 'the most important transaction in Life', goes on to remark that as a result of this Baphometic Fire-Baptism 'perhaps I directly thereupon began to be a Man.'

In *Crime and Punishment* the words 'terror', 'fear', 'afraid' (twice), 'coward', and 'mouse' all appear on the first page of the novel, and, since Raskolnikov goes on to commit a murder, it is hardly surprising that they continue to appear on almost every page. One quotation, which occurs just before the second interview between Raskolnikov and Porfiry, will suffice to illustrate the point:

> Thinking it over carefully now, and preparing himself for the new battle, he became aware suddenly that he was trembling all over, and he could not help feeling indignant with himself at the thought that he was trembling because he was afraid of that hateful Porfiry Petrovich. What he feared most of all was to meet that man again: he hated him savagely, immeasurably, and was even afraid that he might in one way or another give himself away in his hatred.

Another typical characteristic of the adolescent hero is his lack of a clearly defined place in society. The father-figure performs an important and magisterial role in the community: either he is a king like Claudius, the leader of a political party like Hoederer, an examining magistrate like Porfiry, or a person of importance in industry or commerce like Werle or Hugo's father, who is vice-president of the Tosk Coke Manufacturers. The adolescent hero, on the other hand, is an isolated person, an outsider who has not succeeded in finding for himself a satisfactory niche in society. Hamlet, as John Dover Wilson observes, was in the situation of a 'rightful heir to the throne who had been robbed of his inheritance by an uncle whom he himself describes as "a cut-purse of the empire" '[7]; on this view, the crime of Claudius robs Hamlet of a 'social, publicly acceptable *persona*', as it were.[8] Gregers is the son of a wealthy man, but he banishes himself to the obscurity of the works at Hoidal. His father says to him: 'What can be your object in remaining up at the works, year out and year in, drudging away like a common clerk, and not drawing a farthing more than the ordinary monthly wage? It is downright folly.' Raskolnikov is poverty-stricken and unemployed; Razumikhin describes him as 'a poor student, his resistance lowered by poverty and hypochondria . . . suspicious, ambitious, fully conscious of his own worth, a man who's been confined to his room for months without speaking to a single soul—in rags, and without a decent pair of boots' and, towards the end of the novel, Porfiry tells him, 'what you need more than anything else is life and *a definite position* and suitable air' (my italics). Hugo deliberately uproots himself as a protest against the injustice of the class system. But, as an intellectual, he never really gains acceptance in the Proletarian Party, and he remains uprooted. He says to Hoederer: 'I'm not built for living, I don't know what life is and I don't need to know. I'm in the way, I haven't found the right place for myself and I get on everyone's nerves. Nobody loves me, nobody trusts me.'* Teufelsdröckh, in the passage I quoted a few pages ago, calls himself an 'outcast', and Carlyle, who likens his hero to a modern Wandering Jew, suggests one important reason why he cannot find a place in society:

> Nevertheless, in these sick days, when the Born of Heaven first descries himself (about the age of twenty) in a world such as ours, richer than usual in two things, in Truths grown obsolete, and Trades grown obsolete,—what can the fool think but that it is all a Den of Lies, wherein whoso will not speak Lies and act Lies, must stand idle and despair?

It is interesting that Carlyle describes Teufelsdröckh as 'the Born of Heaven' and then in his very next breath calls him a 'fool', thus drawing attention to the profound ambiguity of the adolescent hero.

Another point of contrast between the son and the father is that the son is innocent and the father guilty. However, the innocence of the son is merely the fugitive and cloistered virtue of inexperience.[9] He is like an ugly woman who is virtuous because no one has ever made a proposition to her. Or, perhaps better still, he is like a political party in opposition that vigorously condemns the shortcomings of the government, and, having had no opportunity to touch pitch and be defiled itself, can point complacently to its own immaculate record. However, just as the opposition party seeks to attain power (even at the risk of

* Sartre, whose father died when he was two, has described himself as the False-Bastard.

being corrupted), so the adolescent hero wants to act. Raskolnikov, who reproaches himself for chattering too much, forces himself to act, and acquires dirty hands by murdering the old woman. Hamlet condemns his own procrastination and admires Fortinbras who plunges into action without thinking too precisely on the event. Hugo, as we saw, wants to prove himself as a man of action; Hoederer says to him, 'All intellectuals dream of doing something' and, again, 'What's this mania that you all have to play the assassin?' Sartre himself, whose 'feverish and incessant verbalizing' we have already noted, insists that 'there is no reality except in action', and that man is 'nothing else but the sum of his actions'.[10] Carlyle also praises the father as man-of-action, or Doer, as we saw in the passage from *Past and Present* quoted earlier in this chapter. In *Sartor Resartus*, Carlyle (or the fictitious editor), adapting Aristotle for his own purposes, admonishes Teufelsdröckh: 'Hadst thou not Greek enough to understand thus much: *The end of Man is an Action, and not a Thought*, though it were the noblest?'

The father, for his part, does not sing the praises of action, nor does he *desire* to act. 'Why should the oak tree prove logically that it ought to grow, and will grow?' The abstract desire to act (by which I mean the desire to be an actor, as opposed to the desire to perform some specific action) is a phenomenon of Self-Consciousness: it reflects the attitudinizing of the young man who wishes to impress other people, or to think well of himself. The father does not have the idea that he wants to act, but in the natural course of things, in order to safeguard his enjoyment of his empire and his women ('My crown, mine own ambition, and my queen', as Claudius puts it), he does act.

The adolescent hero is idealistic, yet at the same time he is a destroyer. I discussed the idealistic rectitudinitis of Hamlet and Gregers in the last chapter. Hugo has 'principles' (unlike Hoederer), and his idealism is apparent in the stand he takes against Hoederer over the question of the expediency of collaborating with the bourgeois. Even Raskolnikov, though he is in revolt against his own idealism and strives to imitate the 'realism' of the father, is actually an idealist. We see his idealism in his love for his landlady's daughter, the plain, dowerless girl, who was always ill and who had wanted to enter a nunnery. 'If she'd been lame or a hunchback I believe I'd have loved her better still', he tells his mother. We see his idealism, too, in his reaction to his sister's proposed marriage to Luzhin, in his relationship with Sonia, and in his attitude to Svidrigailov. When Raskolnikov expresses his disgust for the loathsome, depraved sensuality of Svidrigailov, the latter exclaims: '*You* talk to me about vice and aesthetics! *You* are a Schiller! *You* are an idealist!' Then, a little later in the same conversation, Svidrigailov says jeeringly: 'Look at the Schiller! A regular Schiller! So that's where virtue has taken up her abode!'

In spite of his idealism, or perhaps rather because of it, the adolescent hero constitutes a life-denying force for both himself and others. Disgusted and frustrated by an unideal world, he tends to be 'half in love with easeful death', because it seems to offer the only solution to his problems. Hamlet, Raskolnikov and Hugo all contemplate committing suicide, and Gregers hints darkly that he does not expect to live much longer. Carlyle was at one point on the verge of killing himself, and he has Teufelsdröckh say in *Sartor Resartus*: 'From suicide a certain aftershine (*Nachschein*) of Christianity withheld me.' Furthermore, the adolescent hero is a threat to others. Hamlet kills Polonius and then composes a witty epitaph for him. Hugo, as we saw, wants to blow the world up. Raskolnikov, in addition to experiencing paroxysms of fear, undergoes paroxysms of hatred. 'He hated the people he met in the street, he hated their faces, the way they walked, the way they moved. If any man had addressed him now, he would have spat on him or perhaps even bitten him.' Gregers embraces his destiny as a destructive force, as 'the thirteenth at table'. The adolescent hero, moreover, seems to be destructive in a peculiarly futile, haphazard and stupid way. Raskolnikov kills the old woman and Lisaveta, but, except for a trifling sum, neglects to take away the old woman's money. Hamlet needlessly kills Polonius. Gregers achieves nothing by awakening in Hedvig the 'fearless spirit of sacrifice'. Hoederer's death, finally, is the quintessence of futility and fortuitousness: Hoederer with his dying breath calls it a 'goddamn waste', and Hugo says later, 'It wasn't I who killed—it was chance.'

Once again, the father-figure is as different as possible. He is a realist, and the imperfections and intricacies of the real world provide an appropriate setting for him to exercise his talents in. When we think of the skilful diplomacy with which Claudius allays the fury of Laertes, or of the subtle psychology employed by Porfiry against Raskolnikov, or of the compassionate courage of Hoederer, who risks being shot by Hugo rather than humiliate him by having him disarmed, we can see that the ideal world desiderated by the rebellious son would seem to the resourceful father-figure to be lacking in ginger. The father delights in life and its difficulties. If he destroys, then, unlike the adolescent hero, he destroys deliberately and intelligently, and the destruction is a limited evil which serves, in part, a creative purpose— the prosperity of the father himself! Wilson Knight in his 1947 essay on *Hamlet*[11] cites with reference to Claudius a speech of Undershaft, the wealthy arms-manufacturer in Shaw's *Major Barbara*:

> I moralized and starved until one day I swore that I would be a full-fed free man at all costs; that nothing should stop me except a bullet, neither reason nor morals nor the lives of other men. I said, 'Thou shalt starve ere I starve'; and with that word I became free and great. I was a dangerous man until I had my will: now I am a useful, beneficent, kindly person. That is the history of most self-made millionaires, I fancy. When it is the history of every Englishman we shall have an England worth living in.

This description of the young man who is dangerous because he does not have his will (that is, because he is frustrated), who moralizes and starves, either literally or metaphorically, agrees well with the account of the adolescent hero developed in this chapter. So, too, does the portrait of the rich, free, well-fed, satisfied father. However, we should not be seduced by Undershaft's complacency into uncritical admiration of the father. If man lived by bread—or guns—alone, we could wish to see every adolescent hero converted as quickly as possible into a successful arms-manufacturer. But if the adolescent hero is 'Born of Heaven', as Carlyle says, perhaps he has other business in this world. At this point we touch upon what is really the heart of the matter, the ambiguous nature of the idealism of the adolescent hero, which will have to be considered more fully in the final section of this chapter.

Closely associated with the idealism of the adolescent hero is the question of his character as an abstract thinker. The phenomenon of abstract thinking in Raskolnikov, who 'murdered two people for the sake of a theory', we discussed in Chapter Four. Hugo is another abstract thinker; he tells Hoederer, 'There are too many ideas in my head', and it will be remembered that the bodyguard, Slick, complains that Hugo thinks with his head. That Hamlet is distempered with the pale cast of thought hardly needs to be demonstrated at this point; 'Frailty, thy name is woman!' he exclaims in his first soliloquy, not only reaching an inductive generalization apparently on the basis of a single instance, but also transposing his terms, as if to imply that the abstraction *frailty* is the paramount reality, and the function of the woman is merely to illustrate it.[12]

If we ask why the adolescent hero employs abstract reasoning, the obvious answer is that abstract thinking happens to be an important characteristic of post-Renaissance, Faustian man. The advantage of abstract thinking, as we have seen, is that it enables us to detach ourselves from, and achieve mastery over, our environment. For the adolescent hero, the father and his world constitute the environment, so to speak, and the chief virtue of abstract thinking is that it justifies the revolt against the father. Because the actual world is imperfect, subject to human frailty, subject to change and decay, it will inevitably be found wanting when it is weighed in the balance against an ideal, abstract, utopian perfection. The Renaissance and the Reformation, which as we saw earlier ushered in the era of abstract thinking, can in some respects be regarded as the archetypal form of the revolt against the father in the shape of the 'corrupt' church of Rome. (Note, incidentally, the ambiguity of this revolt, which has been seen as the 'new dawn' and as the 'second Fall of Man'!) Since the Renaissance we have been living in a revolutionary period in which abstract thinking has been employed time and again to justify a complete break with the past. The French Revolution is the most obvious case in point; in his attack upon the revolution in *Reflections on the Revolution in France*, Burke says that it is the spirit of 'metaphysical abstraction' which has led the 'airy metaphysicians' of France to despise their predecessors and their works, and to treat their country as *'carte blanche'* on which they may scribble whatever 'geometrical and arithmetical constitution' they please. It is interesting from our present point of view to find that Burke instinctively speaks of the state in imagery borrowed from the father and son relationship. A man, he says, 'should approach to the faults of the state as to the wounds of a father, with pious awe and trembling solicitude', and should 'look with horror on those children of their country who are prompt rashly to hack that aged parent in pieces'. As the rebellious son does not altogether share Burke's solicitude for the aged parent, it is not surprising that he grasps at abstract thinking as the weapon most ready to his hand in his struggle against the father.

One of the great disadvantages of the adolescent in his conflict with the father is his lack of experience. Here, too, abstract thinking recommends itself to him because it does not require experience; on the contrary, its method is to discard every element of the personal so that its results will have universal application, and it therefore discounts experience on the grounds of its subjectivity. In the realm of abstract thinking the young man is the equal of his seniors, and even has an advantage over them because of the freshness and flexibility of his mind. It is a fact that the majority of mathematical and scientific discoveries have been made by men under the age of thirty, whereas great works of art and imagination, which are the fruit of deep experience, are seldom created by the young man. Abstract thinking begets change, and change favours the young and adaptable. I may have a better command of the English language than my son, but if we went to live in a foreign country, he would learn its language more quickly than I. The young man, then, can hope to overcome the disability of his lack of experience by reliance upon abstract reasoning.

Burke, in his polemic against abstract thinking in the *Reflections*, says of the Revolutionists:

> They despise experience as the wisdom of unlettered men; and as for the rest, they have wrought under-ground a mine that will blow up at one grand explosion all examples of antiquity, all precedents, charters, and acts of parliament.

The destructiveness of the rebellious son ('Something they must destroy, or they seem to themselves to exist for no purpose', Burke had said in the previous paragraph) is here expressed in the very same image of blowing up the world that we met earlier in *Dirty Hands* in connection with Hugo.

Third, we must bear in mind that society trains its members to become abstract thinkers. In our society we require the young to devote ten or twelve of the most impressionable years of their lives to books, and the most gifted among them continue their studies for a much longer period. It is very natural, then, that the adolescent should work with the tools that have been given to him, and bring to bear a bookish spirit—in Veblen's term 'trained incapacity'—upon the problems he has to face. But what is the nature of this bookish spirit? Words themselves are abstract and general, and the symbols by which we represent them on the page are an abstraction of an abstraction. More important, works of literature are an abstraction of experience (literature is more philosophical than history, as Aristotle says!), and in several ways they present a distorted image of reality. It is obvious that some books pander to fantasy and wish-fulfilment, or that other books postulate a moral order in which the good are always rewarded and the bad punished, and so create inappropriate expectations about what life is like. Not so immediately obvious is the fact that even where there is a completely faithful representation of the truth of life, the compassionate understanding of the author redeems the brute facts, and renders them intelligible.* When we read of a good

* Cf. Malraux's *The Walnut Trees of Altenburg*: 'To me our art seems to be a rectification of the world, a means of escaping from man's estate'.[13] The same idea is implied in *The Tempest* when Prospero buries his staff and 'drowns' his book.

man suffering martyrdom in a noble cause, under the tutelage of the writer we are united in loving admiration for the martyr. But if in real life I myself suffer martyrdom in some cause, I am alone in my consciousness of the hatred of those who martyr me, and my own doubts as to whether the cause is really noble. When we read a book, what is best and noblest in the writer appeals to what is best and noblest in ourselves. This appeal to our liberty, to borrow Sartre's expression, is one of the chief glories of literature. But the young, exclusively nourished on this rich diet, having leave to feed on this fair mountain, confuse their ordinary selves with their best selves, and lose sight of what is base and ignoble in themselves and in mankind. The most characteristic note of the father is awareness of human fallibility and human frailty. 'History', says Burke, 'consists, for the greater part, of the miseries brought upon the world by pride, ambition, avarice, revenge, lust, sedition, hypocrisy, ungoverned zeal, and all the train of disorderly appetites. . . .' The father accepts the sinful nature of mankind as his premise, and cuts his coat according to that sombre cloth. The young, led astray, in part, like Don Quixote, by their reading (as well as by their hopes, their fears, and their desires) misjudge the material they have to work with, and think that they can build a world closer to the heart's desires, a 'geometrical and arithmetical constitution' (in Burke's phrase) possessing the beauty, the order, and the rationality of abstract perfection.*

To sum up, then, the adolescent hero employs abstract thinking not only because he is a child of his age, but also because abstract thinking justifies his revolt, because it compensates for his lack of experience, because it is what his training has equipped him to do, because it appeals to his idealism, and because it simplifies and renders orderly a world that is complex, frightening, and unintelligible.

I shall now turn, finally, to the topic towards which so much

* In the terminology of Chapter One, the son is a Rousseauistic idealist, while the father is closer to the Augustinian standpoint. Orestes argues in Sartre's *The Flies* that the father exploits the idea of Original Sin to persuade men to obey him.

E

of our discussion has been leading us: the ambiguity of the rebellious son. It should be said at the outset that ambiguity is one of the distinguishing marks of the young. On the one hand, it is agreed that generosity of spirit, devotion to truth, and love of perfection, are more commonly found in the young than in older people. This is Aristotle's view in the *Ethics*. John Stuart Mill, to cite another opinion, remarks in *Utilitarianism* that 'many who begin with youthful enthusiasm for everything noble, as they advance in years sink into indolence and selfishness'. On the other hand, the faults of the young are as remarkable as their virtues; intolerance of human frailty, ignorance of self and of others, insecurity disguised as arrogance, weakness translated into cruelty, these too are more common in the young than in their elders. Here, again, we are dealing with a generally admitted truth. Teufelsdröckh in *Sartor Resartus*, for example, says that he has heard it suggested that young men ought to be 'covered under barrels, or rendered otherwise invisible', from the age of nineteen to twenty-five, and he concedes that 'young gentlemen (*Bübchen*) do then attain their maximum of detestability. Such gawks (*Gecken*) are they; and foolish peacocks, and yet with such a vulturous hunger for self-indulgence; so obstinate, obstreperous, vain-glorious; in all senses, so froward and so forward.'

It is perhaps hardly necessary to argue in support of the truth of what has just been said; however, I do not want to let slip this opportunity to glance for a moment at Dorothea Brooke, the heroine of George Eliot's *Middlemarch*, who is a sort of female first-cousin of the adolescent hero.* Dorothea is a keen reader, who knows many passages of Pascal's *Pensées* and Jeremy Taylor by heart. She is in love with intensity and greatness, and thirsts for martyrdom. Her mind is 'theoretic', and like Don Quixote (the epigraph for Chapter Two is taken from *Don Quixote*), she views life in the light of her experience of literature. 'She felt sure that she would have accepted the judicious Hooker, if she had been born in time to save him from that wretched mistake he made in matrimony; or John Milton

---

* Celia refers to Dorothea's 'Hamlet-like raving'.

when his blindness had come on', we are told. Just as Gregers is clumsy and imperceptive (almost 'stone blind'), so Dorothea is short-sighted, both literally and metaphorically. Commenting on Dorothea's blindness to Sir James Chettam's feelings towards her, Celia says: '. . . you went on as you always do, never looking just where you are, and treading in the wrong place. You always see what nobody else sees; it is impossible to satisfy you; yet you never see what is quite plain. That's your way'. Her relationship with Casaubon, which is based upon George Eliot's own adolescent infatuation with a savant, is deeply ambiguous. Dorothea marries Casaubon not only because she is noble, and possesses 'a mind struggling towards an ideal life', but also because she is blind. ('I cannot help believing in glorious things in a blind sort of way', she says herself.) She misjudges Casaubon, who is by no means a Hooker or a Milton. She misjudges the nature and purpose of marriage: 'For this marriage to Casaubon is as good as going to a nunnery', says Mrs Cadwallader, whose judgement is not clouded by any struggle towards an ideal life. Finally, she fails to take account of the passional element in her own nature, which is revealed to us, for example, by her 'pagan sensous' delight in horse-riding, or by her 'powerful, feminine, maternal hands'. In Dorothea's mixture of nobility, idealism, rashness, obstinacy, ignorance of self and of others, then, we find some of the classical traits of ambiguous youth.

When we turn to the adolescent hero we find that, with the possible exception of Gregers who is accorded a hostile treatment by Ibsen, ambiguity is the characteristic quality of each of them. I discussed the ambiguity of Hamlet and Hugo in the last chapter. Teufelsdröckh, we have just seen, is both 'Born of Heaven' and a 'fool', who might with benefit have been covered under a barrel during his early manhood; in fact, his very name, Diogenes Teufelsdröckh (that is, Born-of Heaven Devil's Dung), is sufficient proof of the equivocalness of his origin and nature. Perhaps *Crime and Punishment* offers the most striking evidence in support of the point I am now making. At their final meeting, Porfiry says of Raskolnikov: 'He has committed a murder, but still regards himself as an honest man, he despises other people, he walks about like a martyr with a pale face.' One could hardly wish for a clearer statement of the ambiguity of the adolescent hero! What is more, we are made to feel that Raskolnikov's attitude to himself is, amazingly enough, a correct one. Porfiry, for example, although he speaks of the murder as a 'sombre affair, a modern one, a case characteristic of our time, when men's hearts have grown rank and foul', yet recognizes the exceptional worth of Raskolnikov. 'What is my opinion of you? Well, in my opinion, you're one of those men who, even if he were disembowelled, would stand and look at his torturers with a smile, provided he had found something to believe in or had found God. Well, find it and you will live.'

The ambiguity of the adolescent hero derives ultimately from the ambiguity of his idealism. Is the adolescent hero 'over-strained' (that is, neurotic), as Werle claims of Gregers, or is it society that is out of joint? Is the adolescent hero trying to restore a sick, corrupt society to sound health, or is he trying to impose on other people the over-exacting demands of his own idealistic rectitudinitis? Is it fear of life or a conscience as yet undefiled by familiarity with evil that inspires him? Is his protest a sign of a religious spirit ('If any man come to me, and hate not his father, and mother, and wife, and children, and brethren, and sisters, yea, and his own life also, he cannot be my disciple'), or is it the sour complaint of a conscience-ridden man who lacks the courage to grasp and enjoy the good things of this life? Although not untrue, it would be evasive to say that the answer to these questions varies from case to case; the real answer surely is that the adolescent hero is unable to judge the world because part of him belongs to the world. Those who are pure in heart, who have nothing within them to fear or disown, can perhaps view the world calmly and dispassionately. But the adolescent hero is *not* pure in heart, and his ambiguity lies precisely in the fact that his condemnation of the world is impure.

From another point of view, we may explain the ambiguity of the adolescent hero in terms of the complex motivation of the revolt against the father? We have seen that the father acts, and the young man wants to act; we have seen that the son, who condemns the destructiveness of the father, is himself a destroyer. Does the adolescent hero, then, wish to reform the father or to *become* the father? Is the idealism of the adolescent hero essentially a device for attacking the father? Is it virtue or envy that makes the son condemn the lechery of the father? Does the adolescent hero, finally, seek the kingdom of heaven, or some *Lebensraum* in the kingdom of this world enjoyed by the father? Here, again, the son who is pure in heart, like Alyosha in *The Brothers Karamazov*, can seek that which belongs to him without judging the father; but the adolescent hero is *not* pure, and in so far as he is partly the son of his father (the apple does not fall far from the tree!), his condemnation of the father is impure and ambiguous.

Finally, the adolescent hero is ambiguous just because he is a young man on the threshold of life. Only time will show whether the adolescent hero is going to emerge in the end as an ugly duckling or a beautiful swan. At their final meeting, Porfiry says to Raskolnikov: 'Don't worry, life will carry you out straight on the shore and put you on your feet. What shore? How do I know? I just believe that you've still many years of life before you.' In reminding ourselves that the adolescent hero is to some extent an unknown quantity because he is just at the beginning of his journey, we are in effect reverting to the point on which we ended the last chapter with Hugo confessing that youth is a bourgeois malady from which many people never recover. In the next chapter, then, we shall take up the problem of how the adolescent hero helps himself over the hump of immaturity.

CHAPTER SEVEN

The Reaction Against Idealism: 1. Spurious Acceptance

It is the act of an ill-instructed man to blame others for his own bad condition; it is the act of one who has begun to be instructed, to lay the blame on himself; and of one whose instruction is completed, neither to blame another, nor himself.

EPICTETUS[1]

We have seen that the adolescent hero judges the father and his society (and himself too) by the severe standards of the puritanical conscience. Idealistic rectitudinitis makes a good stick to beat the father with, but unfortunately its blows alight also on the head of the person who wields it. When the adolescent hero comes to recognize that in attacking the father in the name of conscience, he is merely exchanging one form of servitude for another, he is ready to commence the task of liberating himself from his subjection to a life-denying idealism. The forms that the reaction against idealism takes are varied; one of the most interesting and important of them I shall call spurious acceptance.

It will be convenient to begin our discussion of spurious acceptance with the comparatively simple and familiar variety known as cynicism. The idealistic youth thinks that the world is out of joint, and he undertakes to set it right; cynical acceptance concedes that the world is out of joint, but insists that there is nothing that can be done about it. If the idealistic youth tries to make a silk purse out of a sow's ear, the man at the stage of cynical acceptance holds that the world contains nothing but sows' ears. Cynical acceptance, in fact, adopts in all its rigour the Hamletian belief that evil is ineradicable and ubiquitous, and that there is no vantage ground of purity from which to set about the task of combating it. On this view, the problem is not that of reforming the world, but of coming to terms with it and reconciling oneself to it. After all, if the world is incurably evil, perhaps the evil father-figure is the appropriate person to govern it. In any event, the question of the regulation of this vile world is a matter of small importance, which is certainly no concern of the adolescent hero. 'What business is it of mine?' Raskolnikov asks himself bitterly, regretting his action in calling the policeman to protect the girl from the plump gentleman in the park. 'It's not your business', he says to the policeman, and the phrase, 'It's not our business', occurs again a few pages later in the dream of the mare. Thus where the idealist interferes too much—'Dost thou think, because thou art virtuous, there shall be no more cakes and ale?' Sir Toby Belch says to Malvolio—the man at the stage of cynical acceptance is content to leave ill alone and to mind his own business. The wise man asks much of himself, but little of others; the idealistic youth, being uncertain of himself, asks too much of others, demanding that they reflect back to him his own ideal aspirations; the man who has adopted the posture of cynical acceptance demands nothing of others, and nothing of himself.

From the standpoint of the psychic economy of the young man, the advantages of cynical acceptance are considerable. If he believes that he is virtuous but everyone else is base, he can enjoy the pleasure of looking down upon his fellow-men, like Gulliver looking down upon the diminutive Lilliputians. If (as is more probably the case) he is filled with self-disgust, cynical spurious acceptance assures him that everyone else is as bad as himself, or worse. Then, too, the belief that the world is incurably bad justifies him in doing nothing, and it is safe and agreeable to do nothing. To oppose the rich and powerful father-figure is dangerous, but if the adolescent hero does nothing, remaining motionless, wearing kid gloves (as Hoederer puts it in a passage of *Dirty Hands* quoted earlier), then he can keep his hands clean, and at the same time avoid the risk of suffering defeat at the hands of his more experienced opponent. Thus, in *The Trial*, when Joseph K. loses the woman to authority in the shape of the Examining Magistrate, he reflects that

> . . . he had received the defeat only because he had insisted on giving battle. While he stayed quietly at home and went about his ordinary vocations he remained superior to all these people and could kick any of them out of his path.[2]

(The word *kick* reveals the secret spite that accompanies this renunciation.) The man who runs away from the battle can partly assuage his grief and shame by embracing the cynical belief that there is no cause that is worth fighting for.

We saw in Chapter Five that in *The Wild Duck* Ibsen is attacking idealism. 'Don't use that foreign word: ideals', Relling says to Gregers. 'We have the excellent native word: lies.' We may now profitably observe that Relling himself appears to exhibit many of the characteristics of cynical spurious acceptance. He believes, for example, that most men are sick, and that they need to be supported by crutches in the shape of life-illusions (*livslögnen*, which means literally 'life-lies'). 'Rob the average man of his life-illusion', he declares, 'and you rob him of his happiness at the same stroke.' Accordingly, he shores up the drunkard, Molvik, by concocting for him the illusion that he is 'daemonic', and he supplies Hialmar with the illusion that he is working on a great invention. He himself loses the woman, Mrs Sörby, to the father-figure, Werle; instead of doing battle against the father, he consoles himself for the loss of Mrs Sörby by getting drunk, and makes shift to patch together the creatures that the father has ruined. The depth of his cynicism is revealed by his comment on Hialmar after the tragic death of Hedvig: 'Before a year is over, little Hedvig will be nothing to him but a pretty theme for declamation.' Gregers says that if Relling is right life is not worth living, and Relling replies that 'life would be quite tolerable' if it were not for the demands made upon 'our poverty' by the claims of the ideal. But is 'our poverty' so great that after a short time the deaths of our children mean nothing to us but an excuse for sentimental self-display? It would seem that in repudiating excessive idealism Relling falls into the opposite extreme of denying the ideal altogether, so that he sees man as a beast. What Relling stands for, then, is not a mature acceptance of inescapable fact, but a false and belittling conception of human nature.

How far Ibsen is identified with Relling's spurious acceptance it is difficult to say. Relling's exposition of his philosophy-of-life occupies a place of importance in the decisive fifth Act, and we are obviously expected to endorse his judgements upon Gregers, Hialmar and Molvik. Consequently, Relling must appear to be to some extent a spokesman for Ibsen, and in the theatre the audience will tend to find his views persuasive. Upon reflection, however, we observe that Relling himself is a failure—Mrs Sörby implies that he has 'frittered away all that was good in him'—and it is possible to argue that Ibsen leaves us the option of believing that Relling's cynical view of mankind is itself a self-consolatory 'life-illusion'. (The man who says that mankind is prone to delusions inevitably exposes himself to the *tu quoque* argument that he himself is deluded.) On the other hand, it could equally well be argued that the fact that Relling is 'sick' only serves to confirm the gloomy view of human nature that is communicated by the play, and particularly enforced by the dominant symbol of the crippled wild duck. It is true, of course, that the successful father-figure, Häkon Werle, is never identified with the crippled wild duck, and there is no suggestion that he feels any need to take refuge in the false security of life-illusions; but to admit so much hardly proves that Ibsen is very far removed from the standpoint of cynical acceptance.

A second variety of spurious acceptance, which may be called complaisant acceptance, has for its basic premise the idea that the world is not a bad place, and that one ought to be able to accommodate himself to it. If idealistic rectitudinitis tries to make a silk purse out of a sow's ear, and cynical acceptance denies the existence of silk purses, complaisant acceptance affirms that sows' ears are useful and agreeable in their way, and reminds us that it takes all sorts to make a world. The father-figure, after all, as we have just seen in the case of Werle, is rich, successful, esteemed and happy. From a strict ethical point of view he may seem to have achieved his success by questionable means, but this circumstance has not damaged his reputation, and it does not disturb his tranquil enjoyment of his happiness. If the tree may be known by its fruits, then surely the 'evil' father, who flourishes like the green bay-tree, must be good. 'Is it not passing brave to be a King, / And ride in triumph through Persepolis?' If woman and gold are the chief goods of this earthly existence, then the success of the father in obtaining them is deserving of admiration, and perhaps even of emulation.

Complaisant acceptance appears to constitute something of a volte-face, but it is really easily understood in the light of the adolescent hero's attitude towards himself. While the father is a happy and respected member of the community, the son is 'despised and rejected of men; a man of sorrows, and acquainted with grief': is it then astonishing that the son should falter? In the first place, he doubts his vocation. The passage of the *Divine Comedy* where Dante expresses misgivings about the journey that he alone—*io sol uno*—must undertake, saying that neither he nor others consider him to be worthy to follow in the footsteps of Aeneas and St Paul, constitutes a type of the diffidence and false humility that beset the hero. Second, in casting off vulgar errors, the adolescent falls into such egregious errors himself that he loses faith in his personal judgement.* If, for example, Dorothea Brooke in *Middlemarch* had deferred to the commonsensical views of people like her sister and Sir James Chettam, she would not have made the mistake of marrying Casaubon.[3] After receiving a few hard knocks, the son hesitates to trade 'on his own private stock of reason' (as Burke says), and is instead tempted to avail himself of 'the general bank and capital of nations'. Third, the adolescent hero is suspicious of his own motives, and with good reason. We have frequently had occasion to note that the motivation of the revolt against the father is impure and ambiguous, and that as the adolescent hero reaches an advanced level of Self-Consciousness,

---

* The very word *egregious* warns of the danger of straying from the herd.

he becomes more profoundly aware of this impurity and ambiguity. Knowing his heart, and knowing that he is evil, how dare he pass judgement on the presumptive evil of the father? Fourth, and perhaps most important of all, the reaction against idealism causes the adolescent hero to doubt his own ethical values. It is as if in a boxing-match the father hits below the belt, and the son refuses to copy him, but at the same time feels that the father's contempt for the rules of the game is more in accordance with reality than his own moral fastidiousness. To hit below the belt is a useful and intelligible action, whereas to obey the rules is not, and it seems to the adolescent hero that there is a kind of joyous self-affirmation in the father's criminality which contrasts strongly with his own anxious scrupulosity. Yet if I am filled with anger because a man maltreats his horse, why should I assume that I ought to 'accept' his brutality, but not my anger?[4] The fact is, that in reaction against his phase of idealistic rectitudinitis the young man tends to assume that brutality is more authentic than compassion, and thus is led to betray that which is genuinely moral in his nature. When he is able to see that his moral scrupulousness (whatever its inconveniences) is as natural and valid a form of self-affirmation as the father's criminality, the adolescent hero can be said to be moving in the direction of genuine acceptance. Thus, to paraphrase the quotation from Epictetus that stands at the head of this chapter, idealistic rectitudinitis blames others, the man at the stage of complaisant acceptance if he blames anyone, blames himself, and genuine acceptance blames nobody.

Since the religious and philosophical variety of spurious acceptance is largely inspired by the attempt to imitate or to appropriate the virtue of genuine acceptance, it is necessary at this point to embark upon a brief discussion of genuine acceptance. We are told by the great masters of the human spirit that for those who have reached a certain level of development, everything, absolutely everything, in the created world is good. St Augustine, for example, says that some things appear to be 'evil' because they do not harmonize with other things, but yet they do harmonize with still other things, and in themselves they are good; all the works of God are good, and 'there is no sanity in that man whom anything in creation displeases'. From the standpoint of self, the man who injures me is 'evil', but from the universal standpoint of the wise man or the saint, both friends and enemies are seen to be, at bottom, good and worthy of love. 'Love your enemies, bless them that curse you, do good to them that hate you.' Thus, I suggest, we recognize the authentic note of genuine acceptance in the words of St Lawrence as he was being burned at the stake: 'Turn me over, brothers, I am done sufficiently on this side', or perhaps in Spencer's painting of Christ looking at the scorpion. But, it may be asked, how is it possible to love a murderer? Considered in terms of a scale of excellence, a murderer is 'bad' in comparison to a saint, just as almost all men are 'bad' in relation to ideal goodness; but considered absolutely and in himself, rather than comparatively, then, as the words just quoted from St Augustine imply, the murderer is good and lovely. He who seeks the good (or God), like Hamlet rejects everything in the created world, saying 'This is not it', and 'That is not it'. He who has found the good, accepts everything in the created world, because he recognizes in everything a partial embodiment of the good.

In order to be able to love the murderer without condoning murder, genuine acceptance must distinguish between the man and his action, between the real being and the self, between the essential reality of the man and the accidental, temporary manifestation. 'Love the man, hate the condition', Blake says. 'Love the man, hate the sin that is in the man', says the Christian mystic. This distinction rests in part upon the intuition that all things are ineffably bound together, and that the higher things are contained in embryo in the lower, and the lower in the higher. In *The Tempest* Prospero says of Caliban, 'This thing of darkness I / Acknowledge mine', thereby expressing the truth that every Prospero has a Caliban latent within him, and every Caliban a Prospero. In recognizing 'the *all in each* of human nature' (to borrow a phrase from *Biographia Literaria*), genuine acceptance does not confuse Calibans with Prosperos (for example, by making a Caliban head of state), but it sees that it is sometimes necessary to appeal to the latent (or recessive) Prospero in another man, even at the risk of being crucified by the dominant Caliban in that man. Thus where idealistic rectitudinitis makes the impossible demand that lower things shall exhibit the characteristics of higher things, and cynical and complaisant acceptance too readily accept the lower things at their face value, genuine acceptance sees with clarity the limitations of the material it has to work with, but yet it embraces a faith in—or rather an insight into—the unseen or potential in every man. As Goethe well says: 'When we accept men simply as they are, we make them worse than they are. When we treat them as if they already were what they should be, we make them what they are capable of becoming.'[5]

Genuine acceptance is an idea of such sublimity that it possesses to an extraordinary degree the power that we have seen to be characteristic of all ideals, namely it either inspires men to achieve an authentic self-development that brings them into inner conformity with the ideal, or else it leads them to deceive themselves or others with a sham exhibition of the outward trappings of the ideal. At one end of the scale we have the man who pretends to himself or others that he loves his enemy, so that at one stroke he gains a reputation for sanctity and avoids the danger of fighting his enemy. Near the other end of the scale, we have the man who is so enamoured of the beauty and justice of the idea of genuine acceptance that he persuades himself that he loves his enemy, and by dint of perseverance and self-discipline arrives finally at the point where he truly loves him. It is impossible to determine with certainty whether in another person acceptance is genuine or spurious; one can only try to arrive at a probable conclusion by examining the external evidence. Thus, to take a specific example, in his essay, 'A Dissenting Opinion on Kafka', Edmund Wilson is essentially arguing that Kafka is guilty of spurious acceptance. He writes:

'One must not cheat anybody', says Kafka, in an aphorism which has been much applauded, 'not even the world of its triumph.' But what are we writers here for if it is not to cheat the world of its triumph? In Kafka's case, it was he who was cheated and never lived to get his own back. What he has left us is the half-expressed gasp of a self-doubting soul trampled under. I do not see how one can possibly take him for either a great artist or a moral guide.[6]

Undoubtedly, most of us like to get our own back, and most writers seek to cheat the world of its triumph, adopting Voltaire's motto, '*Écrasez l' infâme*'; but then most of us are not called to the study of perfection, and few writers are to be numbered among the meek who shall inherit the earth. For one man who loves his enemies, there are ten who pretend to love them (and ten thousand who frankly hate them). Thus both our experience and our infirmities dispose us to think that the man who does not try to get his own back is a coward, and this tendency is all the more natural since if spurious acceptance is often weakness masquerading as strength, genuine acceptance is sometimes strength which in its humility mistakes itself for weakness. Is the case, then, that a splendidly pugnacious writer like Edmund Wilson cannot enter imaginatively into the idea of genuine acceptance, or is Kafka cheating himself and us with the specious glamour of spurious acceptance? Only profound experience coupled with literary tact and discrimination could hope to approach even a probable answer to this question.

What Edmund Wilson says about Kafka as a self-doubting, defeated man is really a variation upon the common reproach levelled against Christianity (the principal source of the idea of acceptance in our cultural tradition) that it encourages the servile ideals of humility, self-abnegation, and non-violence, as Machiavelli says, or that it produces 'a low, abject, servile type of character', as Mill says in *On Liberty*. It must be admitted that where the revolt against the father often has revolutionary political implications, the religious and philosophical doctrine of acceptance appears to have the opposite tendency. Thus, for example, the saying, 'The powers that be are ordained of God, he therefore who resisteth those powers resisteth God', seems to command unconditional submission to an evil government. It is of course common knowledge that there are Christian martyrs (such as Dietrich Bonhoeffer) who have resisted the powers that be, and it is probable that the man who is authentic-

ally at the level of genuine acceptance either obeys the 'evil'
civil authority, finding in this obedience a perfect discipline of
the will (and hence a means of salvation), or he resists that
authority, saying in effect: 'The powers that be may be ordained
of God, but my resistance to the powers that be is ordained of
God also.' The man at the level of spurious acceptance, being
incapable of this profound self-acceptance, obeys the letter of
Christ's message, and as a consequence it is indeed true that in
the political sphere spurious acceptance tends to issue in a
doctrine of quietism. An illuminating illustration of this phenomenon is provided by a brilliant essay by Sir Isaiah Berlin on
the Russian critic, Vissarion Grigorievich Belinsky.[7] Belinsky,
like most young Russian intellectuals of his time, began as a
bitter opponent of the autocratic police-state of Nicholas I.
In fact, for most of his life—he died of consumption at the age
of thirty-eight—Belinsky was a leader of the radicals, an
individualist, a Westernizer, an advocate of education, science
and technological progress, and an enemy of religion, mysticism,
ignorance and obscurantism. In a word, he dedicated his life
to a struggle against the 'evil' father—'It is a great pity that
Belinsky is dead:' the chief of police said of him, 'otherwise we
should have had the pleasure of rotting him in one of our
fortresses'—and he appears to have possessed more than a
trace of the idealistic rectitudinitis that is characteristic of the
rebellious son. Sir Isaiah Berlin says of him:

> If ever there lived a man of rigorous, indeed over-rigorous,
> and narrow principle, dominated all his life by a remorseless,
> never-ceasing, fanatical passion for the truth, unable to
> compromise or adapt himself, even for a short time and
> superficially, to anything which he did not wholly and
> utterly believe, it was Belinsky.

Nevertheless, in 1839, when he was about thirty, Belinsky,
after a painful emotional crisis, came under the spell of a
version of Hegelianism which led him to disavow completely
his radical faith. The quietist doctrine that Belinsky now
embraced, Sir Isaiah Berlin describes thus:

> What is, is, because it must be. To understand it, is to

understand the beauty and harmony of everything as it falls
into its own appointed time and place in accordance with
intelligible and necessary laws. Everything has its place in
the vast scheme of nature unrolling its pattern like a great
carpet of history. To criticise is only to show that you are not
adjusted to reality and that you do not sufficiently understand
it. . . . His (or Bakunin's) interpretation of Hegel's doctrine
had convinced him that contemplation and understanding
was an attitude spiritually superior to that of active fighting,
consequently he threw himself into 'acceptance of reality'
with the same frenzy of passion as that with which only two
years later he was to attack the quietists and demand active
resistance to Nicholas I's abominations.

I have quoted this passage at length because it provides such an
admirable summary of the quietist position; note particularly
the idea that contemplation is 'an attitude spiritually superior'
to active fighting, which brings out very clearly the spiritual
acquisitiveness that is at the root of the philosophical and
religious form of spurious acceptance.

Belinsky's defection was a severe blow to the progressive
cause, but in spite of the distress that he was causing his friends,
Belinsky adhered for a year or more to the quietist doctrine.
Then, after another period of acute inner conflict, he repudiated
his Hegelian phase, confessing that his advocacy of submission
to an unjust regime was a hideous error. In a letter about this
time, he wrote:

I abominate my contemptible desire to reconcile myself with
a contemptible reality. . . . I will not make my peace or adjust
myself to vile realities. . . . I am tormented by the thought of
the pleasures I have let go because of the contemptible
idealism and feebleness of my character. God knows what vile,
revolting nonsense I have talked in print. . . . What horrible
zigzags my path towards truth seems to involve.

For the rest of his life Belinsky remained faithful to his role as a
crusading reformer and radical.

This brief sketch of Belinsky's bout of spurious acceptance

serves as a fitting conclusion to these general remarks. One final observation, however, may be made. In the letter I have just quoted Belinsky is understandably severe in his condemnation of his year of aberration, but from our detached standpoint we can clearly see that spurious acceptance does perform a useful function in the evolution of the adolescent hero. Who can doubt, for example, that Belinsky himself was a better writer and a more effective force for good after he had been through the stage of spurious acceptance? The revolt against the father, we have seen, is impure in so far as it is compounded of superficial, book-learned, rationalistic ideas, jealousy of the father, spiritual acquisitiveness, together with genuine idealism. Spurious acceptance brings the young man as close as he can come to an adjustment to the world of the father; if he adjusts successfully, then he has arrived at ordinary conformistic acceptance, and so passes outside the scope of this study; if, on the other hand, he finally discovers that he is incapable of accommodating himself to the values of the 'evil' father, then it is at least probable that this repudiation comes, not from books, but from the authentic reality of his own being. Thus, like a period of drought, spurious acceptance makes a superficial idealism wither for lack of roots, but forces the man of genuine idealism to go down into his own depths in search of a more indubitable source of nourishment.

In order to illustrate the argument of the first half of this chapter, I propose now to examine E. M. Forster's novel, *Howards End*, which was first published in 1910. The date is not without interest, for it is above all as a reaction against the excessive idealism of the Victorians that spurious acceptance is historically significant. Conrad's *Under Western Eyes*, for example, published in 1911, is another distinguished study in this field.[8]

Howards End, like *Pride and Prejudice* or *Women in Love*, is a story about two sisters who are looking for husbands. (The convention lends itself to the purposes of a writer who wishes to scrutinize the quality of the men in his society.) Margaret and Helen Schlegel have a good deal in common with the adolescent hero. They are young; they talk too much ('We lead the lives of gibbering monkeys', Margaret says[9]), and they inhabit the world of ideas: they are musical, literary, and artistic. Like Gregers and Hamlet they are attached to the values of a dead parent, for their father, who was an idealist and a dreamer, the countryman of Hegel and Kant, represents a moral touchstone for them. (When Margaret lets her sister down, she thinks repentantly, 'What would our father have thought of me?') The fact that they are women protects them to some extent from the adolescent hero's painful sense of his own unreality and inadequacy (though at one critical point Margaret is invaded by a 'strong, if erroneous, conviction of her own futility'); nevertheless, they are not immune from the intellectual's tendency to feel that ordinary worldly life is more real than his life of cultured ease: 'This outer life', Margaret says, 'though obviously horrid, often seems the real one—there's grit in it. It does breed character.' Since they have independent means, and do not work, they have little contact with this outer life: if not exactly *étrangers*, they are at least slightly *de trop*. Mrs Wilcox thinks them young and inexperienced, and it can certainly be said that these virginal sisters are barren of deep experience with the opposite sex; Margaret almost screams when Mr Wilcox kisses her for the first time, and after Helen and Paul kiss, Forster tells us (somewhat improbably), 'her life was to bring nothing more intense than the embrace of this boy who played no part in it'. Of course, there are differences between the sisters, which we shall have to consider in a moment, but for the present my purpose is to stress the broad resemblance between the two of them and the adolescent hero.

Henry Wilcox possesses many of the attributes of the father. A man in his fifties, he is 'old enough to be their father', as Margaret in fact observes. Being rich—almost a millionaire— and consequently powerful, he has the self-confidence and optimism that go with worldly success, and the assurance that this is 'a very pleasant world'. (The word 'world', incidentally, crops up very frequently in connection with spurious acceptance: Mr Wilcox calls himself a 'man of the world', and Leonard Bast thinks, correctly, that 'Mr Wilcox was king of this world'.)

Forster describes the 'rather box-like construction of [Charles Wilcox's] forehead', and we are told later that the father's forehead is like the son's. (Here, as elsewhere, the Wilcoxes remind one of Carlyle's 'thick-skinned', 'cloudy-browed', thick-soled' Man of Practice.) Mr Wilcox's adulterous relationship with Jacky Bast is evidence of the lasciviousness that we have seen to be characteristic of the father-figure; Margaret accuses him of being 'A man who ruins a woman for his pleasure, and casts her off to ruin other men', (which is similar to what Gregers says to Werle about 'this woman that you palmed off upon Hialmar Ekdal'). The father loves to look in the bright eyes of danger, and it is noteworthy that Henry Wilcox talks glibly about 'the battle of life' and looks upon himself as a warrior: 'Man is for war, woman for the recreation of the warrior', he thinks. Margaret Schlegel, who is 'keen to derive the modern capitalist from the warriors and hunters of the past', tries to see the Wilcox house in London as 'an ancient guest-hall, where the lord sat at meat among his thanes', but when she hears Miss Avery say that the first Mrs Wilcox ought to have married a 'real soldier', she recognizes the sentimental inadequacy of her own attitude. But by this time, of course, Margaret has married the father who is king of this world.

The episode of Helen's brief romance with Paul Wilcox at the start of *Howards End* establishes the theme of the novel. On a week-end visit to Howards End, Helen is impressed by the energy, strength and competence of the Wilcoxes. Mr Wilcox tells her, with all the authority of his wealth and experience backing up the assertion, that equality is nonsense, and she realizes that she had 'just picked up the notion that equality is good from some book' or from her sister. (The idealistic youth's ideas, which have been acquired but not earned, are easily dislodged.) When Charles Wilcox says that servants do not understand politeness, she does not give the typical Schlegel answer ('If they don't understand it, I do'), but instead vows to be less polite to servants in the future. In effect, the Wilcoxes convince her that things are as they are because they must be so, for the good reason that the existing order of things is perfectly adapted to reality, so that any attempt to alter the *status quo* is mere starry-eyed idealism and quixotism. (Mr Wilcox in fact applies the adjective 'quixotic' to the sisters, and he says condescendingly to Margaret, 'Any new Utopias lately?') Again, while the Wilcoxes are many, she is one and, in retrospect, she sees that her infatuation with Paul was due to 'loneliness'. They are the 'very happiest, jolliest family', and she really falls in love with the entire family: 'To be all day with them in the open air, to sleep at night under their roof, had seemed the supreme joy of life, and had led to that abandonment of personality that is a possible prelude to love.' Falling in love with Paul enables her to find solace and repose upon the strong certainties of these limited men.

After the disaster with Paul, Helen reacts violently against her phase of spurious acceptance, and commits herself with fanatical zeal to the cause of the ideal and the absolute. 'Helen is too relentless', Margaret says. 'One can't deal in her high-handed manner with the world.' Helen champions the cause of the unfortunate Basts, and drags them down to Shropshire to confront the 'evil' father, Mr Wilcox, crying hysterically, 'I'll stand injustice no longer.' Her intervention (like Gregers's intervention in the Ekdal family) only makes matters worse, and in the aftermath of her failure she and Leonard Bast (who seems 'not a man but a cause') make love:

> Helen loved the absolute. Leonard had been ruined absolutely, and had appeared to her as a man apart, isolated from the world . . . she loved him absolutely, perhaps for half an hour.

Helen becomes pregnant and passes through a bitter purgation of sorrow and solitude, which cures her of idealistic rectitudinitis: 'I am less enthusiastic about justice now', she says, and confesses that she had been 'revolting by theory'. Finally, at the end of the novel, she finds peace and a new life at Howards End with her sister and her baby.

Helen Schlegel's melodramatic career provides a kind of crude analogue of the subtly nuanced development of her elder sister. In Helen spurious acceptance is above all a phenomenon of immaturity, in Margaret of maturity. Margaret sees that in this material world, the ideal cannot be entirely detached from the material, and she frankly recognizes the importance of money. For example, discussing Leonard Bast at a dinner-party, she says: 'Independent thoughts are in nine cases out of ten the result of independent means.' When someone asks what it would profit Mr Bast to gain the whole world and lose his soul, she replies: 'Nothing, but he would not gain his soul until he had gained a little of the world.' The grasp of reality and good sense that permit Margaret to see that her money is the basis of her spiritual independence, also enable her to set a proper value upon those who are engaged in the activity of making money. 'More and more do I refuse to draw my income and sneer at those who guarantee it.' Thus we are led to the Wilcoxes.

The Wilcoxes are ordinary businessmen—Henry Wilcox is a 'good average Englishman'—and they are hard-working, energetic, able both to command and obey, neat, polite and competent. Yet on page after page, with consummate skill and deadly accuracy Forster exhibits their thoughts, their words, and their deeds, in a way that shows them to be gross and obtuse where feeling is concerned, and, to this extent, evil. One example will sufficiently establish the point. Here is Forster's account of Mr Wilcox's reaction to the idea that Helen is perhaps mad, at any rate very ill:

Henry began to grow serious. Ill-health was to him something perfectly definite. Generally well himself, he could not realize that we sink to it by slow gradations. The sick had no rights; they were outside the pale; one could lie to them remorselessly. When his first wife was seized, he had promised to take her down into Hertfordshire, but meanwhile arranged with a nursing-home instead. Helen, too, was ill. And the plan that he sketched out for her capture, clever and well-meaning as it was, drew its ethics from the wolf-pack.

The apparently casual mention of the fact that the first Mrs Wilcox, who wished to end her days at her beloved Howards

End, was shunted off into a cold, impersonal nursing-home to die, is singularly effective.*

Margaret Schlegel is not blind to the deficiencies of the Wilcoxes, but she appreciates their sterling qualities, too. 'If Wilcoxes hadn't worked and died in England for thousands of years, you and I couldn't sit here without having our throats cut', she says. 'There would be no trains, no ships to carry us literary people about in, no fields even.' In a sense, the Wilcoxes stand for action, and the Schlegels for thought. Plato says that if a man devotes himself exclusively to gymnastics, he becomes a brute, and if he devotes himself exclusively to music, he becomes effeminate. The Wilcoxes, who are 'keen on all games', represent one extreme, and Tibby, who is fond of music and 'profoundly versed in counterpoint', the other. All the Schlegels are impractical, and Margaret is stimulated and impressed by people who have got their hands on all the ropes, who excel where she is deficient:

> How dare Schlegels despise Wilcoxes, when it takes all sorts to make a world?
> 'Don't brood too much', she wrote to Helen, 'on the superiority of the unseen to the seen. It's true, but to brood on it is medieval. Our business is not to contrast the two, but to reconcile them.'

The truism that it takes all sorts to make a world, and the word 'reconcile' are tell-tale indications of the presence of complaisant acceptance. (Cf. Belinsky's declaration: 'I abominate my contemptible desire to reconcile myself with a contemptible reality. . . . I will not make my peace or adjust myself to vile realities.')

Up to this point, one may suppose, the reader is comparatively sympathetic towards the positions that Margaret has adopted. Even when she says, 'It certainly is a funny world, but so long as men like my husband govern it, I think it'll never be

---

* 'Can what they call civilization be right', Mrs Wilcox had asked, 'if people mayn't die in the room where they were born?' The word *home*, of which 'nursing-home' is a travesty, is important in the novel; Forster, in fact, has suggested whimsically that the subject of *Howards End* is 'a hunt for a home'.

a bad one—never really bad', we are willing to concede the
point (even if we subjoin the comment of Miss Avery, 'No,
better'n nothing'). Nevertheless, the question insistently presents itself: By all means respect the merits of the Wilcoxes,
but why *marry* one of them? Charles Wilcox, for example, a
man of approximately the same calibre as his father, marries
'a rubbishy little creature', and is perfectly content with her.
Why, then, should Mr Wilcox marry a superior woman like
Margaret Schlegel? In his essay on Forster, Dr Leavis discusses
this question with great cogency:

> The Wilcoxes have built the Empire,: they represent the
> 'short-haired executive type'—obtuse, egotistic, unscrupu-
> lous, cowards spiritually, self-deceiving, successful. They are
> shown—shown up, one might say—as having hardly a
> redeeming characteristic, except that they are successful. Yet
> Margaret, the elder of the Schlegel sisters and the more
> mature intelligence, marries Mr Wilcox, the head of the clan;
> does it coolly with open eyes, and we are meant to sympa-
> thize and approve.[10]

Dr Leavis argues that the marriage is not 'credible or acceptable', and he finds Forster guilty of 'a kind of *trahison des clercs*'.
  This argument is a strong one, forcefully presented, yet if I
cannot demolish it, I can at least hope to make a small dent in it!
First, then, we must remember that *Howards End* is above all
concerned with acceptance, with the desire to reconcile oneself
to what the idealist would regard as not 'acceptable'. The
tendency of the mainstream of literature from Jane Austen
onwards is to teach us to discriminate between higher and lower
things, and to ridicule and despise those lower things (such
as Mr Collins or Wickham in *Pride and Prejudice*). But
the religious tradition of acceptance says, 'Judge not, that ye
be not judged', and 'Whosoever shall say, Thou fool, shall
be in danger of hell fire'. The publicans love their friends, and
the idealist loves the good, the true and the beautiful, but
religious acceptance tells us to love our enemies. Forster tells
us that Margaret's allegiance is divided between her sister's
value of Truth (or men as they ought to be) and the opposing

value of Love (or men as they are), but 'on the whole she sided with men as they are'. Thus the inner logic of the drive towards acceptance, in conjunction with other circumstances (such as the 'flight from spinsterhood' mentioned by Dr Leavis, and the charms of wealth and social importance), serves to make her marriage to Mr Wilcox sufficiently credible, at any rate as credible as, say, Dorothea Brooke's marriage to Casaubon. (The parallel is in fact a suggestive one, since both Margaret and Dorothea marry men old enough to be their fathers, but the former marries a man who is 'king of this world', while the latter, with more naïve ideality, marries a man whom the world is inclined to despise; nevertheless, both women exhibit nobility of mind as well as nescience in their choice of a spouse.)

Second, Forster does not ask us to sympathize with or approve of the marriage any more than George Eliot does in Dorothea's case. What he does do is exhibit the consciousness of his heroine without comment or with a minimum of comment, and this restraint is all the more necessary and commendable because, as we saw earlier, only the inner consciousness of the individual himself can really determine whether his acceptance is genuine or spurious. Thus, when Margaret says that she knows all Mr Wilcox's faults, even admitting that spiritually he is not as honest as she is (which of course is a gross under-statement), Forster merely remarks drily that 'she was not far wrong in boasting that she understood her future husband'. Again, after Mr Wilcox has unfeelingly cut short Margaret's annual visit to her aunt at Swanage, Forster writes:

> A wave of tenderness came over her. She put a hand on either shoulder, and looked deeply into the black, bright eyes. What was behind their competent stare? She knew, but was not disquieted.

The words 'competent stare' are quite sufficient to alert us to the attitude that the novelist wishes us to take towards Mr Wilcox; we are ready to interpret the last sentence to mean either that she *thought* she knew or that she ought to have been disquieted, or both.

In the upshot, of course, Margaret Schlegel (or Wilcox, as

she is at this point) herself rejects her husband, and thus implicitly disowns her previous attitude of acceptance. When 'the pack' turns upon Helen, she makes common cause with her sister, and defies the world: 'They would be mad together if the world chose to consider them so.' Shortly afterwards, she attacks her husband furiously:

> Stupid, hypocritical, cruel-oh, contemptible!—a man who insults his wife when she's alive and cants with her memory when she's dead. A man who ruins a woman for his pleasure, and casts her off to ruin other men. And gives bad financial advice, and then says he is not responsible. These men are you. You can't recognize them, because you cannot connect. I've had enough of your unweeded kindness. I've spoilt you long enough.

This is to pronounce judgement with a vengeance! Upon reflection Margaret is 'unrepentant' in approving of everything she had said during the course of this outburst:

> She neither forgave him for his behaviour nor wished to forgive him. Her speech to him seemed perfect. She would not have altered a word. It had to be uttered once in a life, to adjust the lopsidedness of the world.

Earlier, when she found out about Mr Wilcox's affair with Jacky, Margaret had thought, 'Henry must be forgiven, and made better by love.' That she now dismisses Christian charity and forgiveness may be taken as an explicit repudiation of spurious acceptance. Just as Belinsky refused to make his peace or adjust himself to vile realities, so Margaret throws her weight against the world and thus forces it to adjust in some measure its lopsidedness.

The ending of the novel presents peculiar difficulties. The reader is likely to feel that Forster has produced a happy ending by a deliberate piece of contrivance: Margaret has rejected the father-figure and defied the world, but in order that she may enjoy the good things of this world (such as Howards End), the puissant father is suddenly rendered impotent. Nevertheless, a case can be made for the happy ending of *Howards End* based upon the kind of argument that one might employ to defend the miraculous victory of peace and reconciliation at the end of Shakespeare's last plays. In the first place, then, we should note that it is essential to Forster's argument that Henry Wilcox shall be 'saved'. Before their marriage Margaret had wished to help in bringing about his redemption: 'She would only point out the salvation that was latent in his own soul, and in the soul of every man. Only connect! That was the whole of her sermon.' But Mr Wilcox refuses to see any 'connection' that might damage the elaborate self-protective structure upon which his self-esteem and his esteem in the eyes of the world are based. His forehead (which we noticed earlier) is 'a bastion that protected his head from the world'. When Margaret expresses an implied criticism of him, he blots out all consciousness of her meaning, and replies 'straight from his fortress'. After his defences fall momentarily, we are told that he 'continued to feel anger long after he had rebuilt his defences, and was again presenting a bastion to the world'. While we labour unceasingly to adorn and preserve our imaginary being (as Pascal says), we cannot of course experience the salvation that is latent in the soul of every man. It is therefore necessary for Mr Wilcox to become a 'broken Coriolanus' (to borrow a phrase from *The Waste Land*). The imprisonment of Charles brings about this result: 'I'm broken—I'm ended', the father says to Margaret, and Forster comments, 'She did not see that to break him was her only hope',* and a few lines later, 'Then Henry's fortress gave way.' Thus the defeat of Mr Wilcox, far from being a mere device to benefit the heroine, is a necessary part of the comedy of salvation that is enacted in the novel.

Secondly, we can partly justify the ending of *Howards End* by observing that the shape of the novel is determined by the shape of Beethoven's Fifth Symphony. Near the beginning of the novel the Schlegels attend a concert at Queen's Hall, and we are offered an interpretation of the Fifth Symphony as an allegory of human life. In the first movement, there are heroic

---

* *A broken and contrite heart, O God, shalt thou not despise.* But is Mr Wilcox contrite?

figures engaged in titanic struggles; the second movement is
a slow, peaceful intermission; in the third movement goblins
walk over the universe, quietly remarking that 'there was no such
thing as splendour or heroism in the world'. Soon, they appear
again, and repeat this statement. Then, with the transitional
passage on the drums, Beethoven himself enters upon the
scene, the goblins are driven away, and heroic, radiant gods and
demi-gods declare and show forth the glory of the universe.
But then, once again, the goblins return, and with increased
malignity repeat the statement that life is meaningless, sordid,
empty and insignificant. However, 'Beethoven chose to make
all right in the end.' Heroism, magnificence and joy come before
us again, and the Fifth Symphony is brought to a triumphant
end. 'But the goblins were there', Forster concludes. 'They
could return. He had said so bravely, and that is why we can
trust Beethoven when he says other things.'

Near the end of the novel we learn that remorse and suffering
have had a regenerative effect upon Leonard Bast, and have
brought him an insight into the truth of the ultimate goodness
of life: 'It was not the optimism which he had been taught at
school. Again and again must the drums tap, and the goblins
stalk over the universe before joy can be purged of the superficial.' Even though the final phrase is itself, alas, a trifle superficial, this sentence provides unmistakable proof that the Fifth
Symphony serves as a model for the structure of the novel.
Thus Margaret and Helen, like Leonard Bast, have had to
endure 'the racket and the torture' before they can win their
way through to a clear vision. 'Can't it strike you—even for a
moment—that your life has been heroic?' Helen says to
Margaret. We infer that they deserve their happy ending, even
if Forster has to appear in person, like a *deus ex machina*, in
order to drive the goblins away. Note, too, that the goblins are
there, and may return. London is creeping towards Howards
End, and Helen fears its approach: 'Life's going to be melted
down, all over the world.' On the penultimate page of the novel,
Paul Wilcox makes a peculiarly brutal remark—he is accustomed
to natives, and 'a very little shook him out of the Englishman',
Forster explains!—which shows us that Forster knows that the

goblins are still there, and that is why we are not altogether without grounds for trusting him when he allows Margaret and Helen their splendid but fragile victory.

Finally and perhaps most important, we should note that there is no trace of prestidigitation in Forster's account of his heroine's spiritual development. Margaret Wilcox achieves self-knowledge and peace of mind, and she would carry these blessings with her wherever she went, whether to Germany with her sister (as was originally planned) or to Howards End. Forster insists that spiritual growth such as Margaret's bears fruit in the outer life: 'There are moments when the inner life actually "pays", when years of self-scrutiny, conducted for no ulterior motive, are suddenly of practical use.' A hundred pages later, when the estrangement between the sisters is healed, and they present a united front to the world, he says, 'The inner life had paid.' The Wilcoxes, of course, are not interested in the inner life—'I am not a fellow who bothers about my own inside', Mr Wilcox says. If Margaret's triumph shows that self-knowledge can sometimes be 'of practical use', Mr Wilcox's collapse demonstrates that lack of self-knowledge can sometimes be practically disastrous. Although in its context Mr Wilcox's collapse seems improbable and contrived, in general we can easily believe that the Wilcoxes of this world, who adorn the imaginary being and neglect the real one, may go to pieces when their inner emptiness or their inner rottenness (Henry Wilcox is 'rotten at the core') is suddenly exposed; at any rate, it is scarely a *trahison des clercs* on Forster's part to ask us to believe it.

In the last chapters of *Howards End* we are given to understand that Margaret Wilcox has emerged out of spurious acceptance, and entered into the gladness of genuine acceptance. There is an abundance of religious language; words and phrases like 'salvation', 'a new life', 'tranquility', 'regeneration' and 'ultimate harmony' occur. Margaret catches 'glimpses of diviner wheels', and she explains to her sister that 'eternal differences, [are] planted by God in a single family, so that there may always be colour'. Margaret experiences 'the peace of the present, which passes understanding', and is comforted by the knowledge that 'a child would be born into the world'. The word 'comfort' is used in its traditionary religious sense: 'Don't you see that all this leads to comfort in the end?' Margaret says.* A few lines later, Helen picks up a bunch of grass, composed of clover, daisies and bents:

'Is it sweetening yet?' asked Margaret.
'No, only withered.'
'It will sweeten to-morrow.'

The tranquil scene, which has been prepared for by Forster's affectionate portrayal of rural England and of 'the fertility of the soil' of Howards End, effectively invokes the pastoral imagery of the New Testament ('Lift up your eyes, and look on the fields, for they are white already unto harvest!') In almost the last lines of the book, Henry Wilcox asks Margaret if he did wrong to ignore his first wife's dying wish to bequeath Howards End to her, and she replies: 'You didn't, darling. Nothing has been done wrong.' All things work together for good to them that love God, or as St Juliana of Norwich says in lines made famous by T. S. Eliot: 'Sin is behovabil, but all shall be well and all shall be well, and all manner of thing shall be well.'

It will be well to end this chapter on a more circumspect note! In defending the happy ending of *Howards End*, I have paid more attention to Forster's intention than to his performance. Judged by its performance, *Howards End* is a fine novel, but it is really not great enough for its ending to sustain the grand—one is tempted to say, grandiose—intentions of the author. Margaret Wilcox, for example, admirable as she is, and admirably as she is done, evidently does not quite attain to heroic stature (in spite of her sister's claims); for one thing, she is somewhat disembodied, and lacks the animal vitality that is requisite in those who would storm the gates of heaven; for another, it is doubtful whether she (or Forster himself, for that matter) suffered enough for her joy to be altogether purged of the superficial. Then, too, in a story about two sisters who are looking for husbands, it is disquieting to find that the mate of

* The Wilcoxes employ 'comfort' in its usual secular sense: 'I can't stand those people who run down comforts', Mr Wilcox says.

one of them, having performed his progenitive function, is conveniently killed off, while the spouse of the other is conveniently metamorphosed into an exhausted, broken, defeated shadow of a man. (Is there not more rigour in a story like Kafka's 'The Judgement' in which the bed-ridden, declining father at the decisive moment leaps up like a giant awakened, and reasserts his authority with deadly effect?) However, these animadversions, though they may affect our estimate of the ending of the novel, do not seriously diminish our admiration for *Howards End* as a subtle and mature study of spurious acceptance.

CHAPTER EIGHT

The Reaction Against Idealism: 2. The Crime

So far as we are human, what we do must be either evil or good; so far as we do evil or good, we are human; and it is better, in a paradoxical way, to do evil than to do nothing: at least, we exist.

T. S. ELIOT, 'Baudelaire'

We have already seen that the domination of the father is manifested at the literal, moral, political, religious and anagogical levels. The idealistic youth rejects the literal father, but he discovers that in his enslavement to the ideal he has acquired a worse master. The man at the level of spurious acceptance escapes from the domination of the ideal or the over-severe conscience, but in the course of achieving his adjustment to reality, he undermines the basis of his revolt. In accepting the principle that 'Whatever is, is right', he is in effect, as Voltaire saw, capitulating to the father at the literal and political levels. In other words, he is virtually back where he started. When the hero of Consciousness becomes aware of the cowardice and insincerity of spurious acceptance, he perceives that the father is a Hydra-headed monster that must be encountered simultaneously at every level—and slain.

The adolescent hero at the levels of spurious acceptance and idealistic rectitudinitis is bogged down in a kind of sterile inactivity. In the case of spurious acceptance, this inactivity is embraced deliberately; in the case of idealistic rectitudinitis, it is a result of excessive thinking, of thinking too precisely on the event, which means that when action does occur it tends to be unpremeditated, rash and irresponsible. In both idealistic rectitudinitis and spurious acceptance we find that the young man is concerned with himself first and foremost, and only secondly and indirectly with the world. The idea of the self, in effect, represents a mist or a fog that interposes itself between a man and reality, creating a barrier that separates him from the world he has to deal with. Instead of trying to act upon the world with a view to achieving certain results, the man at the level of Self-Consciousness seeks to behave in a way that will permit him to think well of himself. Instead of freely choosing what he wants to do, he thinks about what he *ought* to do, and his experience takes on the significance of a test imposed on him as a result of which he hopes to achieve salvation, or to acquire merit of one kind or another on earth or in heaven. But this need to conform to a 'shadowy ideal of conduct', as Conrad phrases it in *Lord Jim*, is a fatal disability in the contest with the father. The father is interested in political and social power rather than in preserving a gratifying self-image; he is willing to concede to the young man unnumbered victories in the kingdom of the mind, provided he retains his mastery of the kingdom of this world. The young man, for his part, eventually tires of endless shadow-boxing and unprofitable introspection.* Recognizing that it is only by acting that he can prove his manhood and achieve independence of the father, he makes ready to throw himself violently into action.

In so far as the aim of the adolescent hero is to liberate himself from both literal and allegorical father-figures, it is understandable that the form of action that is most likely to recommend itself to him is the crime. To one brought up in subservience to the law, the crime has all the allurement of the forbidden fruit in the Garden of Eden. St Augustine, for example, discussing in his *Confessions* the incident where he stole some pears from a neighbour's garden for the mere love of stealing, suggests that

---

* Since we shall be largely concerned with André Gide in this chapter, a quotation from his *Journal* of August, 1893, is relevant here: 'This perpetual analysis of one's thoughts, this absence of action, this moralizing, are of all things in the world the most wearisome, insipid and almost incomprehensible, once one has got clear of it.'[1]

the theft was a perverse attempt to imitate the freedom and omnipotence of God:

> Perhaps it was the thrill of acting against Your law—at least in appearance, since I had no power to do so in fact, the delight a prisoner might have in making some small gesture of liberty—getting a deceptive sense of omnipotence from doing something forbidden without immediate punishment.[2]

It is, presumably, the thrill of this 'deceptive sense of omnipotence' which accounts for the zest and exuberance of criminal figures such as Shakespeare's Iago, Edmund in *King Lear*, Marlowe's Jew, Jonson's Volpone, or Milton's Satan. But where the omnipotence of God is characteristically revealed in creation, the crime is usually an act of destruction. It takes many years to grow a tree, but the tree can be felled, or its fruits stolen, in a matter of minutes.* As Burke says in *Reflections on the Revolution in France*: 'Rage and phrenzy will pull down more in half an hour, than prudence, deliberation, and foresight can build up in an hundred years.' Thus the young man who is thirsting for action chooses the crime partly because it is the easiest and most striking form of action.

The chief recommendation of the crime of destruction in the eyes of the adolescent hero is that it deals a double blow to the father, who is both the lawmaker and, in his capacity as a property-owner, the chief beneficiary under the law. Moreover, as we saw in Chapters Five and Six, the father is himself a criminal, and the law, which upholds the *status quo*, protects the father in the enjoyment of the fruits of his successful crime. *La propriété c'est le vol.* To disobey the law is to claim the freedom that the father had claimed; to obey the law is to submit to the ideology of the father and his class. As soon as the hero divines that it is only fear that keeps him obedient to the law, he compels himself to defy the law and the father. Thus it is that the *acte gratuit* of Gide, for example, typically takes the form of

---

* One of the *actes gratuits* of Ménalque in Gide's *Les Nourritures terrestres* actually consists of indulging in this particular destructive whim. 'When the autumn came, I had the finest trees cut down and took pleasure in laying waste my domain.'[3]

F

a crime such as that of Lafcadio in *Les Caves du Vatican* who pushes a man off a train simply to show that he is capable of doing it. Similarly, in *Crime and Punishment* one of the reasons offered by Raskolnikov to explain why he murdered the old woman is this: 'I had to find out then, and as quickly as possible, whether I was a louse like the rest or a man. Whether I can step over or not. Whether I dare to stoop or not?' The hero steps over the human law, and stoops under the divine law (by refusing to allow it to browbeat him into being 'good'). By committing a crime, then, the adolescent hero asserts his defiance of all laws and prohibitions, whether of man or of god, and claims to be a law unto himself. The crime is above all a declaration of freedom and independence.

It may be as well at this point to consider an objection that is likely to suggest itself. It will perhaps be said that to rebel against the father is to prove that one is dependent on him, and that to affront society by committing a crime is to pay an inverted compliment to the power and authority of society. Professor A. J. Ayer, for example, in an article entitled 'Philosophy at Absolute Zero: An Enquiry into the Meaning of Nihilism', argues with reference to the Gidean *acte gratuit* that the man who 'sets himself to contravene accepted standards is in fact displaying his acceptance of them, or at least his recognition of their influence'.[4] Setting aside the ambiguous final phrase (for who can fail to recognize the influence of accepted standards?) we have to grant that there is a good deal of force in this criticism. The free man does what he wants to do, and what he wants to do is not determined by obedience to, or rebellion against, the will of other people. The man who is conditioned by the need to do the opposite of what other people tell him to do may be described, in the terminology employed by David Riesman in *The Lonely Crowd*, as *anomic* rather than *autonomous*.[5] Professor Ayer, however, sees little in the *acte gratuit* besides its logical absurdity. For us, the motives behind the gratuitous crime, and the reasoning on which it is based, are relatively unimportant; what matters is whether it *works*. And if we ignore the motives and consider the fruits of the crime, it becomes pretty clear, I think, that the crime can be a road to freedom. I may commit a murder to prove I am capable of it. But, once I have done the murder (and thus proved I am capable of it), the very outrageousness of my act reveals to me, upon reflection, that I am always free to murder or not to murder. It is psychologically impossible for a child of, say, ten to carry out a radical revolt against the parent. Yet there comes a day when the child does some action to assert itself, and thereafter both child and parent recognize that a fundamental change has occurred in their relationship. So, for the adolescent hero, the crime, whatever its logical status, can be the act which proclaims and establishes his freedom and independence with respect to *all* authority.

What, then, does freedom mean? For our present purposes it will perhaps suffice to define freedom in subjective terms and say that to be free means to be conscious that one can do (or attempt to do) whatever one wills. If I am in prison and unable to escape, my freedom consists in the fact that I can *wish* to escape, and act in any way likely to increase my chances of escaping. Expressed negatively, to be free means to be conscious that one is not bound to obey the commands of anything outside oneself, whether man, god, reason, immutable moral law, absolute value, or the like. Freedom, in fact, is the goal of the revolt against the father, and the indispensable condition of the adolescent hero's progress. As Coleridge says in *Biographia Literaria*: 'Where the spirit of man is not filled with the consciousness of freedom (were it only from its restlessness, as of one still struggling in bondage) all spiritual intercourse is interrupted, not only with others but even with himself.' The adolescent hero, indeed, deserves this title, because though struggling in bondage he is a seeker after freedom.

Though freedom has always been an elusive prize that is sought after only by the few, it is perhaps true that it has become exceptionally difficult of attainment in the course of the last century or so. Chief among the forces hostile to freedom is the deterministic outlook of the sciences. The mechanistic physical science of Newton led to the mechanistic psychology of Hartley and others, to the theory that human psychology can be explained in terms of attraction (or pleasure) and repulsion (or pain), and thence to the deterministic psychology that we find today, for example, among the Freudians and the behaviourists. This mechanistic conception of the universe is a source of great distress to the seeker after freedom. Teufelsdröckh in *Sartor Resartus*, for example, cries:

> To me the Universe was all void of Life, of Purpose, of Volition, even of Hostility; it was one huge, dead, immeasurable Steam-engine, rolling on, in its dead indifference, to grind me limb from limb. O, the vast, gloomy, solitary Golgotha, and Mill of Death!

As we have seen already, Teufelsdröckh's victory over the steam-engine philosophy, and his conquest of fear, is achieved through the discovery that, even if all else is but a dead machine, he is free and a 'Child of Freedom'. In Dostoyevsky's *Notes from Underground*, also, there is, beneath the grim humour, an earnest attempt to refute the view that with the advance of scientific knowledge it will become possible to determine what is 'advantageous' to any particular man at any particular time, and thus to predict behaviour:

> So one's own free, unrestrained choice, one's own whim, be it the wildest, one's own fancy, sometimes worked up to a frenzy—that is the most advantageous advantage that cannot be fitted into any table or scale and that causes every system or theory to crumble into dust on contact. . . . But let me repeat to you for the hundredth time that there is one instance when a man can wish upon himself, in full awareness, something harmful, stupid, and even completely idiotic. He will do it in order to *establish his right* to wish for the most idiotic thing and not to be obliged to have only sensible wishes.[6]

Here, of course, the justification of harmful and idiotic acts in the name of freedom is precisely the reasoning that underlies the Gidean *acte gratuit*.

The deterministic view of the world might be less oppressive if it did not have powerful support in the shape of one's consciousness that most men are obviously *not* free. As the Indian sage, Ramakrishna, says somewhere: 'People who live in the world are enslaved by three things: by their masters, by their wives, and by their money.' Here, again, it would seem that our own times provide a soil that is peculiarly unfavourable to the growth of freedom. We are more worldly-minded than men of other periods, and the whole tradition that is implied in the ideas of contemplative detachment or retirement from the world is with us virtually extinct. As we saw in Chapter Three, man's very success in mastering nature has served to enslave him; he compels nature to satisfy his desires instead of executing an inner act of freedom that detaches him from his desires. How can this spoilt child of fortune, who is the slave of his machinery, his comforts, his belief in his right to happiness and in his duty to keep up with the Joneses, know freedom? As Goethe says:

In der Beschränkung zeigt sich erst der Meister
Und das Gesetz nur kann uns Freiheit geben.*

Note, too, that science, which has rendered mankind almost all-powerful, has in some ways created a world in which the individual is less master of his fate than men were in the past. Our lives and our livelihoods are dependent on hydrogen-bombs and economic crises that come to us from distant lands. The complexity of our civilization puts us at the mercy of external regulations. Bertrand Russell has said that freedom as he knew it in his youth is now as out-dated as the crinoline. Not long ago the American who wanted some land and a house simply went off into the woods with his axe; today he needs planning permission to build an outhouse! It may be objected at this point that nothing external to me can prevent me from knowing that I can do (or attempt to do) whatever I wish. This is true; once the lamp of freedom is illuminated, nothing in the external world can put it out. It is also true, however, that whether the intuition of freedom arises in the first instance or not partly depends on external conditions, so that if we are interested in freedom, we have to take account of these conditions.

Having established a broad general framework for our discussion, we may now examine some works of literature in which

---

* It is in working within limits that the master first reveals himself, and only obedience to Law can give us freedom.

the ideas we have been considering in the abstract are explored concretely. One is tempted to begin at the beginning with Adam and Eve in the Garden of Eden. Their 'crime', if not formally (at any rate on Adam's part) a declaration of independence, was nevertheless a 'Fall into Freedom', as Gulley Jimson says in *The Horse's Mouth*. It may be observed, too, that the 'deceptive sense of omnipotence' that St Augustine associates with the crime is evident in Milton's Satan, who 'trusted to have equall'd the most High / If he oppos'd', and also in Eve (of whom Milton says, 'nor was Godhead from her thoughts'). However, the Genesis account is too short to be suitable for detailed critical analysis, and Milton's version of the story, besides being rather too long, is open to the objection that there is some doubt as to whether the poet is on the side of God or of Satan!

In the ordinary way *Crime and Punishment* would naturally suggest itself as appropriate for our present purposes, but we have already examined Dostoyevsky's novel in some detail, and further extensive discussion of it would be otiose. One brief cautionary observation may however be offered at this point. Raskolnikov exhibits some of the characteristics of idealistic youth and of spurious acceptance, although he is above all a representative of the criminal adolescent hero. It is important to note, then, that while it is necessary to distinguish between idealistic rectitudinitis, spurious acceptance, and the crime, and to discuss them separately, it would be an error to think of them as forming discrete stages in an irreversible, chronological sequence; a more just view would be to regard the total complex that constitutes the adolescent hero as analogous to a landscape in which different geological eras are simultaneously visible.

We have already seen that Sartre's writings merit the close attention of those who wish to understand the phenomenon of the rebellious son. Since we shall be concerned with Sartre again in the next chapter, it will suffice here to note briefly that his play, *The Flies*, is an admirable study of the revolt against the father in all his manifestations. In the play, Orestes has returned to Argos to avenge the murder of Agamemnon by slaying Clytemnestra and her paramour, King Aegisthus. Orestes kills the literal father (or, rather, step-father), and, since Aegisthus is the king—the 'father of his country'[7]—in killing him, Orestes at the same time proclaims his defiance of society. The slaying of Aegisthus also involves Orestes in disobedience to the will of the gods, for Zeus regards Aegisthus as a natural ally, saying to him: 'A king is a god on earth, glorious and terrifying as a god.' When, therefore, Orestes prays to Zeus for guidance, Zeus sends a sign forbidding him to kill Aegisthus; Orestes, however, refuses to obey his 'fatherly old friend' (as Electra ironically calls Zeus), saying 'from now on I'll take no one's orders, neither man's nor god's'. Then, after the crime of murder has been committed, the Furies, symbolizing the voice of conscience, are sent to plague Orestes, but he defies them, too. 'I am free. Beyond anguish, beyond remorse. Free. And at one with myself', he says. And, again, 'The most cowardly of murderers is he who feels remorse.' *The Flies*, then, is an account of the slaying of that polymorphous and protean monster, the father-figure.

If we are not permitted to talk about Dostoyevsky and Sartre, then André Gide, who looks back to the one and forward to the other, is the obvious choice to illustrate the argument of this chapter. We have already seen that the *acte gratuit* of Lafcadio in *Les Caves du Vatican* takes the form of a crime that is performed deliberately, spontaneously, gaily, and without motivation; in *The Immoralist* there is a crime which is not a crime, which is performed undeliberately, sorrowfully, and with unconscious motivation; for this very reason the latter work offers the more profound and valuable insights into the nature of the crime of the rebellious son. It is to *The Immoralist*, then, that we must now turn our attention.

Michel, the hero of *The Immoralist*, possesses many of the characteristic traits of the young adolescent hero. His instruction at the hands of his father in Hebrew, Sanskrit, Persian and Arabic, as well as Latin and Greek, reminds one of John Stuart Mill's formidable education. Michel follows his father into his profession, and at an early age writes an erudite treatise that entitles him to be received on terms of equality by the most learned scholars. 'And so I reached the age of twenty-five, having barely cast a glance at anything but books and ruins and knowing nothing of life.'[8] Largely in order to please his father, who is dying, Michel marries a girl whom he has known since childhood, the daughter of old friends of the family. He is a virgin when he marries Marceline and the marriage is not consummated until some months after the wedding-day. In the first days of the marriage, Michel treats his wife with 'a kind of frigid gallantry', which is somewhat reminiscent of Casaubon's courtship of Dorothea Brooke in *Middlemarch*, and, in fact, he seems to comport himself rather in the manner of a dry middle-aged scholar than of a young man. The idealism of the adolescent hero manifests itself in Michel in a strain of Puritanism, which, we are told, is a consequence of the austere moral training that he had received at the hands of his Huguenot mother. At the start of the novel, the friend who records Michel's narrative, describing the change in him, observes: 'He was no longer the learned Puritan of old days, whose behaviour was made awkward by his very earnestness, whose clear and simple gaze had so often checked the looseness of our talk.' Of these friends, who, apart from books and ruins, were the chief element in his life before his marriage, Michel says revealingly:

> I loved a few friends (you were among them), but it was not so much my friends I loved as friendship—it was a craving for high-mindedness that made my devotion to them so great; I cherished in myself each and all of my fine feelings.

Here, in a manner characteristic of the abstract thinker, what is valued is the ideal of friendship in the abstract, rather than the concrete, flesh-and-blood men in whom the friendship is embodied. We have seen that the adolescent hero broods over the idea of committing suicide; the flow of life in Michel is too languid for him to contemplate so positive an action as suicide, but when he becomes seriously ill with tuberculosis, satisfied that he has worked hard and done his duty, Michel feels no real desire to resist the onslaught of death: 'After all, what had life to offer?'

Thanks to the loving care of Marceline, Michel does not die, and during his convalescence he is surprised to discover that a 'new self' is beginning to awaken in him. It may be observed that a grave illness often precipitates a change of heart and a kind of rebirth. For one thing, the forced cessation of one's ordinary occupations breaks the tyranny of habit, and creates a gap in which there is room for new things to appear. Then, too, the nearness of death induces one to distinguish between what is important and what is unimportant. Very often the man who has been close to death and then recovers, feels obscurely that his illness was both a punishment for wrong living and a warning: 'Behold, thou art made whole—sin no more lest a worse thing befall thee.' During his convalescence, then, Michel begins to love life, and, inspired by the healthy, animal, unconscious vitality of the Arab boys, whose tongues are as pink as a cat's, he deliberately puts himself in a state of hostility, and prepares to fight for life and health.

It should be said at this point that the history of Michel is very nearly the same as that of André Gide himself. There are, however, a few significant differences that should be noted. It was his cousin on his mother's side, Madeleine Rondeaux, and not a childhood friend that Gide married in 1895. In the novel, Michel successfully defends his wife in a fight with a drunken carriage-driver, and finally consummates his marriage that same night; in real life Gide never had sexual relations with his wife. Whereas Marceline dies of tuberculosis at the end of *The Immoralist* (which was published in 1902), Gide's wife lived until 1938. The most important difference is this: in the novel Michel marries Marceline as it were to please his dying father, but, in fact, it was in the period of panic that followed immediately upon the death of his *mother* that Gide married his cousin. As M. Jean Delay observes in *La Jeunesse d'André Gide*, Gide was 'the only child of an ill-assorted household in which the father played a minor role and the authority of head of the household was exercised by a powerful and tyrannical mother'.[9] Furthermore, Gide's father died when he was eleven, and he was brought up entirely by his straitlaced, masculine, moralistic mother. Obviously, then, in Gide's case it is the mother who is the moral authority, and we shall see that the 'immoralism' of Gide and of his hero has the character of a revolt against the mother.

The 'new self' that emerges during Michel's convalescence proves to be the antithesis of the old. Where the old Michel devoted himself to books, Puritan high-mindedness, and the pleasures of the mind, the 'new self' gives its allegiance to life and action, immorality, and the pleasures of the body. Books are a record of the past, and the past is dead. As his enjoyment of the present grows, Michel comes to despise learning, and to believe that an 'abstract and neutral acquaintance with the past' is mere vanity. We have seen in previous chapters that the bookish adolescent hero develops his intellectual powers at the expense of his powers of sensation. The old Michel, whom Ménalque described as 'the blindfolded scholar, the learned bookworm', had been so buried in books that he knew nothing of life. It is only on his honeymoon that he notices for the first time that his wife is pretty. 'I reproached myself for not having noticed it sooner.' During his convalescence, however, the life of the senses begins to awaken in Michel: 'Up till that day, so it seemed to me, I had felt so little and thought so much that now I was astonished to find my sensations had become as strong as my thoughts.' In due course, he discovers that his senses have not so much awakened as reawakened; they had been alive in childhood, but had been buried during his adolescence. When he and Marceline go to stay in a house where he had spent many summers as a child, Michel smells the scent of the grass and hears the piercing cries of the swallows, and the whole of the buried past comes alive in him again.

On their return to Paris, Michel finds that his colleagues in the field of archaeology and philology, and also the poets and novelists, philosophers and mathematicians of his acquaintance, are all boring and unalive. 'They are all alike', he tells Marceline, 'When I talk to one, I feel as if I were talking to the whole lot.' As Ménalque explains later, it is fear, especially the fear of finding themselves alone, that has led these people to follow the path of conformity. 'It is his own self that each of them is most afraid of resembling.' The hero, Michel decides, must reject the secondary, artificial creature produced by culture and instruction, and rediscover 'that authentic creature, "the old Adam", whom the Gospel had repudiated, whom everything about me—books, masters, parents, and I myself— had begun by attempting to suppress'. Michel's rebellion, then, is directed against books, masters, parents, his old self, and the Gospel that had been taught to him as a child. He tells Marceline not to pray for him:

'Why not?' she asked, a little troubled.

'I don't want favors.'

'Do you reject the help of God?'

'He would have a right to my gratitude afterwards. It entails obligations. I don't like them.'

Michel applies to modern civilization the insights he has gained as a result of his own experience. He argues that culture, which arises spontaneously from the superabundance of life, soon stiffens and hardens into an imprisoning mould, so that it ends by destroying life. He begins to admire the 'savage grandeur and nobility' of the Goths, who destroyed culture, and in particular he interests himself in the young king Athalaric 'worked on in secret by the Goths, *in revolt against his mother Amalasontha,* rebelling against his Latin education and flinging aside his culture, as a restive horse shakes off a troublesome harness' (my italics). The image of the restive horse is a fine one, and, indeed, it is a natural one for expressing the resurgence of the animal side of man's nature, as we see, for example, in the figure of the centaur,* or in the film *Extase,* or in Lawrence's *St Mawr.* We may note, too, that the revolt against culture is an important theme in the Romantic tradition which links Gide with Rousseau, Nietzsche, Rimbaud, and others.

Michel's changed attitude towards books, conformity, and culture is accompanied by a revolution in his attitude towards morality. The emergence of the 'old Adam' in him is illustrated by the incident when the Arab boy, Moktir, steals a pair of scissors belonging to Marceline. Michel, who happens to witness the theft, does not feel the righteous indignation of the wronged

* Compare, for example, *King Lear:* 'Down from the waist they are centaurs, though women all above. But to the girdle do the gods inherit, beneath is all the fiend's'.

property-owner, but instead is delighted, and Moktir from that time becomes his favourite. (It is no doubt relevant that the 'crime' was committed against Marceline; and, bearing in mind that Gide as a boy was threatened with castration for masturbating, it is perhaps not altogether far-fetched to attach a special significance to the scissors.) Michel's interest in Athalaric, which we have already noticed, also illustrates his revolt against morality. He pictures Athalaric 'plunging for a few years into a life of violent and unbridled pleasure with rude companions of his own age and dying at eighteen, rotten and sodden with debauchery'. Michel obviously identifies himself with this debauched boy, who rebelled against his mother, for he says 'in Athalaric's horrible death, I did my best to read a lesson'. Clearly, even Athalaric's fate did not discourage Michel from wishing to follow in his footsteps.

Although Michel does not in fact plunge into vice quite so spectacularly as Athalaric, he devotes himself with Puritan zeal to the task of 'systematically condemning and suppressing everything which I believed I owed to my past education and early moral beliefs', seeking to uncover the dark treasures within himself that are 'smothered by culture and decency and morality'. On his property at La Morinière, Michel creeps out of the house at night to help the poacher, Alcide, to outwit his own bailiff (Alcide's father) and steal from himself. This inversion of the natural order of things—'I stole out of doors as a thief steals in'—seems appropriately paradoxical in the learned young Puritan who turns from virtue to vice, from light to darkness, from ascent to descent. It is at La Morinière, too, that he discovers that some of the country people, in particular the Heurtevants, possess the primitive savageness and licentiousness that he had admired in the Goths. Old man Heurtevant, who has fathered two children upon his own daughter, on one occasion held a girl down by force while his eldest son raped her. 'My imagination began to circle round the lurid attractions of Heurtevant's house like a blow-fly round a putrid piece of meat,' Michel remarks. The image happily reflects the blend of fascination and revulsion that the lapsed Puritan often feels towards the delicious pleasures of depravity.

It is, of course, the 'crime' of Michel that primarily concerns us in this chapter. Michel's crime—he invites his hearers to use the term, for he speaks of 'my crime—if you choose to call it that'—is that he is indirectly the cause of his wife's death. Marceline, no doubt as a consequence of nursing Michel, becomes ill with tuberculosis and she needs rest, but he drags her on a nightmare journey across France, Switzerland, Italy and North Africa, and, finally, to Touggourt, where she dies. It is made plain that Michel loves his wife ('Oh, perhaps you will think I did not love Marceline. I swear I loved her passionately'), and the reasons why he illuses her are obscure. 'Some irresistible demon goaded me on', he says, and, again, 'No longer do I know what dark mysterious god I serve.' This obscurity serves Gide's artistic purposes in the novel, and it is also faithful to Gide's own experience, since he himself at the time of his marriage had only a very confused notion of what he was about. As he writes in his autobiography, *Si le grain ne meurt*, 'The secret motive of our acts—I mean of the most decisive ones—escapes us.'[10]

We can throw some light on the more cognizable reasons for Michel's conduct by glancing at Ménalque, who has preceded Michel along the path of self-fulfilment, sensual enjoyment and immoralism, and thus constitutes for Michel a kind of elder brother in the spirit or infernal counsellor. Ménalque regards a wife as an encumbrance. When Michel refuses his invitation to dinner, reminding him that he is married, Ménalque replies: 'The frank cordiality with which you were not afraid to greet me made me think you might be free.' On another occasion Ménalque, who has embraced a sort of apostolic poverty and non-attachment to earthly possessions for the sake of freedom,* draws attention to the numerous responsibilities that Michel has taken upon his shoulders: he has an estate in Normandy and a luxurious apartment in Paris: he is lecturing at the Collège de France; he is married and his wife is expecting a baby. Later,

* Ménalque, as mentioned above, also appears in *Les Nourritures terrestres*, where he says: 'I sold absolutely everything, being determined to have no *personal* possession on this earth—not the smallest relic of the past.'[11]

Michel confesses that he sometimes thinks that the tranquil happiness of the married state is strangling him, and Ménalque comments: 'One imagines one possesses and in reality one is possessed.' On the eve of his departure from Paris (and the novel), Ménalque's parting words to Michel are highly significant:

> I don't like looking backwards and I leave my past behind me as the bird leaves his shade to fly away. Oh, Michel! every joy is always awaiting us, but it must always be the only one; it insists on finding the bed empty and demands from us *a widower's welcome*.

(My italics)

In due course, Marceline has a miscarriage, and Michel disburdens himself of his lectureship, his Paris apartment, and his Normandy estate; then, in the company of his sick wife, he embarks on the nomadic existence recommended by Ménalque, and by the end of the novel he is indeed a widower. It seems, then, that it is his adoption of the gospel of Ménalque that inspires Michel to jeopardize his wife's life, and to claim his freedom to do as he wills, which means, among other things, to explore the homosexual interests of which he becomes gradually aware as the novel progresses. The last pages of the novel confirm this view. At the end of his narration, Michel tells his friends: 'I have freed myself'; and, in the final paragraph of the book there is a fairly overt reference to homosexuality when Michel confesses that he has given up a woman to please the native boy who brings his food.

In his preface to *The Immoralist* written some years after the novel was published, Gide remarks: 'It was not in vain that I had adorned Marceline with so many virtues; they [readers of the novel] could not forgive Michel for not preferring her to himself.' Gide appears to be arguing on Michel's behalf that one has to choose between self-fulfilment and self-abnegation; if public opinion condemns the former choice, then the hero must have the courage to disregard public opinion ('I care little for the approbation or disapprobation of men', Ménalque had said to Michel), and do as he pleases. We may recall here the speech of Undershaft in *Major Barbara* quoted in Chapter Six:

> I moralized and starved until one day I swore that I would be a full-fed free man at all costs; that nothing should stop me except a bullet, neither reason nor morals nor the lives of other men. I said, 'Thou shalt starve ere I starve'; and with that word I became free and great.

Michel makes the same claim to freedom and greatness ('Are you worth no more than this, you make-believe great man?' he reproaches himself when he feels pangs of anxiety about Marceline), and he chooses to feed himself—that is, to wander over the earth in search of experience and self-fulfilment—and to sacrifice his wife. We must, however, distinguish between Michel and Undershaft, not only because Michel's starvation is merely metaphorical, but also because of an obvious point that Gide, perhaps disingenuously, overlooks: namely, that Michel could perfectly well have travelled abroad on his own without dragging his wife along with him! The difference between the two men, in fact, illustrates the difference between the destructiveness of the father and that of the son that we discussed in Chapter Six. Undershaft is prepared to commit a crime if need be, in order to achieve the rational goal of feeding himself. Michel, on the other hand, resembles Raskolnikov in that his 'gratuitous' crime has a concealed and equivocal meaning that he himself does not really understand.

At a deeper level, we have to recognize that Michel's crime has the significance of a symbolical destruction of the parent-figure. Gide, who, as we have seen, married Madeleine Rondeaux immediately upon his mother's death, turned his cousin into a parent-figure, and fought against her his battle against the moralistic, tyrannical mother. As M. Delay says, 'The struggle which he began to wage against his wife—it is this that constitutes the very theme of *The Immoralist*—was simply an unconscious repetition of the fight that he had carried on against his mother.'[12] Since the wife corresponds to the mother, and the mother exercises the authority of the father, it is apparent that Michel's crime against Marceline is precisely equivalent to the crimes of patricide that we have examined already. *The Immoralist*, then, inasmuch as it unites the themes of the destruction of the parent-figure, the attack upon culture and morality, and the quest for freedom and self-fulfilment, may properly be described as an account of the revolt against the father at the literal and allegorical levels.

Two topics remain. We have already seen that one of the characteristics of the adolescent hero is that he does not have a satisfactory physical and emotional relationship with a woman. It seems appropriate at this point, then, to say something on the subject of Gide's failure to consummate his marriage, and to mention, briefly, some psychoanalytical contributions to the understanding of the meaning of the crime of the adolescent hero. M. Delay, who is himself a psychiatrist as well as a member of the Académie Française, argues in *La Jeunesse d'André Gide* that Gide's failure to consummate his marriage was due to his identification of his wife with his mother, which meant that he gave his wife a 'pure' spiritual love, and expressed his sensual love with men. (In his autobiography, Gide speaks of 'that fundamental incapacity for mixing the spirit with the senses, which is, I believe, somewhat peculiar to me'.[13]) The emergence in Gide of a philosophy akin to that of the Nietzschean superman, M. Delay explains in Adlerian terms as a *compensation* for Gide's sexual failure with his wife. He interprets Gide's hostility towards his mother, not in Oedipal terms, but in terms of the ambivalent feelings of love and hate that an over-protected child feels towards the parent-figure who is both his guardian and his gaoler. The layman is likely to prefer this interpretation (which in fact agrees very well with the position adopted here) to the Freudian view, because the latter does more violence to our everyday notions of human psychology. However, as far as I am able to judge, the two systems are not necessarily incompatible, and we are at liberty to combine them eclectically, deriving what light we can from each. In *Civilization and its Discontents*, Freud says that the prohibition of incest was 'perhaps the most drastic mutilation which man's erotic life has in all time experienced'.[14] The powerful ambivalent feelings of the Oedipal son can be attributed to the fact that he both loves his mother and, because she denies him, hates her. On the Freudian view, then, it would seem that the crime of the rebellious son is partly a symbolical substitute for the Oedipal crime, partly a means of retaliating against the parent and the society that have frustrated him, and partly (in most cases) a means of bringing punishment on himself, and assuaging his guilt for having entertained the forbidden desire.[15]

Before we leave the subject of psychoanalysis, it is worth mentioning that both Gide and Sartre, in *The Counterfeiters* and *Being and Nothingness* especially, have expressed opinions highly critical of the teachings of Freud. One hesitates to make common cause with those who interpret every criticism of Freud as a sign of *resistance*, but at the same time it is difficult to deny that both Gide and Sartre seem to simply cry for a Freudian interpretation. Both of them lost their fathers during their childhood, and were brought up by doting mothers. Both men make freedom the cornerstone of their thinking, and, as we have seen, are committed to a revolt against the father, and a fierce rejection of the aid and divine consolation of God the Father. Both men flout the sexual mores of their class: Gide by his avowed homosexuality, and Sartre by his less blatant, but equally notorious, rejection of bourgeois marriage in his relationship with Simone de Beauvoir. Sartre, whose mother 'betrays' him by marrying again, does not marry, and has no children.* Gide, whose mother did not marry again, is 'faithful' to her in the sense that he marries only in name, not in the flesh. Sartre writes an existential analysis of Baudelaire, in which he argues that the remarriage of the poet's mother was the decisive event of his life; he also writes a play about an Orestes, who kills his mother and her second husband, and refuses to repent

---

* A passage from *Existentialism* seems to justify the inference that, for Sartre, to choose infertility for himself is to choose it for all, and thus to will the destruction of mankind: 'To take a more individual matter, if I want to marry, to have children . . . I am involving all mankind in monogamy and not merely myself. Therefore, I am responsible for myself and for everyone else. I am creating a certain image of man of my own choosing. In choosing myself, I choose man.'[16]

of his crime. Gide, for his part, writes a play depicting an Oedipus who kills his father and marries his mother, and also refuses to repent of his crime. Gide, a homosexual, writes *The Immoralist;* though not a homosexual, Sartre evidently dislikes women,[17] and he writes a book in praise of Jean Genet, who is (like Gide's Lafcadio) a homosexual, a bastard, and a criminal. It would be interesting to pursue this comparison further, but to do so would carry us quite beyond the scope of the present inquiry into the realms of comparative psycho-biography!

Our final task is to assess the role of the crime in the progress of the adolescent hero. On the positive side we may say that the crime takes the hero out of his study, and involves him in action; it teaches him that he is free; it brings to a successful conclusion the revolt against authority; and, more generally, it may be said that the carrying out of the crime is the culminating step along the path of self-assertion and self-realization. To kill a man to indulge a mere whim—it is impossible to conceive a more perfect devotion to the self and its desires! Porfiry, indeed, consoles Raskolnikov with this very thought. 'At least you haven't been deceiving yourself long', he tells him, 'You've reached the end of the road all at once.'

However, beside each of the above points we have to set a qualifying rider. No doubt the crime involves the hero in action, but the action he performs—for example, the murder committed by Raskolnikov or Lafcadio—is not carried out so much because the adolescent hero genuinely wants to do that particular act, as because he wants to prove that he is capable of doing it. In other words, the crime is still to a greater or lesser extent tainted by the self-preoccupation and the desire for self-esteem that we noted as characteristic of idealistic rectitudinitis and spurious acceptance. Then, again, the crime certainly teaches the hero that he is free, but since in reality his freedom is inalienable and immortal, it is obvious that he was just as free before the crime as after. To commit a crime to demonstrate that you are free is like entering your house by breaking down the front-door with an axe, when you have the door-key in your pocket all the time!

It is true, also, that the crime completes the radical revolt against the authority of the father. It would be difficult to overestimate the importance of this achievement, which is in fact the indispensable condition of the hero's progress, but even here we must acknowledge that the invincible father that the hero is wrestling with is largely a monster of his own creation. Moreover, since the father is not immortal, the son needed only to wait patiently to achieve victory without bloodshed or guilt. In Gide's play, *Oedipus*, written when he was sixty-two, the hero says: 'I was a king's son without knowing it. I had no need to kill to become a king, but merely to wait.'[18]

Finally, it must be conceded that the crime marks the end of a road. But what kind of a road is this? St Augustine, reflecting on his own 'gratuitous' crime—the theft of pears referred to earlier in this chapter—exclaims: 'Would any man commit a murder for no cause, for the sheer delight of murdering? The thing would be incredible.'[19] The crime of the adolescent hero is, in the last analysis, an absurd or insane act of destruction, which exacts an inevitable penalty. At the end of *The Immoralist* Michel declares that his strength is exhausted, and something in his will is broken: 'O taste of ashes! O deadly lassitude! O the sadness of superhuman effort!' he cries. It requires great strength and resolution to follow the road of self-assertion and self-realization to the bitter end. The man who possesses 'the unconquerable Will / And study of revenge, immortal hate, / And courage never to submit or yield' that we find, say, in Heathcliff in *Wuthering Heights*, can perhaps follow this path of excess until he arrives at the palace of wisdom. For those with less than superhuman strength, the way of crime leads to the weariness and torpor of Michel, to the delirium of Raskolnikov, or to the death of Kurtz in Conrad's *Heart of Darkness* after he has pronounced judgement on his own crimes with his dying words, 'The horror! The horror!'

This discussion of the crime completes our account of the adolescent hero, and of the 'horrible zigzags [his] path towards truth seems to involve' (to borrow the words of Belinsky quoted in Chapter Seven); the chapters that follow will be concerned with the spiritual odyssey of the mature hero of Consciousness. In T. S. Eliot's *The Cocktail Party* Sir Harcourt-Reilly shrewdly observes that 'All cases are unique, and very similar to others.' If the adolescent hero has to discover that he is unique and free, the hero of Consciousness has to achieve insight into the truth contained in the second half of Sir Harcourt-Reilly's aphorism: in other words, he must learn to know and feel not only that he is very much like everyone else, but also that everyone else is very much like him. '*Hypocrite lecteur!—mon semblable,—mon frère!*'

PART III

THE HERO OF
CONSCIOUSNESS

CHAPTER NINE

The Descent into Solitude

The strongest man in the world is the man who stands alone.
IBSEN, *An Enemy of the People*

The more our soul finds itself in perfect solitude, the fitter does it become to approach and reach up to its Creator and Lord.
IGNATIUS LOYOLA, *The Spiritual Exercises*[1]

The commission of a crime can be a means of escaping from the domination of the father, but the crime is a dark, paradoxical, and anomalous road to freedom. In this chapter we shall see that it is possible for the hero to achieve freedom, without violence to others, by cutting the umbilical cord which binds him to other men and entering into the solitude of his own depths. By means of a radical descent into solitude, the hero of Consciousness (that is, the hero struggling to pass from Self-Consciousness to Consciousness) can throw off the old, uneasy dependence on other people based upon money and fear and the desire for approval, and open the way to genuine, creative relationship.

Where the Calvinist divides men into the elect and the damned, Sartre, a latter-day Puritan (like Gide), divides them into the free and the enslaved. The problem of human enslavement is the central theme of many of Sartre's plays. In *The Respectful Prostitute*, for example, a white man in a southern town of the United States has shot a Negro. In order to clear him, his friends assert that two Negroes were trying to rape a white woman, and that the murderer shot one of them in her defence. They then try to persuade the woman, the respectful prostitute, to confirm their story, but she refuses to help to frame the other Negro. The white-haired Senator comes on the scene and paints her a heart-rending picture of the grief and shame of the white boy's dear old mother. She is touched, and says charmingly:

> As things stand, it's too bad the nigger didn't really rape me. . . . It would have meant so much to you, and it would have been so little trouble for me.[2]

The Senator then gives such an inspiring eulogy of the murderer —'one hundred per-cent American . . . Harvard . . . a firm bulwark against the Communists, labor unions, and the Jews'— that she is persuaded into signing the statement. Afterwards she repents, and when the Negro appears at her door she agrees to hide him from the lynching party. She urges him to fight, but he replies, 'I can't shoot white folks', and refuses. A short while later, she herself tries to shoot one of the guilty whites who comes to see her. She fails. He says to her: 'A girl like you *can't* shoot a man like me. Who are you? What do you do in the world? Do you even know who your grandfather was? I have a right to live.' And the play ends as the woman, a respectful prostitute, submits to his embraces.

As to the white man who says he has a right to live, Sartre, of course, asserts that human life is wholly contingent, *de trop*, or absurd in the existentialist sense, and that it is only a kind of fearful self-deception (or *mauvaise foi*) that makes a man persuade himself or others that he has a right to live. The Negro is the type of all oppressed people. His enslavement is evident in the fact that, even when he is in peril of his life, he says, 'I can't shoot white folks'; that is, he submits to the ideology of the dominant group.[3] The prostitute, who also ends by submitting, is the type of all of us. (And how characteristic it is of Sartre to represent mankind in general by the symbol of the respectful prostitute, that is, the prostitute who is a conformist!) Because she is vaguely aware of the claims of human decency, she refuses at first to bear false witness against the Negro, but she flees from her human responsibility—'I hate trouble, don't you understand?'—and so instead of making common cause with those who are oppressed, she yields to the desire to establish herself in the eyes of the people who really count, and ends up, uneasily, in the arms of the oppressor.

In *No Exit* we have Sartre's most powerful representation of the suffering which results from our dependence on other people, from our need to see a favourable reflection of ourselves in the eyes of others. The action takes place in Hell, and the three protagonists, who are newly dead, are locked together in a room, where they act out a curious variation upon the theme of the eternal triangle. Estelle, who in her life had betrayed her lover and made away with the child of their love, now has to 'justify' herself and distract herself by winning the love of Garcin. Garcin, who has been guilty of a shameful act of cowardice, now feels impelled to 'justify' himself by winning the respect of the cynical Inez. And Inez, a woman of masculine intelligence, is a Lesbian who seeks to escape her unbearable loneliness by winning the love of Estelle. Each refuses the respect, love or pity that the others crave, and every attempt by two of them to set up a mutual self-deluding and self-gratifying relationship is shattered by the third who ruthlessly holds up before them the mirror in which they see 'such black and grained spots / As will not leave their tinct'. (There are, significantly, no real mirrors in Hell; the protagonists are obliged to see themselves through the eyes of others—a situation I shall have more to say about later.) They wait, meanwhile, for the punishments of Hell to start, but they finally realize that they are creating their own hells for each other; in other words, they perceive that 'Hell is—other people', a conclusion that expresses with forceful exactitude the plight of man at the level of Self-Consciousness.

The task of the hero of Consciousness is to free himself from dependence on other people, and to enter into the solitude of his own depths. This process tends to be characterized by feelings of contempt and hatred towards other men. It is, of course, precisely because he is dependent on other men that the hero hates them, and the function of his hatred is to wrench him violently free from a degrading dependence on other people; once this has been accomplished, the hatred evaporates. To show the applicability of these generalizations to Sartre's work, we must turn to his first novel, *Nausea*.

The hero of *Nausea*, Antoine Roquentin, is a young man of independent means; as he is not under the necessity of working, is not married, and has no links with the past in the shape of family or friends, his connection with the rest of mankind is extremely tenuous. 'I have no troubles, I have money like a capitalist, no boss, no wife, no children: I exist, that's all', Roquentin says.[4] He watches, detached and aloof, as his fellow creatures perform their various antics, carry out the rites of salutation in the fashionable street of a Sunday morning, or, sleepy and full-bellied after Sunday lunch, wait inertly for the day of freedom to pass away. Sartre's most bitter attacks are reserved for the more successful and influential members of the bourgeoisie. For example, at the end of Roquentin's visit to the portrait-gallery, where the great men of Bouville are enshrined, there is a passage of devastating irony:

> Farewell, beautiful lilies, elegant in your painted little sanctuaries, good-bye, lovely lilies, our pride and reason for existing, good-bye you bastards!

The common people, on the other hand, inspire Roquentin with disgust rather than with hatred. The card-players in the café, for example, when viewed without compassion and from a strictly exterior viewpoint, are both ridiculous and disgusting:

> Smiles. His teeth are rotten. The red hand does not belong to him, it is his neighbor's, a fellow with a black moustache. The fellow with the moustache has enormous nostrils that could pump air for a whole family and that eat up half his face, but in spite of that he breathes through his mouth, gasping a little. With them there is also a young man with a face like a dog. I cannot make out the fourth player.

As he watches the hands being raised and withdrawn, and the cards falling, Roquentin recognizes that card-playing is simply a painless way of killing time. The need to kill time, to distract oneself and hide one's emptiness, necessarily involves one with other people. The café proprietor, for example, slides into unconsciousness as the café closes: 'When this man is lonely he sleeps.' And his customers are like him. 'In order to exist, they also must consort with others.' Even their solitude is corrupted by the invisible presence of others. 'People who live in society have learned how to see themselves in mirrors as they appear to their friends.' And this compulsion to see ourselves as others see us, as we shall see more clearly in a moment, is the root of the malady of Self-Conscious man.

Death, which means the annihilation of the self, is of course the real enemy that the bulk of mankind seeks to escape, or, at least, to ignore. When Roquentin visits the Bouville museum, he is fascinated by a painting called 'The Bachelor's Death'. It depicts the death of a bachelor, in squalor and misery, while his mistress robs him before his body is even cold, and a cat in the corner laps milk indifferently. The moral of the painting is obvious: marry, have children, get into line, or you will die in loneliness and neglect. Here we perceive the absurdity and pathos of man at the level of Self-Consciousness, who is so dependent on others that he even needs their presence to lend dignity and reality to the experience of dying.

The idea expressed by the painting is reinforced by the story of the Self-Taught Man who confesses that he joined the Socialist Party to escape from an unendurable solitude that was driving him to suicide:

Before taking this decision I felt myself in a solitude so frightful that I contemplated suicide. What held me back was the idea that no one, absolutely no one, would be moved by my death, that I would be even more alone in death than in life.

And, in a terrifying passage, Sartre shows that the doctor who prides himself on his 'experience' (a form of acquisition that he would like to believe is immune against decay) is in fact merely seeking to blot out from his consciousness the thought of death:

The truth stares me in the face: this man is going to die soon. He surely knows; he need only look in the glass: each day he looks a little more like the corpse he will become. That's what their experience leads to, that's why I tell myself so often that they smell of death: . . . And this terrible corpse's face! To be able to stand the sight of it in the glass he makes himself believe that the lessons of experience are graven on it.

It would be easy to multiply quotations tending in the same direction as those cited in the last few paragraphs, but this is not really necessary. Enough has been said to illustrate Sartre's 'misanthropy'—he, or, to be precise, the writer of the diary, prefers to express it more negatively, and say that he does not love mankind—and to suggest his diagnosis of the sickness of man at the level of Self-Consciousness. We must now turn to consider how Roquentin attempts to free himself from the bonds that shackle other men.

Early in the diary we find the statement, 'I live alone, entirely alone. I never speak to anyone, never.' Professor Champigny aptly sums up the situation of Roquentin, when he remarks, 'The only concrete relations he undertakes are those purely hygienic rapports he has with the proprietress of the "Rendez-vous des Cheminots".'[5] His loneliness is thrown into heightened relief by the conformity and sociability of those around him:

I am alone in the midst of these happy, reasonable voices. All these creatures spend their time explaining, realizing happily that they agree with each other. In Heaven's name, why is it so important to think the same things all together.

Looking back on the past, Roquentin realizes that previously he had only toyed with solitude for the sake of cultivating certain emotional experiences, where now he is entering into his own depths in earnest:

You must be just a little lonely in order to feel them, [these emotional experiences], just lonely enough to get rid of plausibility at the proper time. But I remained close to people, on the surface of solitude, quite resolved to take refuge in their midst in case of emergency. Up to now I was an amateur at heart.

As he penetrates deeper into the heart of his loneliness, Roquentin begins to be frightened by it; he recalls how, when he was a child, he and the other children instinctively fled from the lonely man that used to sit in the park, and he wonders if he is heading for the same fate. The fear of this happening makes him want to see again Anny, the woman he had formerly loved. We may note, incidentally, that it is generally true that as a man's isolation from society grows, his dependence on the woman increases. Thus Othello, the black man in a society of whites, seeks refuge in Desdemona, 'When I love thee not, / Chaos is come again'; and Matthew Arnold, in 'Dover Beach' passes naturally from lamenting the decay of religion, the cement of society, to an appeal to the woman: 'Ah, love, let us be true / To one another!' In our own century, the relationship between D. H. Lawrence and Frieda Lawrence provides a classical demonstration of the truth that the writer or intellectual who is cut off from society seeks refuge in the woman. In his darker moments, then, Roquentin's thoughts turn to Anny, but when after about a hundred and fifty pages without having any real contact with another human being, he does actually see her, he finds that she has travelled along the same paths as himself, and they have both gone too far into solitude for there to be the slightest possibility for them to re-establish their old relationship. 'I . . . I outlive myself', says Anny, with infinite weariness. The reunion, then, leads only to the inevitable and irrevocable parting, and Roquentin is cast once again, and yet more firmly, into his own inescapable solitude.

The descent into profound loneliness has a purpose and it brings a reward: it enables Roquentin to make the discovery that he exists, and that he is free. But what do these words mean? Sartre, of course, is perfectly well aware that the words 'freedom' and 'existence' are not entirely determinate and unequivocal, but he is forced to make use of them as the best tools that are available to him.* How, then, should we interpret them? In subjective terms, we may say that the statement that man is

---

* 'Indefinable and unnameable, is freedom also indescribable?' he asks in *Being and Nothingness*.[6]

free means that he is not, or does not have to be, dependent on other people. We can express the matter in philosophical language and say that there is no God, or that existence precedes essence, or that there are no eternal values inscribed on the universe, but all these ideas involve the question of dependence on other people, for, in Sartre's view, these absolutes, essences and eternal values are created by other people, and we are all enslaved by the monsters that others have created. (William Blake understood this when he said, 'I must create my own system or be enslaved by another's.') Though the bald statement that freedom means that one is not dependent on other people sounds somewhat pedestrian, it is clear that the inner experience or intuition of freedom has something of the character of a religious revelation. Thus when Roquentin looks at the roots of the chestnut tree and discovers the reality of his freedom, he cries out ecstatically:

> . . . contingency is not a delusion, a probability which can be dissipated: it is the absolute, consequently, the perfect free gift. All is free, this park, this city, and myself. When you realize that, it turns your heart upside down and everything begins to float. . . .*

When we turn to consider Sartre's use of the term 'existence', we find that it also is concerned with this same problem of dependence on other people. What brings on Roquentin's attacks of 'nausea' is the fact that objects in man's world—the puddle of yellow beer, the café proprietor's suspenders, the seat of the car—escape from the tyranny of usefulness and meaningfulness that man imposes on them, and reveal themselves as simply existing:

> Things are divorced from their names. They are there, grotesque, headstrong, gigantic, and it seems ridiculous to call them seats or say anything at all about them: I am in the midst of things, nameless things. Alone, without words,

* Cf. the Zen experience of *satori*, as described by Professor D. T. Suzuki: 'Just like ordinary everyday experience, except about two inches off the ground!'[7]

defenceless, they surround me, are beneath me, behind me, above me. They demand nothing, they don't impose themselves: they are there.

When we cease to organize the universe in terms of utility, ignoring those objects that are not useful, and seeing everything in terms of our own ends and purposes, the rich thingy-ness of creation reveals itself as overwhelming, frightening, and alive. The hero of *Nausea* has so far dissociated himself from mankind and its projects that objects reveal themselves to him in their naked existence, and thus cause him to experience nausea. But the rediscovery of reality at a pre-verbal level—'Things are divorced from their names'—necessarily involves the rediscovery of the self, subjectively experienced as existing also at the pre-verbal level.

The self when experienced at the verbal level, at the level of Self-Consciousness, is already tainted by dependence on others, since words come to us from other people, and when I *think myself* through words, I can do so only through the eyes and ideas of other people, and thus my concept of myself flickers and changes as other people promote me or demote me in their esteem; and since, in order to have a stable and gratifying idea of myself, I have to assure myself of their esteem, I have to bribe them by good behaviour, and this puts me at their mercy. But the hero in his loneliness discovers that he exists, that he possesses existence (*Dasein*), an existence real, certain, and incurable (at this present moment, that is), an existence prior to the Cartesian *cogito*, prior to all verbal formulations—'I thought without words, *on* things, *with* things' Roquentin says— prior to all efforts of the self to protect itself, to esteem itself, and to justify itself. In short, through the descent into solitude the hero regains that pristine, subjective knowledge of himself that he possessed prior to the emergence of the self with its concomitant dependence on other people. 'Except ye become as little children, ye shall in no wise enter into the kingdom of heaven', or, as Sartre puts it in *Being and Nothingness*, it is necessary to achieve a 'self-recovery of being which was previously corrupted.'[8] What we are speaking of here has to be experienced rather than described, since words are traitors to us from the start, belonging as they do to the public, objective world rather than to the world of subjectivity. The withdrawal from society and the consequent falling away of almost all forms of activity—'I'm not hungry but I'm going to eat to pass the time' Roquentin says—can be likened to the peeling of an onion. As one pulls off one piece of the onion-skin after another, it seems to the outsider, and to oneself because one sees with the same eyes as the outsider, that one is being stripped and reduced to nothing. At this point, there is the temptation to turn back to the hell that is other people, that is, to the hell that one knows rather than to the hell that one doesn't know. But the man who has the courage or pride, stubbornness or intellectual rigour, to continue the journey and complete the experiment, finds that as the onion shrinks away almost to nothing, there is a sudden jump, and in a flash he is aware that he is inside the onion, at the heart of the subjective. There is in Indian literature a story of a wise man who came to the king and offered to sell him eight books of wisdom for a very great sum. The king refused, and the wise man burnt four of the books, and offered him the remainder at the original price for eight. The king again refused, and the sage burnt two more books. Finally, there was only one book left, and the king was offered this for the same sum that he had before regarded as exorbitant for eight, and now he accepted. Only when we are in danger of losing everything does it become possible for us to understand the one thing that is needful. So Antoine Roquentin, denuded of social position, usefulness, honour, love and troops of friends, once he knows that he exists, is stronger than the rest of mankind who exist precariously, at the caprice of other people.

We have now seen that the hero of Sartre must undertake the descent into solitude in order to free himself from dependence on others; like the ancient Israelites he can escape from bondage in Egypt only by undertaking a long and painful journey through the wilderness. We have next to consider how far he succeeds in reaching the Promised Land of 'deliverance and salvation' of which Sartre speaks in *Being and Nothingness*.

The misanthropy of the hero, as we noted earlier, was a result of his dependence on others; when the hero discovers that he is rooted in freedom and existence, he is cured of misanthropy, because he now has nothing to fear from others and nothing to hope from them. 'He that is without fear and hate can walk untouched among the things of fear and hate', as the *Bhagavad-Gita* expresses it. Furthermore, when he knows that he exists and that he is free, he discovers by the same token that all men exist and are free, even though they hide their freedom from themselves. This discovery has two consequences. First, he feels love and pity for his brother, recognizing in him the free and sovereign being that is hidden by the self-protective, fearful mask of man at the level of Self-Consciousness. Second, perceiving that he has discovered a truth of inestimable value and importance, he feels impelled to try to teach this truth to as many other men as will receive it.

Even in *Nausea*, which is of course primarily concerned with the descent into solitude, we see clear indications of the commencement of the hero's journey back to mankind. At the end of the book, Roquentin decides to leave Bouville and go to live in Paris; in other words, he abandons his lonely, unproductive life in the provinces, and rejoins mankind in the metropolis. Then, before he departs, he asks the waitress in the café to play for the last time his favourite record, 'Some of These Days', and his heart is filled with tenderness for the Jew who wrote it and the Negro who sings it: 'Yet no one could think of me as I think of them, with such gentleness.' Listening to the song, he perceives that as a work of art it reflects man's freedom in its purest form, and he resolves himself to create a work of art, a novel, which will tell men what he has discovered. As hope begins to bud in him again, Roquentin says of himself: 'But I am like a man completely frozen after a trek through the snow and who suddenly comes into a warm room.' The image reminds one irresistibly of the last canto of the 'Inferno', when Dante departs from the frozen lake of Cocytus and emerges to glimpse again the stars of our human world; and the comparison with the 'Inferno' is in fact appropriate, since *Nausea* is precisely concerned with the descent of the hero into the hell of solitude

G

which paves the way for the recovery of human life. In the splendid words that Sartre gives to Orestes in *The Flies*: 'Human life begins on the far side of despair.'

It is clear that the last pages of *Nausea* foreshadow the main lines of Sartre's future development. I remarked that the man who is beginning the descent into solitude hates other men, but the hero who has completed the descent feels love and compassion toward them. This point can be well illustrated by a passage from *Dirty Hands*:

> *Hoederer*: You don't love men, Hugo. You love only principles.
>
> *Hugo*: Men? Why should I love them? Do they love me? . . . As for men, it's not what they are that interests me, but what they can become.
>
> *Hoederer*: And I, I love them for what they are. With all their filth and all their vices. I love their voices and their grasping hands, and their skin, the nudest skin of all, and their uneasy glances, and the desperate struggle each has to pursue against anguish and against death.

Hugo, as we have already seen, is in the classic Hamletian stage of misanthropy and rebellion against domination by the father and by father-substitutes; Hoederer, on the other hand, is one of Sartre's most successful attempts to portray the man who has achieved freedom and salvation.

I noted, too, with respect to Roquentin, that the man who has completed the descent into solitude has something of vital importance to say. That Sartre feels that he has an important message may be seen from this jubilant and apocalyptic passage which occurs at the end of *Being and Nothingness*:

> Existential psychoanalysis is going to reveal to man the real goal of his pursuit . . . existential psychoanalysis is going to acquaint man with his passion. In truth there are many men who have not waited to learn its principles in order to make use of them as a means of deliverance and salvation.[9]

Hazel Barnes, in her introduction to *Being and Nothingness*, has said that of all the novels *Nausea* 'is richest in philosophical content. In fact one might truthfully say that the only full exposition of its meaning would be the total volume of *Being and Nothingness*.'[10] We may perhaps go as far as to say that all of Sartre's work has its ultimate basis in the experience recorded in *Nausea*, although in fairness it is necessary to add that in some of his later work there is a falling away from the austere optimism and the unsentimental love of men that we get a glimpse of at the end of *Nausea*. For the moment, however, it is not Sartre's failures that concern us, but the triumphant demonstration in *Nausea* that the descent into solitude can be a road to 'deliverance and salvation'.

It would be easy to demonstrate the importance of the theme of the descent into solitude in any of a dozen or more modern writers, from Dostoyevsky (whose *Notes from Underground* is probably the direct literary ancestor of *Nausea*) down to Camus or Samuel Beckett in our own day. Carlyle, who was born a quarter of a century before Dostoyevsky, seems to me particularly significant because he grasped the existential truth that it is above all the death or disappearance of God that makes the descent necessary. Without religion, Teufelsdröckh says in *Sartor Resartus*, society would become a 'dead carcass,— deserving to be buried. Men were not longer Social, but Gregarious: which latter state also could not continue, but must gradually issue in universal selfish discord, hatred, savage isolation, and dispersion.' Teufelsdröckh's descent into solitude, then, like that of Roquentin, is a repudiation of the gregarious- ness and inauthenticity of the lonely crowd, and a quest for identity and freedom. 'I was alone, alone!' Teufelsdröckh cries, and a few pages later, he exclaims:

I kept a lock upon my lips: why should I speak much with that shifting variety of so-called Friends, in whose withered, vain and too-hungry souls Friendship was but an incredible tradition? . . . Now when I look back, it was a strange isolation I then lived in. . . . In midst of their crowded streets and assemblages, I walked solitary: and (except as it was my own heart, not another's, that I kept devouring) savage also, as the tiger in his jungle.

Teufelsdröckh, again like Roquentin, emerges briefly from his solitude to attempt to enter into a relationship with a woman, the fair Blumine, but Blumine rejects him on prudential grounds, and Teufelsdröckh is thrown back again into his embittered and embattled solitude. Then, in the crucial passage of the chapter, 'The Everlasting No', that we looked at in Chapter Six, there occurs the exultant moment of liberation when Teufelsdröckh realises that, even if all else is enslaved, he is free and a 'Child of Freedom, though outcast'. Later, he says: 'Our Life is compassed round with Necessity: yet is the meaning of Life itself no other than Freedom, than Voluntary Force.' What is this distinction between Necessity and Freedom but a nineteenth-century equivalent of Sartre's *Être-en-soi* (In-Itself) and *Être-pour-soi* (For-Itself), a distinction which is likewise the child of an inner experience or intuition of freedom? Like Roquentin again, Teufelsdröckh, after his illumination, finds that the bitterness and contempt that he had felt towards others, and especially towards the rich, powerful, and self-satisfied,[11] is changed into compassion:

> With other eyes, too, could I now look upon my fellow man; with an infinite Love, an infinite Pity. Poor wandering, wayward man! Art thou not tired, and beaten with stripes, even as I am? Ever, whether thou bear the royal mantle or the beggar's gabardine, art thou not so weary, so heavy-laden; and thy Bed of Rest is but a Grave. O my Brother, my Brother, why cannot I shelter thee in my bosom, and wipe away all tears from thy eyes!

Clearly, provided we make due allowance for the difference between the nineteenth-century sentimental, baroque, quasi-biblical rhetoric of Carlyle, and the astringent, ironic, quasi-philosophical language of Sartre, the parallel between *Sartor Resartus* and *Nausea* is unmistakable, for both books are spiritual autobiographies, thinly disguised as fiction, in which, through the device of a diary, we are told how a young man, a middle-class intellectual, overcomes the problem of isolation and alienation by employing the strategy of a descent into solitude.

Since at first sight there appears to be a touch of paradoxicality in the very idea of comparing Carlyle and Sartre, a word should be said about the important differences between them. Carlyle, after passing through 'The Everlasting No' of protest and revolt, emerges with the conviction expressed by Teufelsdröckh in 'The Everlasting Yea' that 'the Universe is not dead and demoniacal, a charnel-house with spectres; but godlike, and my Father's!' Carlyle, in other words, finally reposes on the fatherhood of God, while Sartre denies the existence of God, and takes his stand on the brotherhood of man, or human solidarity. This is a difference of some magnitude. Consistently with their respective ultimate allegiances, Carlyle is, in politics, an authoritarian of the right, while Sartre is of course on the extreme left. Predictably, again, Carlyle—in *Past and Present*, for example—lashes out at the unheroic present by contrasting it with the England of the past; Sartre, on the other hand, looks to the future, the future of the socialist revolution, for a cure for the evils of the present. (He says in *Anti-Semite and Jew*, for instance, that anti-Semitism is a bourgeois phenomenon that will not occur in a classless society.*) The differences between these two writers, and the resemblances between them, can be to some extent reconciled if we say that Carlyle is a Puritan of authoritarian stamp, a Presbyterian, while Sartre is a Puritan of the equalitarian variety, a Leveller or Independent.[12]

The final point that I want to make about the descent into solitude can be conveniently illustrated by a further comparison between Carlyle and Sartre. It is generally acknowledged that *Sartor Resartus* is Carlyle's best book, and it will be granted that *Nausea* is at any rate Sartre's best novel. It is not without significance that these early books should have been in many ways their best books, and that both Carlyle and Sartre towards the end of their careers seem to have become increasingly

---

* Cf. the sentimental Utopianism of the progressive Lebezyatnikov in *Crime and Punishment*: '. . . people ought not to have any fights and in the society of the future any sort of violence is unthinkable'.

rigid, pessimistic, and embittered. Part of the explanation lies in their Puritanism. The Puritan has a strong predisposition to separate men into the sheep and the goats, the elect and the damned, the free and the enslaved, or the hero and the mass of ordinary blockheads (to borrow a word that Carlyle employs even more frequently than Sartre uses the word *salaud*). The descent into solitude is liable to reinforce this predisposition, because it provides assurance that one is oneself of the elect, having experienced a 'Spiritual New-birth, or Baphometic Fire-baptism' (as Teufelsdröckh claims) or achieved a 'self-recovery of being which was previously corrupted' (as Sartre puts it). Now, this arbitrary division of mankind into the elect and the damned, and so on, is a dangerous falsehood. It is not true, as Sartre suggests, that one man achieves a final conquest of 'deliverance and salvation' while another remains wholly trapped in relationships of competitive sado-masochistic exploitation. Nor is it true, as Carlyle would have us believe, that the hero has a capacity (altogether lacking in the blockhead) of infallibly perceiving the Reality that underlies the flux of appearance. The real truth is that we are all free at some times and in some situations, and unfree in others, and each of us is part blockhead and part hero. As George Herbert says in 'The Temper':

> Although there were some fourtie heav'ns or more,
>> Sometimes I peer above them all;
>> Sometimes I hardly reach a score,
>> Sometimes to hell I fall.

We saw that through the descent into solitude the hero learns to feel love and pity for his fellow-men, and discovers his vocation for imparting to others the truths that he has learnt. But, in so far as men are blockheads, how can one love them or reasonably aspire to convert them? Or, conversely, since most men remain obdurately unregenerate in the face of all attempts to convert them, how can they be anything else but blockheads? (It is to be noted here that Carlyle and Sartre are alike in being actively involved in contemporary political issues, and profoundly disappointed in their political hopes.) Thus in Carlyle and Sartre the impulse to love and pity is constantly at odds with a Puritan tendency to separate men into sheep and goats, and to pronounce severe judgements on the goats.[13] By the time of 'Shooting Niagara' or 'The Nigger Question' and, to a less degree, *Critique de la raison dialectique* or *Morts sans sépulture*, Puritan rigidity and moroseness have overcome the fundamentally optimistic vision of *Sartor Resartus* and *Nausea*. In the final analysis, then, Carlyle and Sartre demonstrate that the gains achieved by the descent into solitude are not a perpetual, irrevocable possession; one recalls the words that the 'lost leader' Wordsworth used of himself: 'I see by glimpses now; when age comes on, / May scarcely see at all.'[14] Pascal, again, says: '*Ces grands efforts d'esprit, où l'âme touche quelquefois, sont choses où elle ne se tient pas; elle y saute seulement, non comme sur le trône, pour toujours, mais pour un instant seulement.*'*

To sum up, then, we may say that the descent into solitude carries the hero a stage beyond the crime, yet the dividing line between them is in some respects fairly thin. The crime, as a breach of faith with the community, itself constitutes a species of descent into solitude. The descent into solitude, on the other hand, is also a breach with the community, which tends to produce feelings of *Angst* and guilt. (In *Sartor Resartus*, the editor says of Teufelsdröckh: 'Thus must he, in the temper of ancient Cain, or of the modern Wandering Jew,—save only that he feels himself not guilty and but suffering the pains of guilt,— wend to and fro with aimless speed.') Moreover, if, as I suggested, the crime is a dark and paradoxical road to freedom, surely the descent into solitude is a paradoxical and anomalous road to freedom and genuine, creative relationship! The chief differences between the two are, first that the crime is a kind of *reductio ad absurdum* of the spirit of self-assertiveness, while the descent into solitude is not primarily a phenomenon of self-assertiveness, but, rather, a desperate expedient arising out of the breakdown of relationship at the level of Self-Consciousness; second, the descent into solitude, to a much greater

* The soul is unable to sustain those great spiritual efforts of which it is sometimes capable; it attains them, not as if it were mounting a throne for ever, but for a moment only.

extent than the crime, can lead to an illumination—brilliant and exciting, though not necessarily permanent—into freedom and existence, and thus bring release from self-assertion, and misanthropy, and other symptoms of dependence on other people.

CHAPTER TEN

The Encounter with Death

Three types of men have made all beautiful things. Aristo-
cracies have made beautiful manners, because their place in
the world puts them above the fear of life, and the countrymen
have made beautiful stories and beliefs, because they have
nothing to lose and so do not fear, and the artists have made
all the rest, because Providence has filled them with
recklessness.

W. B. YEATS, *Poetry and Tradition*

As we saw at the end of the last chapter, the crime and the
descent into solitude are anomalous means of achieving love and
relationship, for what do the crime and the descent into solitude
essentially represent if not the annihilation of the Other, either
literally or symbolically? Then, too, it is from his vantage-
point in solitude that the hero feels love and pity for his fellow-
man, and recognizes him as a brother; as soon as he rejoins
humankind in the metropolis, he encounters once again the
selfishness, the competitiveness and the hatred that prompted
his withdrawal. His very success in accomplishing the descent
into solitude seems to emphasize the gulf between him and
other people.* If the hero of Consciousness has to learn to know
and feel that *all cases are unique, and very similar to others*, then
it is plain that the crime and the descent into solitude are
admirably qualified for teaching the first half of this truth, but
not so well equipped for teaching the second. How, then, does

* Even at the end of *Nausea*, for example, we find Roquentin
looking down on other people: 'I feel so far away from them, on the
top of this hill. It seems as though I belong to another species'.

the hero of Consciousness obtain a firm grasp of the truth that all men are very similar? It is to this problem that we must now turn our attention.

One of the most instructive studies of the evolution of the Hamletian hero is the portrait of Pierre Bezukhov in Tolstoy's *War and Peace*. When we first make his acquaintance, Bezukhov is presented as a vacillating, corpulent, ungainly young man who is entirely lacking in will-power and decision. His weak good nature makes him the dupe of every rogue he meets; his stewards rob him, his friends impose upon him, and he allows himself to be manoeuvred into marrying a woman he does not love. Like Hamlet, he is a man who cannot make up his mind, but in his case the chief result of his lack of a centre of gravity in himself is that he is left at the mercy of other people and their desires. This is brilliantly illustrated in the account of his 'courtship' of Hélène:

> . . . when he had decided that to marry Hélène would be a calamity and that he ought to avoid her and go away, Pierre, despite that decision had not left Prince Vasili's and felt with terror that in people's eyes he was every day more and more connected with her . . . and that though it would be a terrible thing he would have to unite his fate with hers.[1]

So, under pressure from other people, Pierre Bezukhov drifts into marriage; later he finds himself involved in a duel; then, a chance encounter makes him decide to become a Freemason. His life, in short, is determined by the accidents that happen to him, and, again like Hamlet, he is a 'pipe for fortune's finger / To sound what stop she please'. This is one of the classical traits of Self-Conscious man.

In the course of time, during the Napoleonic wars when the French armies are nearing Moscow, Bezukhov decides that it is his 'mission' to assassinate Napoleon. (Again we may note that it is characteristic of the adolescent hero that he seeks to destroy the evildoer, or the evil father, in order to set to rights a world that is out of joint.) As an indirect consequence of his absurd efforts to carry out this fantasy, Bezukhov is arrested on suspicion of being an incendiary, and he is carried off by the

French in their retreat from Moscow. In this experience he has to endure great physical privation and intense suffering, and narrowly escapes being executed by a firing-squad. He witnesses brutality, inhumanity and death, and he sees the peasants, who undergo the same sufferings as himself, endure their afflictions patiently. (Compare Hamlet's encounter with death in the graveyard scene, and his reflections upon the stoicism of the grave-diggers.)

In this ordeal, Pierre Bezukhov is transformed. As he walks along with his bare feet covered with sores, he experiences the peace, joy and inner tranquillity that he had sought in vain in philosophy, in Freemasonry, in dissipation, and in sentimental, ineffectual philanthropy. He is changed physically. 'The look of his eyes was resolute, calm and animatedly alert, as never before.' When he returns to his own world, he proceeds, without hesitation and without fuss, to put his affairs into order. He finds that he now knows for certain what ought and what ought not to be done; he is no longer at the mercy of the toadies and flatterers who had burdened him; he takes proper control of his finances. Tolstoy writes of him:

> Formerly he had appeared to be a kind-hearted but unhappy man and so people had been inclined to avoid him. Now a smile of the joy of life always played round his lips . . . and people felt pleased by his presence.

Where before he was weak and distracted, pulled hither and thither by many currents, he is now clear, simple and resolute. In other words, he has emerged out of the doubt and indecision of Hamletian man, and obtained at least a glimpse of the Promised Land of Consciousness.

There are three main elements in Pierre Bezukhov's transformation: the peasants, his experience of suffering, and his encounter with death. About the importance of the peasants in Tolstoy's life and imagination a good deal is known. One calls to mind, for example, the famous scene in *Anna Karenina* when Levin, who corresponds to Tolstoy himself, works beside the peasants mowing in the fields. Levin envies the healthy, happy peasants, and he dreams of changing 'his wearisome, idle, and artificial personal life for that hard-working, pure, and delightful life'.[2] Of his own fame and greatness as a writer Tolstoy used to say that it counted for nothing with the peasants and so had no real existence. In his short story *The Death of Ivan Ilych* (which we shall consider at length later) only the peasant, Gerasim, feels a human, brotherly, instinctive compassion for Ivan Ilych, while his friends and family react to the dying man's suffering from their own purely selfish viewpoints. As far as Pierre Bezukhov is concerned, it is the example of the peasants, and particularly of the holy little man, Platon Karataev,* that enables him to see the folly and vanity of his past life. In the prisoners belonging to his own class he sees a reflection of his own limitations, of everything in himself that he dislikes, while through the peasants he rediscovers the inexhaustible, creative wonder of life itself.

What, then, is the significance of the peasant? The Hamletian hero, who is sickened by the egoism and competitiveness that he finds in himself and in other men of his own class, admires the peasant as a man who is not stricken by the malady of Self-Consciousness. Because he still dwells in the Garden of Eden of Unconsciousness, the peasant is not alienated from himself by the need to conform to a gratifying self-image, nor is he alienated from his fellow-men by the partitive demands of the self. (Thus Tolstoy writes of Karataev: 'But his life as he regarded it, had no meaning as a separate thing. It had meaning only as part of a whole of which he was always conscious.') In the eyes of the hero of Consciousness, Self-Conscious man is guilt-ridden, devitalized and anxious, while the man at the level of Unconsciousness is endowed with innocence, spontaneity and fullness of being; the one is sick, self-divided and rootless, while the other is healthy, whole and rooted in life; the one is an embodiment of individualistic acquisitiveness, the other of social co-operation and solidarity.

It may be argued that the virtues that the hero of Consciousness discerns in the peasant are imaginary. In *Rousseau and Romantic-*

---

* In *Sartor Resartus* Teufelsdröckh says: 'Sublimer in this world know I nothing than a Peasant Saint, could such now anywhere be met with. Such a one will take thee back to Nazareth itself.'

ism Irving Babbitt observes ironically of romanticism: 'The whole movement is filled with the praise of ignorance and of those who still enjoy its inappreciable advantages—the savage, the peasant and above all the child.'[3] If it is true that a great deal of sentimental nonsense has been written about the Noble Savage, it is also true that the decided verdict of a great movement like romanticism (which includes in its ranks men of the stature of Rousseau, Wordsworth and Tolstoy), though it may sometimes be partly wrong, must always be partly right, and bear witness to a real and substantial truth. We must approach this topic, then, without sentimentality, but also without condescending irony. What is justly admired in the peasant is his authenticity; he lives, spontaneously and unself-consciously, in accordance with the law of his real being. The error that many Romantics commit consists in the assumption that because the peasant is free from Self-Consciousness, and therefore lacks some of the vices they detest, he must also by the same token possess all the virtues that they admire. Nothing could be farther from the truth; one of the main reasons why the peasant lacks certain of the vices of Self-Consciousness is that he does not at all aspire to the virtues that Self-Conscious man values. Experience and reason both confirm that the peasant, who usually holds a fairly humble rank in the scale of creation, can be cruel, drunken or bestial. It can of course be said that the peasant's 'vices' are authentic; he indulges in them because he really enjoys them, not because he wants to think well of himself or to have others think well of him. Where Self-Conscious man, like the young Princess Victoria, says 'I will be good', Unconscious man lives his life without reference to (or at least with no more than the most fleeting reference to) ideal or moralistic goals. Thus when Unconscious man experiences negative feelings, such as hatred or envy, he lives out these feelings, and then has done with them. As Blake writes in 'A Poison Tree':

> I was angry with my friend:
> I told my wrath, my wrath did end.
> I was angry with my foe:
> I told it not, my wrath did grow.

Unconscious man tells his wrath—or acts it. Self-Conscious man hides his wrath from friend and foe, either out of prudence or out of a desire to avoid the sin of *ira*, and his buried wrath grows inwardly. When his heart is full of suppressed violence, Self-Conscious man has all the more reason to disguise and disown his feelings, with the result that the gulf between inward feeling and outward behaviour becomes ever wider. In Unconscious man, no shadow falls 'Between the desire / And the spasm', and he feels no motiveless malignity towards a mysterious Other who has robbed him of his life. Thus it can be said of Unconscious man that though he may be capable of barbarous cruelty towards his enemies, at least he does not rejoice in the misfortunes of his friends.

Since all created things, with the exception of man at a certain stage of his development, spontaneously obey the law of their own nature, it follows that what I have said about the peasant could be applied with equal appropriateness, not only to the savage and the child, but also to other living things. Tolstoy's choice of similes to describe Platon Karataev illustrates this point; he tells us that when Karataev wakes up, he is wholly awake instantly, just *as children are*; Karataev sings, not like a trained singer, but *like a bird*: he speaks and acts as spontaneously as a *flower* exhales its fragrance. The whole of the creation, in fact, by its obedience to the will of God, proclaims fallen man's guilt. The tree, for example, because it stands upright and has roots in the earth and branches in the heavens, is an apt symbol of that integrity of being which man has lost. Women have often been successfully used as symbols of Unconsciousness, because they are (or used to be) more instinctive creatures than men, and because traditionally they have been less thoroughly indoctrinated than men with the ideology of their society. Animals, too, are frequently employed to shadow forth the innocence and spontaneity of pre-lapsarian man, or to provide a backdrop against which the vices of Self-Conscious man show up more clearly. The Houyhyhnms serve the latter purpose in *Gulliver's Travels*. In *Hard Times* Dickens uses the faithful dog, Merrylegs, to confound the *laissez-faire* economists by showing, as Mr Sleary expresses it, that 'there ith a love in the world, not all Thelf-interetht after all, but thomething very different'. Near the end of *The Horse's Mouth* a haughty cat is introduced as a symbol of solitude and individuality in contrast to the gregarious human-beings who are so anxious to be liked. ('The cat turned its head away with a dignity you can't get in humans. They try too hard. And they're so sympathetic', Gulley Jimson notes.[4]) Consider, again Whitman's popular poem, 'Animals':

> I think I could turn and live with animals, they are so
>   placid and self-contained;
> I stand and look at them long and long.
> They do not sweat and whine about their condition;
> They do not lie awake in the dark and weep for their
>   sins;
> They do not make me sick discussing their duty to God;
> Not one is dissatisfied—not one is demented with the
>   mania of owning things;
> Not one kneels to another, nor to his kind that lived
>   Thousands of years ago;
> Not one is respectable or industrious over the whole earth.

One could adduce volumes of quotations along these lines, but it must already be clear that the biblical view that a man is better than a sheep is not universally accepted; on the contrary, it is sometimes considered to be a compliment to a man to raise him up to the dignity of an animal. Thus Melville says of his hero Billy Budd, who (we are told) has not eaten of the questionable apple of knowledge: 'Of self-consciousness he seemed to have little or none, or about as much as we may reasonably impute to a dog of St Bernard's breed.'

We are now in a position to attempt to strike a balance. It is natural that the man at an advanced stage of Self-Consciousness, in his sickness and despair, should admire the innocence, health and animal spirits of the peasant. The spontaneity and unselfconsciousness of the peasant exhibit, on a lower plane, an authentic image of the excellence that the hero of Consciousness is in quest of. The peasant does not consciously know that *all cases are unique, and very similar to others*, but since he is not blinded by self-love, he instinctively recognizes the truth expressed in this aphorism, and acts and feels in accordance with it. Unconsciousness and Consciousness, in fact, by reason of their fidelity to the real being, are alike diametrically opposed to Self-Consciousness. The quotation from Yeats that stands at the head of this chapter indirectly affirms this fact: the peasant and the artist can create beautiful things because they are free from the self-protective anxieties of man at the level of Self-Consciousness. Pascal, who is far from being a romantic, says in the *Pensées*:

> *Le monde juge bien des choses, car il est dans l'ignorance naturelle, qui est le vrai siège de l'homme. Les sciences ont deux extrémités qui se touchent. La première est la pure ignorance naturelle où se trouvent les hommes en naissant. L'autre extrémité est celle où arrivent les grandes âmes, qui, ayant parcouru tout ce que les hommes peuvent savoir, trouvent qu'ils ne savent rien, et se rencontrent en cette même ignorance d'où ils étaient partis; mais c'est une ignorance savante qui se connaît. Ceux d'entre eux, qui sont sortis de l'ignorance naturelle, et n'ont pu arriver à l'autre, ont quelque teinture de cette science suffisante, et font les entendus. Ceux-là troublent le monde, et jugent mal de tout.**

A little knowledge puffeth up, but the wise man and the peasant are both humble. The hero of Consciousness, then, has reason to feel an affinity with the peasant. At the same time, it must be confessed that there are serious limitations to the value of the peasant as a symbol. In the first place, the Tolstoyan peasant

---

* The common people are good judges of things, because they are in the state of natural ignorance, which is the true condition of man. Knowledge has two extremes that meet. The first is the pure natural ignorance in which all men find themselves at birth. The other extreme is that attained by great spirits, who, having exhausted all that men can know, discover that they know nothing, and find themselves once again in that same state of ignorance from which they had set out; but theirs is an educated ignorance, which is conscious of itself. Those between these two extremes, who have emerged out of natural ignorance, and have not been able to arrive at the other, possess a mere tincture of this competent knowledge, and pretend to be wise. They bring trouble to the world, and are bad judges of everything.

belongs to a species that is almost extinct; in our times the labouring classes almost everywhere receive a middle-class education and acquire the stable ego of the man at the level of Self-Consciousness, with the result that that state of ignorance which Pascal says is the true condition of man, has been virtually abolished. It is worth observing parenthetically that this assimilation of the labouring classes into the middle classes helps to explain why contemporary writers, like Faulkner or the Steinbeck of *Tortilla Flat*, draw their characters from the lowest dregs of humanity, from social outcasts, degenerates and imbeciles. It is only at this level that they can find the truly Unconscious man who will enable them to satisfy their nostalgia for a lost innocence, or provide them with a stick with which to beat their Self-Conscious readers' backs. E. M. Forster's Italians and Greeks, D. H. Lawrence's gypsies and North American Indians, and Samuel Beckett's tramps, all obviously perform the same function.

Second, he who has not passed through the hell of Self-Consciousness does not understand mankind. Such ignorance is excusable in the peasant, but it is an intolerable deficiency in the seeker after truth. Thus Pascal, after demonstrating in the passage just quoted that the common people have a right view of the world, in his very next proposition overturns that judgement, saying:

> *Mais il faut détruire maintenant cette dernière proposition, et montrer qu'il demeure toujours vrai que le peuple est vain, quioque ses opinions soient saines: parce qu'il n'en sent pas la vérité où elle est, et que, la mettant où elle n'est pas, ses opinions sont toujours très fausses at très mal saines.**

It may very well be argued that the perfection of the peasant is of a lower order than the imperfection of Self-Conscious man. In any case, it is impossible for Hamletian man to revert to the

---

* But it is necessary now to destroy this last proposition, and show that it is always true that the common people are deluded, even though their opinions are sound: because they do not perceive the truth to be where it is, and place it where it is not, their opinions are always wholly false and unsound.

level of Unconsciousness, or to recover a lost ignorance. Thus though the hero's heart may be cheered and refreshed by the peasant or the child, he must not attempt to emulate them. The saying 'Except ye become as little children, ye shall not enter into the kingdom of heaven' is misleading unless it is coupled with the injunction, 'Be ye therefore wise as serpents, and harmless as doves.' Only by passing from Self-Consciousness into Consciousnses can Hamletian man regain Paradise.

We have spoken about the peasants, and we have next to consider the role of suffering in Pierre Bezukhov's transformation. Let us begin with the simplest and most tangible form of suffering—pain. We saw that while he was in captivity Pierre Bezukhov had to sleep on the cold, damp ground, and to endure hunger and thirst and foot-sores, and that it was in the midst of these hardships that he achieved peace of mind and a feeling of vigour and *joie de vivre* such as he had never known before. The use of pain is that it brings us into contact with reality. In the cloistered security of my own mind, I can harbour the belief that I am a great man, or imagine that it is my appointed task to assassinate Napoleon, but pain easily disabuses me of these illusions. King Lear learns this lesson in the storm: 'They told me I was everything. 'Tis a lie: I am not ague-proof.' Even the mildly painful labour of digging a ditch brings home to us concretely the limitations that the nature of things imposes upon us. 'This is the monstrosity in love, lady', says Shakespeare's Troilus, 'that the will is infinite and the execution confined; that the desire is boundless, and the act a slave to limit.' Viewed from the standpoint of youthful idealism and its pretensions, the limitations of the material world are an affront to human dignity, but from the standpoint of maturity (as we see, for example, in a film like *Woman of the Dunes*), it is the painful struggle against these limitations that brings about the creative encounter with reality. As Simone Weil finely observes: 'Each time that we have some pain to go through we can say to ourselves quite truly that it is the universe, the order and beauty of the world, and the obedience of the creation to God which are entering our body.'[5]

Where pain teaches us the limitations that we must acknowledge in the physical world, suffering teaches us that our desires are not omnipotent in the inner world either. And what is it that we desire? In *Sartor Resartus* Teufelsdröckh asks and answers this question in the climactic chapter, 'The Everlasting Yea':

> What is this that, ever since earliest years, thou hast been fretting and fuming, and lamenting and self-tormenting, on account of? Say it in a word: is it not because thou are not HAPPY? Because the THOU (sweet gentleman) is not sufficiently honoured, nourished, soft-bedded and lovingly cared for?

In this passage Carlyle lays his finger upon the most characteristic trait of modern man: his belief in his inalienable right to happiness. The utilitarian claims that the greatest happiness of the greatest number is the end of life. The romantic eagerly or greedily pursues his own private happiness, and asks plaintively, 'Wherefore am I not happy?' The merchant assumes that money procures happiness, so that for him money becomes the mediate object of life. (We may note parenthetically that there is a profound analogy between the merchant and the utilitarian: just as the merchant seeks to make abstract money, and the concrete means by which he obtains money are merely instrumental, so the utilitarian fixes his eyes on the abstract goal of happiness, and the concrete content of this happiness—for instance, the water with which I quench my thirst—is likewise merely instrumental.) Men of all creeds, then, find a common ground in the universal clamour after happiness. Now, if happiness is the end of life, Self-Conscious man's competitive attitude towards other people must above all express itself with respect to the quest for happiness. Accordingly, Self-Conscious man wants to believe in, and convince others of, the superiority of his own happiness; so he rejoices in the misfortunes of his friends because they help to improve his own standing in the happiness charts. In the interests of self, then, there is the attempt to grasp happiness and to escape from suffering. But suffering is an inevitable part of life ('Man was made for joy and woe', as Blake says), and the attempt to evade suffering increases still farther the gulf between the unreasonable demands of the self and the real nature of things. As a result, a vicious circle is created. We try to interfere with the natural movement of life in the hope of procuring for ourselves more happiness and less suffering. This interference creates more suffering. This suffering creates still more desperate attempts to escape. And so on. When suffering reaches a sufficient degree of intensity, the futility of the acquisitive pursuit of happiness becomes evident. Immediately after the passage just quoted from *Sartor Resartus*, Teufelsdröckh rounds upon himself scornfully:

> Foolish soul! What Act of Legislature was there that *thou* shouldst be Happy? A little while ago thou hadst no right to *be* at all. What if thou wert born and predestined not to be Happy, but to be Unhappy! Art thou nothing other than a Vulture, then, that fliest through the Universe seeking after somewhat to *eat*; and shrieking dolefully because carrion enough is not given thee?

Because the quest for happiness is at the heart of the endeavour of the self, to renounce the idea that one has a right to be happy (or a right to exist*) is an important step on the road towards renouncing the self and its aspirations altogether. Thus Teufelsdröckh goes on, in language very much like that which the orthodox Christian might use, to express his gratitude for the 'manifold merciful Afflictions' which were necessary because 'the Self in thee needed to be annihilated'. Born of the desire to evade suffering, the self is finally annihilated by the suffering that it brings upon itself; like a scorpion it stings itself to death. Pierre Bezukhov achieves a similar insight into the positive value of suffering when a voice in a dream says to him: 'If there were no such thing as suffering, man would know no limits to his own will—he would not know himself.' Suffering, then, is a means of achieving self-knowledge or, rather, self-identity. Itself a particular mode of the descent into solitude (since, as Tolstoy notes in connection with Pierre Bezukhov, men instinctively avoid the unhappy man), suffering thrusts the hero into the immediate reality of his own unique

---

* Compare Sartre's view of those who think that they have a right to live.

life at the same time that it initiates him into the wide fellowship of suffering men. Once he knows that he is unique and very similar to everyone else, the hero is able to look upon other men compassionately rather than competitively, so that he becomes like Edgar in *King Lear*,

> A most poor man, made tame to fortune's blows,
> Who, by the art of known and feeling sorrows,
> [is] pregnant to good pity.

We may add that the 'most poor man' who has been taught by fortune's blows to know who he is and to understand his proper place in the scale of creation is in fact rich, just as at the end of the play Lear and Cordelia in prison are richer than the packs and sects of great ones who ebb and flow by the moon.

Our discussion up to this point might appear to suggest that suffering is desirable because it curbs the lust for happiness, but this conclusion is an over-simplification in two important respects. First, the desire for happiness is not necessarily reprehensible. At one point in the course of his discussion of happiness, Carlyle has Teufelsdröckh say:

> . . . there is in man a HIGHER than Love of Happiness: he can do without Happiness, and instead thereof find Blessedness!

Carlyle here appears to be groping towards the truth that there is a right happiness and a wrong happiness. There is the happiness that consists in living an 'imaginary life in the opinion of other people', as Pascal expresses it (that is to say, the happiness that lies in the gratification of the self), and on the other hand there is the right happiness—or 'Blessedness', as Carlyle calls it—of the real being, which is a proper object of desire. If life is a blessing, then simply to live is to be blessed or happy; as Father Zossima says in *The Brothers Karamazov*: '. . . men are made for happiness, and anyone who is completely happy has a right to say to himself: "I am doing God's will on earth." All the righteous, all the saints, all the holy martyrs were happy.'[6]

Second, the belief that suffering is desirable can be dangerous, because it makes suffering an object of spiritual acquisitiveness. When it is said, as for example Nietzsche says in *Beyond Good and Evil*, that the depth of a man's suffering is almost a measure of his worth, the Hamletian hero naturally wants to establish his claim to a distinguished place in the first rank of sufferers. 'What's better—cheap happiness or lofty suffering?' Dostoyevsky's Underground Man asks.[7] Needless to say, the substitution of the greedy pursuit of suffering for the greedy pursuit of happiness does nothing to diminish the gulf between the unreasonable demands of the self and the real nature of things. When you bang your head against a wall, the pain that you experience warns you to stop; he who thinks that suffering enriches the soul is in the position of a man who goes on doggedly banging his head against a wall in the belief that the pain is good for him. Then again, one of the great virtues of suffering is that it teaches humility, but if suffering is considered to be a prerogative of the spiritually elect, it will beget pride instead of humility. Thus it may be seen that the acquisitive desire for suffering prevents men from understanding the meaning of their suffering, and so exposes them to yet more fruitless sorrow.

When we turn to consider the significance of death for the hero of Consciousness, we find that nearly everything that can be said about suffering applies *a fortiori* to death, which is the final and irrefutable demonstration of the impotence of the self. It will be remembered that Pierre Bezukhov, like Dostoyevksy in real life, was led out before a firing-squad to be (as he supposed) shot. In point of fact, he was not himself one of the men selected for execution, but he was forced to watch the gratuitous, cold-blooded slaughter of some of his fellow-prisoners, and this sight, Tolstoy says, extinguished his faith in the goodness of creation, in his own soul, and in the existence of God. This descent into anguish and despair is a necessary prelude to his regeneration, for it destroys the shaky edifice of a faith that was based on sentimentality and unreality, and prepares the ground for the experience with the peasant, Platon Karataev, which enables Pierre's soul to be resurrected on 'immovable foundations'. Death, then, is a touchstone which enables us to distinguish what is real from what is sham, what belongs to the real being from what belongs to the self. This is well illustrated in the novel by Prince Andrew Bolkonsky, who, on the eve of the battle of Borodino, sees in the light of death the essential insignificance of the passions—patriotism, the desire for glory, love of a woman—that had governed his life: 'Yes, I see them all,—a series of delusive images which cheated my excited fancy! thought he, looking at them in the cold relentless glare cast by the presence of death.'

From the point of view of our present inquiry, we should consider death in relation to two topics: the future and the descent into solitude. It is the nature of Self-Conscious man to sacrifice the present to the future. The future can be seen either as a danger against which he must prepare himself as best he can (for example, by putting money away for a rainy day) or as a land of milk and honey which can be reached only through effort and sacrifice now. In either event, the present is fully absorbed in preparing for this future, and thus the present itself—which is, of course, the only thing that really exists at all —is forever being swallowed up in the maw of an ever-vanishing future. Pascal expresses this truth with beautiful clarity in the *Pensées*:

> *Que chacun examine ses pensées, il les trouvera toutes occupées au passé et à l'avenir. Nous ne pensons presque point au présent; et, si nous y pensons, ce n'est que pour en prendre la lumière pour disposer de l'avenir. Le présent n'est jamais notre fin: le passé et le présent sont nos moyens; le seul avenir est notre fin. Ainsi nous ne vivons jamais, mais nous espérons de vivre; et, nous disposant toujours à être heureux, il est inévitable que nous ne le soyons jamais.**

Let us consider a specific example. When man at the level of Self-Consciousness feels, say, anger against someone like his

* If each person examines his thoughts, he will find them entirely occupied with the past and the future. We practically never think of the present; and if we do think of it, it is only with the object of obtaining insight from it in order to control the future. The present is never our goal: the past and the present are our means; the future alone is our goal. Thus we never live, but only look forward to living; and, since we are always preparing to be happy, it is inevitable that we never are.

employer, he inhibits this anger lest the person in authority do him an injury at some time in the future. As a result, his anger works inwardly like a poison, or it is discharged in other circumstances (for instance, onto his wife when he gets home from the office) where it does not belong. Thus two situations are perverted: the original situation in which the anger is repressed, and the later situation in which it is improperly discharged. In both cases the lesson that the experience had to offer is lost. Man at the level of Self-Consciousness, then, preserves his life, but his life is emptied of its real significance; in seeking to save his life he loses it, where man at the level of Consciousness takes no thought for the morrow, and so loses his life to save it. The contrast can be well illustrated by a short passage from *Antony and Cleopatra* which occurs when Lepidus is trying to enlist the aid of Enobarbus in bringing about a reconciliation between Caesar and Antony:

> *Lepidus*:   'Tis not a time
>   For private stomaching.
> *Enobarbus*:   Every time
>   Serves for the matter that is then born in't.

Lepidus, like Self-Conscious man, endeavours to regulate his behaviour in the present with the object of achieving some future goal, while Enobarbus is ready to give the reality of the moment its due.

When a man is brought face to face with death, he discovers that this endless stream of tomorrows is a mirage. (R. P. Blackmur, incidentally, is quite wrong to suggest that 'Today, and today, and today' would do just as well as 'Tomorrow, and tomorrow, and tomorrow' in Macbeth's famous speech; it is the future that corrupts Macbeth's strong imagination.) The tomorrow when we mean to begin to live never comes. Camus makes this point effectively in *The Myth of Sisyphus*:

> We live on the future: 'tomorrow', 'later on', 'when you have made your way', 'you will understand when you are old enough'. Such irrelevancies are wonderful, for, after all, it's a matter of dying. Yet a day comes when a man notices or

says that he is thirty . . . He belongs to time, and by the horror that seizes him he recognizes his worst enemy. Tomorrow, he was longing for tomorrow, whereas everything in him ought to reject it. That revolt of the flesh is the absurd.[8]

Anxiety about the future robs us of the present, but in the moment of confrontation with death there *is* no future. The imaginative confrontation with death, therefore, allows the present to be reborn in all its beauty and truth and terror.

We must now turn to a consideration of death and solitude. It is a characteristic trait of man at the level of Self-Consciousness that he is unable to endure solitude; in order to esteem himself, in order to be reassured of his own existence, he must seek a favourable reflection of himself in the eyes of other people. This dependence on other people, this fear of being forced to be alone, puts Self-Conscious man at the mercy of other people, so that he is forced to laugh when they say laugh and weep when they say weep (as we observed in connection with Pierre Bezukhov). But 'other people' cannot save us from death, and death forces us to face our solitude. Thus it is only at the end of *Scarlet and Black* that Julien Sorel, as he awaits death in prison, finally achieves peace of mind and deliverance from bondage to other people: 'Leave me to enjoy my ideal life of dreams [*ma vie idéale*]', he exclaims. 'What do I care for *other people?* My relations with *other people* are soon to be abruptly severed.'[9] The encounter with death, then, is a species of descent into solitude, but, unlike the simple descent into solitude or even the experience of suffering, it does not afford any encouragement to feelings of pride and superiority. When I know and feel that I must die alone, I know, too, that all men must die alone: '*on mourra seul*', as Pascal says. What sophistry could find grounds for self-conceit in this universal and inescapable truth about the human condition? Thus death (or, rather, the contemplation of death) is the most effective means of teaching the hero of Consciousness that *all cases are unique, and very similar to others.*

At this point it may be useful to say a few words about Tolstoy's short story, *The Death of Ivan Ilych*, which is a remarkable account of the impact of death on the pretensions and evasions of man at the level of Self-Consciousness. Ivan Ilych is a typical Russian bureaucrat, a capable, sociable, conformistic member of his class. He lives comfortably and respectably, enjoying above all other things a good game of bridge. He does not love his wife, but, by transferring the centre of gravity of his life to his work, he succeeds in arranging his affairs so that her existence does not incommode him too much. He has cultivated the art of pleasing, and his pleasant, conventional personality has smoothed his path through life. He has prospered in the legal profession because he has found a way of simplifying all the problems he has to deal with; his method is 'to exclude everything fresh and vital, which always disturbs the regular course of official business'.[10] Near the beginning of the story, Tolstoy says of his hero: 'Ivan Ilych's life had been most simple and most ordinary and therefore most terrible.' The function of the *death* of Ivan Ilych is to bring the truth of this statement home to Ivan Ilych himself.

When Ivan Ilych becomes seriously ill, the agreeable and decorous life to which he considers himself entitled is interrupted. Illness makes him irritable and depressed. He can no longer enjoy his games of bridge. His doctors are exponents of his own method; they treat him as an object, discussing his illness in technical terms, but ignoring the suffering, anxious man. For his colleagues and subordinates the chief interest of Ivan Ilych's illness lies in the possibility of his post becoming vacant. His wife wants him to die, because he is a burden upon her, but at the same time she wants him to go on living, because he is still drawing a salary. The indifference of others casts him into solitude, and his solitude is deepend by the knowledge that he alone is going to die, while they are all going to go on living. Tolstoy writes:

Latterly during that loneliness in which he found himself as he lay facing the back of the sofa, a loneliness in the midst of a populous town and surrounded by numerous acquaintances and relations but that yet could not have been more complete anywhere—either at the bottom of the sea or under the earth—during that terrible loneliness Ivan Ilych had lived only in memories of the past.

Reflection upon the past reveals to him that his childhood was a joyful time, and that there was some good in his youth and a little good in his early manhood, but that as time went on his efforts to live decorously and in conformity with the ideas of highly placed people had filled his life with falsity and sterility. (It is the history recorded in the 'Intimations Ode': the child sports by the sunlit ocean, and even the youth 'by the vision splendid / Is on his way attended', but at length all fades into the light of common day.) He thinks to himself:

'It is as if I had been going downhill while I imagined I was going up. And that is really what it was. I was going up in public opinion, but to the same extent life was ebbing away from me. And now it is all done and there is only death.'

In short, death teaches Ivan Ilych the truth of Pascal's statement that we sacrifice our real life for the sake of living an imaginary life in the opinions of other people.

As his condition grows worse, Ivan Ilych's rage and resentment increase. He is offended by the health and energy of others, and derives a bitter satisfaction from the thought that they too will sooner or later meet the same fate as him. He loathes his wife: 'While she was kissing him he hated her from the bottom of his soul and with difficulty refrained from pushing her away.' However, as death approaches and all hope vanishes, his hatred evaporates. (We hate other people because we think they constitute a threat to us. What has a man who is on the point of death got to protect?) Just as Prince Andrew Bolkonsky in *War and Peace*, as he is dying, at last truly understands the meaning of the command to love those that hate you, so near the very end, Ivan Ilych's feelings are softened and he feels pity, first for his son, and then for his wife also:

With a look at his wife he indicated his son and said: 'Take him away . . . sorry for him . . . sorry for you too. . . .' He tried to add, 'forgive me', but said 'forego' and waved his hand, knowing that He whose understanding mattered would understand.

Thus the imminence of death (or the imaginative contemplation of death) reveals the impotence of the self and the futility of one's self-protective activities, and so opens the way to the recovery of authenticity and genuine, creative relationship. Even though Ivan Ilych's final victory over death ('There was no fear because there was no death. In place of death there was light.') is unconvincing, it does very little to impair Tolstoy's achievement; *The Death of Ivan Ilych* remains a wholly convincing and magnificently successful demonstration of the value of the imaginative contemplation of death.

In conclusion, we should note that it is not a mere accident that suffering, death and the peasants should all play a part in Pierre Bezukhov's journey towards Consciousness. The connection between suffering and death we have already established; but there is a natural connection, too, between the peasants and suffering. The middle classes think that they have a right to be happy, but the peasants know that suffering and sorrow are part of life. (Thus Platon Karataev says to Pierre Bezukhov: 'Suffering lasts only an hour, but life goes on for ever.'[11]) The money of the middle classes shields them from many of life's troubles, but the peasants' condition makes them a natural prey to every kind of misfortune. As Simone Weil says:

> Peasants and workmen possess a nearness to God of incomparable savour which is found in the depths of poverty, in the absence of social consideration, and in the endurance of long drawn-out sufferings.[12]

The peasant's attitude to death, moreover, is very different from that of Self-Conscious man. In *The Death of Ivan Ilych*, for example, the members of Ivan Ilych's own class are afraid of death, and avert their eyes from the awful reality of his dying; it is only the peasant, Gerasim, who can treat his master with compassion, and face the fact of death quite simply, saying: 'It is God's will. We shall all come to it some day.' Similarly, in *Moby Dick*, when Queequeg, who is manifestly a symbol of man at the level of Unconsciousness, falls ill, he tranquilly prepares himself to die, and even orders his coffin and tests it for size; then he suddenly remembers a duty ashore that he has not performed, so he decides not to die. 'In a word, it was Queequeg's conceit', Melville tells us, 'that if a man made up his mind to live, mere sickness could not kill him.' Self-Conscious man dreads suffering and death above all because they cause him to lose face in the eyes of other people; as a character in Orwell's *Nineteen Eighty-Four* says, 'every human being is doomed to die, which is the greatest of all failures'. Unconscious man, who lives from within, instinctively knows that life is a manifestation of energy, and that when there is no energy, life departs. What is so dreadful about this? Thus the ultimate significance of Pierre Bezukhov's experience in captivity is that suffering, death and the peasants teach him to live from within, to achieve 'a self-recovery of being which was previously corrupted' (as Sartre says), so that he is able to discover 'another new and comforting truth—that there is nothing in the world to be dreaded.'[11]

CHAPTER ELEVEN

The Return to Sensation

O for a life of Sensations rather than of Thoughts!
JOHN KEATS, 'Letter to Benjamin Bailey'

Goethe says somewhere that the young poet ought to do some violence to himself in order to escape from mere general ideas. Many of the topics that we have been considering, such as the crime or the descent into solitude, can very well be considered as violent attempts on the part of the hero to escape from mere general ideas or from abstract thinking. Once the habit of abstract thinking is acquired, however, it is not easily shaken off. To preserve and consolidate what he has gained, the hero needs to develop a mode of consciousness or a function (in Jung's sense of the word) that will provide him with a permanent bulwark against abstract thinking. It is to this problem that we must now turn our attention.

Since a disproportionate stress on thinking tends to produce a desiccation of the feelings, it is understandable that *feeling* should first have suggested itself as the natural antidote against abstract thinking. John Stuart Mill's *Autobiography* provides the classic illustration of this truth. Mill received at the hands of his father, whose 'teachings tended to the undervaluing of feeling', a rigidly Benthamite education as a mere reasoning machine. At the age of twenty, Mill went through a mental crisis during which he came to believe that all feeling was dead within him; the part played in his recovery by the poetry of Wordsworth is told in Chapter Five of the *Autobiography*:

> What made Wordsworth's poems a medicine for my state of mind [Mill writes], was that they expressed, not mere outward beauty, but states of feeling, and of thought coloured

by feeling, under the excitement of beauty. They seemed to be the very culture of the feelings, which I was in quest of.

Mill, then, had his own painful experience as authority for his conclusion that a one-sided development of the analytical spirit 'has a tendency to wear away the feelings',[1] and for his belief that a corrective is to be found in the culture of the feelings.

That Mill's experience was in its main outlines representative can be seen from the frequency with which the theme of a movement from thought to feeling occurs in the literature of the period. Goethe's Faust, for example, rebels against the academic world and his role as a teacher (that is, as a disseminator of abstract ideas), and embraces the creed of feeling— Gefühl ist alles. In The Sorrows of Young Werther, also, the hero turns to feeling as a refuge from the abstract and impersonal. 'The things I know, every man can know', says Werther, 'but, oh, my heart is mine alone!'[2] In Crime and Punishment, as we have seen, Raskolnikov finally rejects thinking in favour of the value of feeling embodied in Sonia: 'Besides, now he would hardly have been able to solve any of his problems consciously; he could only feel. Life had taken the place of dialectics, and something quite different had to work itself out in his mind.' In Anna Karenina, we have on the one hand a number of people, such as Karenin and Koznyshev, who fail because they are unable to escape from the yoke of abstract thinking, and on the other hand we see the hero, Levin, achieve salvation through a conversion to feeling that is very similar to Raskolnikov's. At one point, an anguished consciousness of the meaninglessness of life drives Levin to the verge of suicide; then, in the final chapters of the novel, a remark made by a peasant brings him enlightenment, and he suddenly becomes aware that the answer which had eluded his powers of reason, had all along been known intuitively to his heart and his feelings, and so he renounces what he calls the pride of intellect, the stupidity and dishonesty of intellect:

'I looked for an answer to my question [he says to himself]. But reason could not give me the answer, for it is incommensurable with the answer. Life itself has given me the answer, in my knowledge of what is good and what is evil.'[3]

The Tolstoyan moralistic emphasis aside, the similarity to the ending of *Crime and Punishment* is unmistakable. Thus it appears that the two great Russian novelists shared Coleridge's view, expressed in *Biographia Literaria*, that 'all the products of the mere reflective faculty partook of death', and agreed in finding a remedy for the evil in a return to feeling.[4]

At the same time it is obvious, as the history of romanticism indeed shows, that in the long run feeling could not provide a satisfactory solution to the problem of dissociation. The point about man at the level of Self-Consciousness is that he looks at himself from the outside, and thus is dissociated from his feelings. But if a man either has no feelings, or is alienated from his feelings, how is he helped by hearing the praises of feeling sung? This difficulty is aggravated by the ambiguities inherent in the word *feeling*. I feel awe when I see the sun rise above a mountain-top, and I feel chagrin when I am not invited to an acquaintance's party. Am I to cultivate both these 'feelings' indiscriminately? In the *Autobiography*, shortly before the passage about Wordsworth that I quoted a moment ago, Mill reports that he first had recourse to Byron, 'a poet, whose peculiar department was supposed to be that of the intenser feelings', but that he got no good, only harm, from his reading of this poet. It is indeed notorious that the Byronic or Wertherian hero is a self-pitying egoist indulging his feelings; yet the gospel of feeling in itself is unable to provide the criteria by means of which we may discriminate between desirable and undesirable feelings.

There is another difficulty connected with the gospel of feeling; the propagation of the *idea* that intensity of feeling is praiseworthy brings to birth an anxious self-consciousness. Instead of simply admiring the sunset, I look at myself to make sure that I am admiring it. In due course, as Jane Austen shows in *Sense and Sensibility*, feeling becomes an instrument of self-assertion and competitiveness. Each competitor in the 'sensibility stakes' (to borrow a happy expression of Stephen Spender's) tries to show that his feelings are bigger and better than his neighbour's. We can see this phenomenon, indeed, in the sentence quoted a short while ago from *The Sorrows of Young Werther*: 'The things I know, every man can know, but, oh, my heart is mine alone!' Here, evidently, feeling is used to emphasise the speaker's sense of his own uniqueness and importance. Thus, instead of bringing men home to themselves, and instead of teaching them to know and feel what they feel, the cult of feeling ends by creating a new form of dissociation: the tyranny of good sense, of the *sens commun*, is simply replaced by a tyranny of the other that manifests itself in the form of an injunction to feel strongly.

Perhaps the most serious objection to feeling is that it does not provide a sufficiently radical solution to the problem of dissociation. We saw in Chapter Three that our feelings are grounded in our physical relationship with the material world, and acquire substance and reality from our daily contacts with things. If we lose touch with things, then our feelings too become disconnected or detached; in other words, dissociation of the senses inevitably leads to dissociation of the feelings. When dissociation of the senses has reached an acute stage (as is generally the case today), the cult of feeling is merely an ineffectual attempt to deal with the symptom instead of going to the root of the problem. It will be seen, then, that the function that requires to be developed to counteract the effects of abstract thinking and provide a valid solution to the problem of dissociation is not feeling but sensation.

The chief merit of sensation is that it is not self-conscious, but is directed outwards upon the object. If I am listening to a clock striking the hour, it is necessary for me to concentrate my attention upon the sound, for if I fall into reverie or become conscious of myself listening, the message that the clock brings to me is lost. This dispassionate awareness—'*pas de cris, pas de convulsion, rien que la fixité d'un regard pensif*', as Flaubert expresses it—provides a means of evading the dual errors of self-assertion and self-abnegation. When I obtrude myself and my desires, I cannot see the object as it really is, even as Dorothea Brooke, because she is looking for a Milton to revere, cannot

H

really see poor Casaubon. But if I deliberately suppress my desires, then I am selfishly denying the object the tribute of desire or admiration that it rightfully claims from me. Dispassionate awareness, on the contrary, means a right relation between subject and object: I am present in sensation in the form of voluntary attention to the object—it is my desire that brings the sound of the clock to birth—yet at the same time my awareness is uncontaminated by self-consciousness or acquisitiveness. We may say, then, that it is the nature of sensation to be centred-in-self (that is, in the life of the real being) but not self-centred.

The point can be well illustrated if we revert to our earlier discussion of the contrast between the adolescent hero and the father. The adolescent hero exploits the object or the other person as a means of gratifying and fortifying his idea of himself. In *Scarlet and Black*, when Julien Sorel becomes the lover of the adorable Madame de Rênal, he is unable to enjoy her because he is too preoccupied with his own efforts to 'play the part of a man accustomed to subduing women to his will'.[5] Stendhal's description of Julien as a lover is a classic account of the psychology of the adolescent hero:

> When he might have been attentive to the transports he aroused, and the remorse that only served to heighten their eager ecstasy, he kept the idea of *a duty to himself* unceasingly before his eyes. He was afraid of feeling terrible regret and of making himself for ever ridiculous if he departed from the model of perfection he had resolved to follow. In a word, what made Julien a superior being was the very thing that prevented him from enjoying this happiness right in front of his eyes.*

The education of Julien is achieved by means of a series of picaresque adventures which bring him into contact with every level of society in France, and finally to his death. Julien shoots Madame de Rênal because she has betrayed him. Then, as he awaits death in prison, he is purged of ambition, role-playing,

* In his obstinate imitation of an external model, Julien is like Raskolnikov. They are alike, too, in their admiration of Napoleon.

and the desire for future happiness. He is now overjoyed to learn that he has not killed Madame de Rênal, and, in the last chapter of the novel, he achieves happiness with her through a love that is free from the taint of self-seeking or self-centredness:

> 'In the past', Julien said to her, 'when I might have been so happy during our walks in the woods of Vergy, my fiery ambition carried my mind away into imaginary countries. Instead of clasping to my heart this lovely arm which was so close to my lips, I let the future bear me away from you. I was deep in the countless battles I should have to fight to carve for myself a glorious career. . . . No, I should have died without knowing what happiness meant, if you had not come to see me in this prison.'

Thus, instead of being preoccupied with his own idea of himself (*duty*) or other people's idea of him (*ambition*), Julien learns to look out at the created world and enjoy it at its true worth. *Scarlet and Black*, then, shows the adolescent hero achieving manhood by means of a love that is rooted in the senses, but not self-centred.

Another significant characteristic of sensation is that it belongs in the world rather than in the mind. The cult of feeling encourages men to value themselves on account of the supposed superiority of their feelings: Werther, for example, in the early, untroubled period of his love for Lotte, writes: 'I am experiencing the kind of happiness that God dispenses only to his saints.' Such boasts about one's inner state are of course not easily substantiated, but then, again, neither are they easily refuted. Sensation, on the other hand, characteristically manifests itself in the form of actions that can be scrutinized. If, in my study, I entertain the delusion that I can run a mile in a minute, it is a simple matter to go to the running-track and put my pretensions to the proof. Action-in-the-world quickly establishes the fact that some men can run a mile in four minutes, while other men need six or seven minutes, and compels me to acknowledge that my own performance falls somewhere within this scale. Sensation, then, makes me recognize my limits, and teaches me that I am a man among men. If we remember that the crux of the problem of Self-Consciousness lies in the gap between a man's real worth and his exaggerated pretensions, the importance of this aspect of sensation will be evident.

However it would be wrong to suggest that sensation lends itself to measurement. Measurement is above all associated with abstract thinking, which strips objects of their concrete particularity in order to manipulate them the more easily. Sensation resists the abstract and impersonal character of thought. I can say that two plus two equals four, but I cannot say that two horses plus two cows equals four horses, nor can I say that two Jersey cows plus two Ayrshire cows equals four Jersey cows. Indeed, I cannot say that any living thing equals any other.[6] To sensation, which does not strip the object of the concrete particularities that constitute it, each living thing is unique and strictly incomparable (with a uniqueness and incomparability that my abstract and impersonal words cannot of course render). The falsely competitive attitude of Self-Consciousness, as we have seen, gives rise to a state of affairs in which it can be correctly said by La Rochefoucauld that each of us takes pleasure in the misfortunes of his best friends. Here, again, sensation provides the true answer to Self-Consciousness because it invalidates this false competitiveness by showing that each living thing—including myself—is unique, and therefore incommensurable with any other thing.

It may appear paradoxical to argue that a man can be compared with other people (in so far as it takes him between four and seven minutes to run a mile), and at the same time to assert that each man is unique and incomparable. We can, however, shed light on this paradox (if it is one) by recalling a sentence quoted earlier from *The Cocktail Party:* 'All cases are unique, and very similar to others.' If feeling stresses the first half of this proposition, and abstract thinking the second ('The things I know every man can know, but, oh, my heart is mine alone'), sensation permits us to keep the whole truth concretely before us. Thus where thinking swallows up the individual in the universal, and feeling proclaims a chaotic, isolated individualism, sensation regards the object with an attentive, dispassionate eye, and so keeps in view both its uniqueness and its representative quality. Each fingerprint is unique, and yet one hand is pretty much like another.

At this point it is as well to pause to consider a difficulty; it may be objected that the gospel of sensation is as liable to misinterpretation or distortion as any other doctrine, and that an uncritical admiration for the life of the senses serves to encourage the aesthete (glutting his sorrow on a rose!), the hedonist, or the crude sensationalist. It is of course true that any doctrine is liable to be received in an inauthentic, acquisitive, and external spirit by the dissociated man. Yet we cannot impose a universal silence just because every doctrine or creed is capable of being travestied. It is sometimes necessary to speak out, even at the risk of being misunderstood. At least, sensation is less liable than feeling to be distorted: it is more practicable to ask a man to join you on a twenty-mile hike than to ask him to share your fine feelings. As far as our immediate interests are concerned, the best safeguard against misinterpretation is to insist that our discussion of the return to sensation has to be understood in the context of the journey of the hero of Consciousness. A brief review will make it plain that the theme of the return to sensation is intimately related to the topics of the last few chapters. We have seen that the adolescent hero is characteristically at home in the world of books, but a stranger in the 'real' world of the senses. Thus in *The Immoralist*, the earlier puritanical Michel is a 'blindfolded scholar' and a 'learned bookworm', and his reawakening and self-discovery is achieved through a return to sensation. 'O joys of the body!' he cries, 'unerring rhythm of the muscles! health! . . .' In the descent into solitude, again, we get this same note of a return to sensation. Words, as I have several times observed, come to us from other people, and writing is an abstract representation of signs (or motions of air) that represent abstractions. Sensation, on the other hand, is obstinately concrete and particular, and has for its foundation the unique body in a particular situation at a particular time. In the Notes to *The Waste Land*, T. S. Eliot quotes this sentence from F. H. Bradley's *Appearance and Reality:* 'My external sensations are no less private to myself than are my thoughts or my feelings.' No less private! They are more private. What is private about my thoughts about the square of the hypotenuse on a right-angled triangle, or my feelings about countries I have never visited and public figures that I have never seen or touched? (It is worth remembering at this point that Jung in *Psychological Types* assigns feeling and thinking to the category of the rational and universal, and sensation and intuition to that of the irrational.) These very things that I see in front of me at this moment have never been seen before by any man, and will never be seen again. Sensation, then, engulfs me in my solitude and contingency. As we saw in connection with *Nausea*, it is the escape from the tyranny of words—'Things are divorced from their names' and 'I thought without words, *on* things, *with* things'—and the shock of sensation in the encounter with the roots of the chestnut-tree that crowns Roquentin's descent into solitude with success.

The peasant is a man of sensation both because of his lack of verbal training and because of his work, which is primarily concerned with things and not with people. In an interesting passage of *Anti-Semite and Jew* Sartre makes the relevant distinction:

> Whether a man is a lawyer or a haberdasher, his clientele comes if he is pleasing. It follows that the vocations of which we are speaking are full of ceremonies; it is necessary to seduce, to captivate, and to retain confidence. Correctness of costume, apparent severity of conduct, honour, all are based on these ceremonies, on the thousand little dance steps it is necessary to take in order to attract a customer. Thus what counts above all else is reputation. A man *makes* himself a reputation, he lives on it; that means that basically he is completely dependent on other men, whereas the peasant has primarily to do with his land, the worker with his materials and tools.[7]

This distinction between the middle-class man (a forerunner of Riesman's 'other-directed' man) and the peasant is indeed a popular theme of the romantic criticism of modern society. In *Anna Karenina*, for example, the joyful physical labour of the peasants—Levin uses the term, *Arbeitskur*, in connection with it—is contrasted with the time-serving and sycophancy of the town-dwelling nobility, who get paid handsomely for doing useless office-work for which the chief qualifications are the right connections and the ability to please. Again, in Arthur Miller's *Death of a Salesman*, the choice lies between the executive or salesman (who depends on being 'well-liked'), and the carpenter or farmhand who can whistle in an elevator without damaging his 'image'. As Biff Loman says '. . . we don't belong in this nuthouse of a city! We should be mixing cement on some open plain or—or carpenters. A carpenter is allowed to whistle!'[8] Thus it may be seen that the peasant or worker stands as a representative of the life of sensation in the eyes of the city-dwelling middle-class person who is dissociated from the senses.

The connection between death and sensation can be easily and quickly established. Man at the level of Self-Consciousness treats the present from a utilitarian point of view, as an instrument for achieving the goal of security or satisfaction in the future; at the same time, he adopts a utilitarian attitude towards objects, exploiting them as subordinate means to ulterior ends. The encounter with death makes him realize that there *is* no future, with the result that he learns to give the present its due, and develops an attitude of disinterested attention to, and enjoyment of, the objects that are immediately present to his senses. The encounter with death, then, is linked with the return to sensation in that it brings deliverance from the Midas-spell which transforms objects into instruments or intermediate agents of profit, and restores to reality its original transcendent brightness.

Enough has now been said to make it clear that the return to sensation is not an invitation to men to revert to walking on all fours (as Voltaire said of Rousseau), but a doctrine of genuine significance, provided it is properly understood in the context of the journey of the hero. Man at the level of Unconsciousness, as I suggested earlier, is drowned in sensation, and he needs ideas in order to free himself from bondage to the flux of moment-to-moment sensation, while the hero struggling towards Consciousness needs to free himself from ideas, in order to open himself to sensation, to the immediate, so that he can achieve a dispassionate enjoyment of reality. With this distinction firmly established, then, we can safely turn to consider the treatment of the theme of the return to sensation in literature.

If the romantics were primarily concerned with combating dissociation of the feelings, and stressed the holiness of the heart's affections rather than the body's, nevertheless, the seeds of a doctrine of sensation are all potentially present in romanticism; in Goethe, indeed, the potentiality is fulfilled, and he presents us with the classical development from romantic feeling in the *Sturm und Drang* period to the triumphant enthronement of sensation in the Italian journey. During the course of the nineteenth century, dissociation of the senses becomes more and more prevalent, and we encounter ever more fervent pleas on behalf of the body. Here, for example, is a reasonably representative passage:

> . . . during the civilization-period, the body being systematically wrapped in clothes, the *head* alone represents man—the little finnikin, intellectual, self-conscious man in contradistinction to the cosmical man represented by the entirety of the bodily organs. The body has to be delivered from its swathings in order that the cosmical consciousness may once more reside in the human breast.[9]

The thought and to some extent even the tone of this passage call to mind D. H. Lawrence, though the quotation is, in fact, from Edward Carpenter's essay, *Civilization—its Cause and Cure*, published in 1893. As we move into the twentieth century, the call for a return to sensation becomes almost a universal chorus. Since D. H. Lawrence is undoubtedly the major prophet of the gospel of the return to sensation, it is fitting that his work should illustrate the argument of this chapter.

Lawrence's short story, *The Blind Man*, although not an entirely successful piece of fiction, provides what is from our present point of view the most convenient point of entry into the world of Lawrence's thought. In the story, Maurice Pervin, who has been blinded in Flanders, has returned from the war, and is living with his wife, Isabel, at a country house belonging to him, which has a rented farm at the back of it. The Pervins live almost entirely alone together in a 'wonderful and unspeakable intimacy', a rich, profound relationship of 'dark, palpable joy'.[10] Pervin finds compensation for the disability of his blindness in the new mode of consciousness that it brings to birth in him:

> He seemed to know the presence of objects before he touched them. It was a pleasure to him to rock thus through a world of things, carried on the flood in a sort of blood-prescience. He did not think much or trouble much. So long as he kept this sheer immediacy of blood-contact with the substantial world he was happy, he wanted no intervention of visual consciousness.

(The last sentence, incidentally, with its irritatingly abstract authorial intrusiveness, reveals the somewhat tired, second-rate quality of the story. Can one imagine Pervin *saying*: 'I want no intervention of visual consciousness'?*) At the same time, because he is isolated from other human-beings by his blindness and by his absorbing intimacy with his wife, Pervin occasionally suffers from 'devastating fits of depression, which seemed to lay waste his whole being'.

In order to give her husband some further connection with the world, and so avert his black moods of depression, Isabel sometimes invites people to stay with them. The action of the story, then, concerns a visit paid to the Grange by Bertie Reid, an old friend and distant relation of Isabel's. Bertie Reid is a Scotsman, a brilliant barrister and *littérateur*, a bachelor who adores women from a distance, but is incapable of approaching them physically. Isabel stands at a sort of mid-point between her husband and her friend; she can enter into the profound, mindless intimacy with her husband, and she also enjoys the

---

* Nevertheless, the point about visual consciousness is well taken. Compare this passage from *Nausea*: 'I did not simply *see* this black [of the root of the chestnut tree]: sight is an abstract invention, a simplified idea, one of man's ideas. That black, amorphous, weakly presence, far surpassed sight, smell and taste.'

brisk, verbal relationship with Bertie. The two men, on the other hand, are not at ease together. Bertie is afraid of the erect, inscrutable blind man, and Pervin, who feels excluded from the complacent verbal rapport that exists between the lawyer and his wife, seizes an opportunity after their first meal together to go out to the farm. After a while, Isabel becomes anxious about Pervin, and Bertie goes out in the rain and darkness to fetch him. Bertie finds Pervin in a barn, among the cattle, untroubled by the darkness, at home in his world, tranquilly pulping turnip-roots. A remarkable Lawrentian scene occurs. Pervin says that they do not really know each other, and then asks suddenly:

'Do you mind if I touch you?'
The lawyer shrank away instinctively. And yet, out of very philanthropy, he said, in a small voice: 'Not at all.'

(The abstract word 'philanthropy' is here beautifully appropriate, for it reveals the gulf between instinct and attitude in the dissociated man.) The blind man runs his hand over the skull, then over the closed eyes, and over the rest of the face of the other man. Then he tells Bertie to touch his own eyes, and when Bertie obeys, he grasps the lawyer's hand and presses the fingers against his disfigured eye-sockets:

He remained thus for a minute or more, whilst Bertie stood as if in a swoon, unconscious, imprisoned.

Then suddenly Maurice removed the hand of the other man from his brow, and stood holding it in his own.

'Oh, my God', he said, 'we shall know each other now, shan't we? We shall know each other now.'

Bertie could not answer. He gazed mute and terror-struck, overcome by his weakness. He knew he could not answer. He had an unreasonable fear, lest the other man should suddenly destroy him. Whereas Maurice was actually filled with hot, poignant love, the passion of friendship, perhaps it was this very passion of friendship which Bertie shrank from most.

They return to the house, and Pervin tells Isabel that they have become friends, but she can *see* the fear and revulsion in Bertie:

> But she was watching Bertie. She knew that he had one desire—to escape from this intimacy, this friendship, which had been thrust upon him. He could not bear it that he had been touched by the blind man, his insane reserve broken in. He was like a mollusc whose shell is broken.

At this point, the story abruptly ends.

Maurice Pervin and Bertie Reid are antithetical. The polar opposition between the two men is explicitly indicated, for Lawrence writes: 'He [Pervin] was very sensitive to his own mental slowness, his feelings being quick and acute. So that he was just the opposite to Bertie, whose mind was much quicker than his emotions, which were not so very fine.' As the story develops, the contrast between the two men is in fact enforced somewhat schematically. Pervin is tall; he has large, reddish hands and powerful, muscular legs. Bertie is small; his hands are thin and white, and his legs short. Pervin has crisp, brown hair and a small head; Bertie has thin, wispy hair and a big forehead. The taciturn Englishman works on a farm, while the Scotsman is a lawyer, or man of words. Pervin is at home in the world of nature; he is at ease in the rain and darkness, and a half-wild cat rubs itself against him. Bertie, on the other hand, hates the wet, and fears the dark, and a dog barks violently at him. Most important of all, Pervin has a profound, dark relationship with a woman, while Bertie is incapable of intimacy of any kind.

If Pervin and Bertie Reid represent antithetical principles or modes of being, then it is evident that Bertie stands for the head alone, or what Carpenter calls 'the little finnikin, intellectual, self-conscious man', while the blind man, who is *dark and powerful*, *a strange colossus*, and a *tower of darkness*, appears to correspond to what Carpenter calls 'the cosmical man represented by the entirety of the bodily organs'. In his 'Introduction to his Paintings', Lawrence writes: 'The history of our era is the nauseating and repulsive history of the crucifixion of the procreative body for the glorification of the spirit, the mental consciousness.'[11] In Lawrentian terms, then, Pervin stands for the procreative body (Isabel is pregnant at the time of Bertie's visit), and Bertie Reid stands for mental consciousness.

It is obvious too, I think, that Bertie possesses many of the traits that we have noted in the adolescent hero. He cannot, for instance, approach women physically; he is afraid ('At the centre of him he was afraid, helplessly and even brutally afraid', Lawrence writes); and he lacks a secure sense of his own reality ('At the centre he felt himself neuter, nothing.'). On the other hand, Bertie is not in revolt against society—he is a successful lawyer and *littérateur*—and he is resigned to his condition ('He had given up hope, had ceased to expect any more that he could escape his own weakness'). In fact, then, Bertie shares the limitations of the adolescent hero, but not his heroic efforts to overcome those limitations. Pervin, for his part, evidently possesses some of the characteristics of man at the level of Consciousness. Isabel, trying to describe to Bertie the change that has taken place in her husband since his blindness, says: 'I don't know—it's awfully hard to define it—but something strong and immediate.' This absence of mediation, this *immediacy* of sensual apprehension is a characteristic note of Consciousness, just as anxiety about the future is of Self-Consciousness. (Pervin tells Bertie that one of the compensations of blindness is that 'You cease to bother about a great many things.') At the same time, Pervin differs from Conscious man in that, like Lawrence himself, he feels an agonized sense of his isolation from other men. It is presumably the passionate desire to escape from this isolation that causes him to fall into delusion regarding the nature of the experience in the barn with Bertie. In the last analysis, then, Pervin is revealed to be both literally and metaphorically blind.

It would be easy to show that the relationship between Pervin, Bertie and Isabel contains the germ of the ideas that are more fully developed later in the figures of Mellors, Sir Clifford and Lady Chatterley in *Lady Chatterley's Lover*, but the demonstration, just because it would be easy, is perhaps not really required.[12] It will perhaps be more interesting and instructive to approach *Lady Chatterley's Lover* by way of an attempt to show that Lawrence's development from *Sons and Lovers* to *Lady Chatterley's Lover* is in essentials parallel to that of Shakespeare from *Hamlet* to *Antony and Cleopatra*. It may at any rate be claimed on behalf of this comparison (provided it can be successfully accomplished) that it 'makes my circle just, / And makes me end where I begun'.

Hamlet and *Sons and Lovers* can be dealt with fairly briefly. Paul Morel possesses many of the classical traits of the adolescent hero in revolt against the father. He gives his allegiance to the middle-class, ambitious, moralistic mother ('She was a puritan, like her father, high-minded, and really stern'[13]) and rejects the sensual, working-class father, just as Hamlet and Gregers side with the moralistic parent against the earthy, sensual father. Hamlet calls Claudius a 'remorseless, treacherous, lecherous, kindless villain', and Lawrence writes:

> Paul hated his father so. The collier's small, mean head, with its black hair slightly soiled with grey, lay on the bare arms, and the face, dirty and inflamed, with a fleshy nose and thin, paltry brows, was turned sideways, asleep with beer and weariness and nasty temper.

(At this point the small head is a sign of meanness, whereas by the time of *The Blind Man* it will be a sign of blood-prescience as opposed to mental consciousness.)

The hatred of the father contains a strong element of sexual rivalry. Although Hamlet makes a violent tirade against sex, and Paul and his mother play out a love-scene together,* there is a curious similarity between the scene in which Hamlet kills the eavesdropping Polonius (a figure associated with the father) and the chapter in which Paul fights with his father, who has returned home to find his wife and son embracing. Both sons plead with the mother to reject the father as lover—'Go not to mine uncle's bed', Hamlet cries, and Paul says, 'Sleep with Annie, Mother, not with him'—both repeat their admonition a second time, and both depart saying, 'Good-night, mother'.

Just as Gide gives his spiritual love to his wife and his

---

* 'He stroked his mother's hair, and his mouth was on her throat. . . . His mother kissed him a long, fervent kiss', and so forth.

physical love to men, so Paul Morel gives his spiritual love to
Miriam and his physical love to Clara; in other words, Paul
Morel shares the characteristic inability of the adolescent hero
to achieve wholeness and fulfilment in his relations with women.
His frustration reveals itself in that longing for death which
we have often noted already in the adolescent hero ('Why did
the thought of death, the after-life, seem so sweet and con-
soling?') and it reveals itself, too, in spiteful aggressiveness
towards the woman; in the chapter 'Defeat of Miriam' which
immediately follows that of the fight with his father, Paul says
to Miriam:

> 'You don't want to love—your eternal and abnormal craving
> is to be loved. You aren't positive, you're negative. You
> absorb, absorb, as if you must fill yourself up with love,
> because you've got a shortage somewhere.'

Shortly after, he sends her a cruel farewell-letter:

> May I speak of our old, worn love, this last time. It, too, is
> changing, is it not? Say, has not the body of that love died,
> and left you its invulnerable soul? You see, I can give you a
> spirit love, I have given it you this long, long time; but not
> embodied passion. See, you are a nun. I have given you what
> I would give a holy nun—as a mystic monk to a holy nun.
> . . . In all our relations no body enters. I do not talk to you
> through the senses—rather through the spirit.

Though the idiom is different, are we not here in the presence of
the same rage of destructiveness that inspires Michel's crime
against Marceline in *The Immoralist* or Hamlet's 'Get thee to a
nunnery' speech? Or, consider Hugo Barine's complaint to
Jessica in *Dirty Hands*: 'Your body is cold and you have no
warmth to give me . . . when I took you in my arms and asked
you to be my wife, you weren't up to it.' Paul, like Hugo, shifts
the blame for his own inadequacies onto the woman.

As the last two quotations from *Sons and Lovers* indicate,
Paul resembles the adolescent hero in that he talks too much.
Furthermore, he knows that he talks too much: 'What a ranter
I am', he writes to Miriam. In this connection we may

perhaps adduce a passage of *Lady Chatterley's Lover*, which certainly applies to D. H. Lawrence and Jessie Chambers, and therefore almost certainly applies to Paul and Miriam. Mellors is giving a brief history of his life; he describes himself at the age of twenty-one as a 'prig' and a 'young curate', and says of his first love:

> She was the romantic sort that hated commonness. She egged me on to poetry and reading: in a way, she made a man of me. I read and thought like a house on fire, for her. . . . And about *everything* I talked to her: but everything. We talked ourselves into Persepolis and Timbuctoo. We were the most literary cultured couple in ten counties. I held out with rapture to her, positively with rapture. I simply went up in smoke. And she adored me. The serpent in the grass was sex. She somehow didn't have any; at least, not where it's supposed to be.[14]

Here, the connection between talking and not making love is explicit. The words 'prig' and 'young curate', it will be noted, serve as a hint that there was in the young Lawrence a trace of the idealistic rectitudinitis of the adolescent hero.

Can it also be said that Paul Morel, like Hamlet, is an abstract thinker? Probably not. We noted earlier Hugo's statement that immaturity is a middle-class disease, and the same thing is largely true of abstract thinking. Paul Morel indeed tells his mother that 'from the middle classes one gets ideas, and from the common people—life itself, warmth', and he says that he himself belongs to the common people. His mother, however, retorts that his friends among the common people are precisely those who are interested in ideas, like the middle classes. The exchange is significant. As far as Lawrence is concerned, we may remark that while it would appear to be an advantage to be partly inoculated against the middle-class disease of abstract thinking, for a major writer it is really a misfortune to be in a measure isolated from an important aspect of the experience of his society. One sometimes feels that Lawrence approaches the phenomenon of abstract thinking from the outside, that is to say, abstractly! As we see, say, from the example of St Augustine and the Manicheans, it is best to conquer the devil in your own flesh before you begin to practise as an exorcist. As far as Paul Morel is concerned, it must be conceded that if he is not really an abstract thinker, he is only partly a Hamletian figure. The resemblance between Paul Morel and Hamlet, in fact, need not be pressed further than is warranted by the identity of their situations as young men in revolt against the father. For our present purposes, this resemblance itself is sufficiently significant.

When we turn to *Antony and Cleopatra* and *Lady Chatterley's Lover*, we find that instead of identifying ourselves with the young son in his revolt against the father, we are required to lend our sympathies to an older man who is in conflict with a younger man. Expressed in the simplest terms, the equations— 'moralistic youth = good, sensual father = bad'—are inverted. Antony, like Claudius, is a middle-aged man, a fornicator, an adulterer, a lover of feasting and drinking, and a ruler of men. Mellors, also, is a middle-aged man, a fornicator and an adulterer. Where Paul Morel is on his way up into the middle classes, Mellors has voluntarily descended to the working-class level; Mellors 'talks broad' like Walter Morel; like Walter Morel he has been employed in the mine; his name, as several critics have noted, is approximately an anagram of Morel. Yet where Claudius and Walter Morel are cast in the role of the villain, Shakespeare and Lawrence use all the resources of language at their command to ennoble Antony and Mellors, or, at any rate, to present them, with all their faults, as images of quintessential manhood. In both *Antony and Cleopatra* and *Lady Chatterley's Lover*, the older man wins the woman, but suffers defeat in a worldly sense, while the younger man loses the woman, but gains money, power and fame.

The conflict in *Antony and Cleopatra* is defined in terms of the opposition between reason and will, that in *Lady Chatterley's Lover* in terms of the opposition between will and touch; since Shakespeare appears to approve of will, while Lawrence violently disapproves of it, one might at first glance suppose that their values are antithetical. In fact, however, behind the contrasting terminology lies an essential similarity of viewpoint. For Shakespeare, *will* is associated with obedience to natural impulse (the heart) rather than the dictates of reason or 'policy'; for Lawrence, on the contrary, the will is the servant of the ego-orientated mental life (or the head).* In effect, then, both works are concerned with what may be broadly described as the conflict between head and heart, with Octavius Caesar and Sir Clifford representing the life-denying values of the head, while Antony and Mellors are associated with the life-affirming values of the heart. Antony has a 'captain's heart'; he calls Cleopatra 'the armourer of my heart', and tells her 'my full heart / Remains in use with you'. Caesar, on the other hand, 'gets money where / He loses hearts'. (The word 'heart' occurs forty-seven times in *Antony and Cleopatra*—more frequently than in any of Shakespeare's other plays except *King Lear*.) The opposition between head and heart may be illustrated by Enobarbus's comment on Antony's recovery of hope after his first defeat:

>   I see still
> A diminution of our captain's *brain*
> Restores his *heart*. When valour preys on reason,
> It eats the sword it fights with. I will seek
> Some way to leave him.
>
>   (My italics)

Enobarbus's desertion to Caesar's camp and subsequent death elicit this excellent observation of Wilson Knight's: 'Enobarbus has throughout been a common-sense commentary on the action: this is the action's commentary on common sense.'[15] In our terms, Enobarbus's death establishes the superiority of the heart-values embodied in Antony and Cleopatra over the head-values embodied in Octavius.

The moralistic youth tends to indulge in self-righteous

* The shift is connected with a cultural change of immense significance. As John Stuart Mill says in *On Liberty:* 'There has been a time when the element of spontaneity and individuality was in excess, and the social principle had a hard struggle with it. . . . But society has now fairly got the better of individuality; and the danger which threatens human nature is not the excess, but the deficiency, of personal impulses and preferences.'

condemnation of the sensual father.[16] Thus Octavius Caesar says contemptuously of Antony:

> Let us grant it is not
> Amiss to tumble on the bed of Ptolemy,
> To give a kingdom for a mirth, to sit
> And keep the turn of tippling with a slave,
> To reel the streets at noon, and stand the buffet
> With knaves that smell of sweat.

Sir Clifford, when he discovers that his wife is in love with his game-keeper and is with child by him, cries out:

> 'That scum! That bumptious lout! That miserable cad! And carrying on with him all the time while you were here and he was one of my servants! My God, my God, is there any end to the beastly lowness of women!'

The moralistic youth, of course, is not given to tumbling on beds with women. Sir Clifford is sexually impotent. As for Caesar, at his brief meeting with Cleopatra near the end of the play, he tells her, 'Feed and sleep', as if he were fattening a pig for market, or talking to Sancho Panza.[17] In the world of the play, the man who is not captivated by Cleopatra is not a man, so that we are entitled to conclude that 'scarce-bearded Caesar' (as Cleopatra calls him) is also incapable of deep relationship with a woman.* Instead of making love to a woman, Caesar and Sir Clifford make money, or, as Lawrence puts it, they prostitute themselves to the bitch-goddess, Success. After his wife has left him, Sir Clifford regresses to an infantile level in his personal life, but his worldly affairs prosper. 'This perverted child-man', Lawrence writes, 'was now a *real* businessman; when it was a question of affairs, he was an absolute he-man, sharp as a needle, and impervious as a bit of steel'. I have already quoted the telling comment, 'Caesar gets money where / He loses hearts'. Both of them, in fact, exhibit the rational values of a puritanical merchant, while Antony and Mellors stand for the generous feeling-values of the soldier or cavalier.

* What Cleopatra says to Seleucus—'Wert thou a man, / Thou wouldst have mercy on me'—is certainly applicable to Caesar, too.

The heart is associated with warmth, and the head with cold calculation or cold virtue. Enobarbus points out that 'Octavia is of a holy, cold, and still conversation', and he deduces that since Mark Antony is the reverse, 'He will to his Egyptian dish again.' Octavius Caesar, when obliged to speak in praise of Antony, commends him in a 'cold and sickly' fashion. Cleopatra speaks disparagingly of 'My salad days, / When I was green in judgement, cold in blood.' When Antony and Cleopatra quarrel, he at first speaks angrily of her 'hotter hours' of lust, but a few moments later he reproaches her:

> *Antony*:   Cold-hearted towards me?
> *Cleopatra*:   Ah, dear, if I be so,
> From my cold heart let heaven engender hail,
> And poison it in the source, and the first stone
> Drop in my neck.

In *Lady Chatterley's Lover*, one of Mellor's more important statements of his creed is expressed in similar language:

> I believe in being warm-hearted. I believe especially in being warm-hearted in love, in fucking with a warm heart. I believe if men could fuck with warm hearts, and the women take it warm-heartedly, everything would come all right. It's all this cold-hearted fucking that is death and idiocy.

Tommy Dukes, who is the spokesman for Lawrentian doctrines that Mellors later *enacts* (we are told that they look somewhat alike), early in the novel expresses his credo also in terms of the heart and sexuality: 'Oh, intellectually I believe in having a good heart, a chirpy penis, a lively intelligence, and the courage to say "shit!" in front of a lady.' Mellors in due course proves to possess all these attributes.

In spite of these references to warm-heartedness, it is not feeling but rather *touch* that provides the essential clue to the argument of *Lady Chatterley's Lover*. (This circumstance accords with the view expressed earlier in this chapter that where dissociation of the senses is far advanced, true feeling can only be recovered indirectly, by way of a return to sensation.) In the novel, then, a gospel of sensation is proclaimed.

The theme is first stated early in the novel by Tommy Dukes:

> 'Give me the resurrection of the body!' said Dukes. 'But it'll come, in time, when we've shoved the cerebral stone away a bit, the money and the rest. Then we'll get a democracy of *touch*, instead of a democracy of pocket.'

(My italics)

Then, at the end of the novel, Mellors restates with the authority of realized experience the creed of touch that Dukes was only able to formulate intellectually:

> And he realized as he went into her that this was the thing he had to do, to come into tender touch, without losing his pride or his dignity or his integrity as a man. . . . 'I stand for the touch of bodily awareness between human beings', he said to himself, 'and the touch of tenderness. And she is my mate. And it is a battle against the money, and the machine, and the insentient ideal monkeyishness of the world.'

(Only a Lawrentian hero could address himself in this way while he is making love, just as only a Lawrentian paragraph contains so many sentences beginning with 'and'!)

The core of the book is concerned with the initiation of Constance Chatterley into the truth of the values embodied in Mellors. At the beginning of the book, Connie's malaise is conveyed by means of frequent reiteration of expressions like 'disconnection', 'out of touch', and 'out of contact'. Even her walks in the woods around the estate are unreal:

> But it was all a dream; or rather it was like the simulacrum of reality. The oak-leaves were to her oak-leaves seen ruffling in a mirror, she herself was a figure somebody had read about, picking primroses that were only shadows or memories, or words. No substance to her or anything . . . no touch, no contact!*

* Sartre, in *Nausea*, describes a similar condition by means of an apt theatrical simile: 'Even when I looked at things, I was miles from dreaming that they existed: they looked like scenery to me. I picked them up in my hands, they served me as tool, I foresaw their resistance. But that all happened on the surface.'

On her arrival at Wragby Hall, Connie quickly perceives that Sir Clifford is cut off from Tevershall village and from his miners—'He was remotely interested; but like a man looking down a microscope, or up a telescope. He was not in touch'— but she pities him, and does not hold him to blame for her own sufferings. Gradually, however, as her insight grows, her feelings change:

> And yet was he not in a way to blame? This lack of warmth, this lack of the simple, warm, physical contact, was he not to blame for that? He was never really warm, nor even kind, only thoughtful, considerate, in a well-bred, cold sort of way!

She sees, too, that the coldness and aloofness of Sir Clifford are the characteristic marks of his class. 'They were all inwardly hard and separate, and warmth to them was just bad taste.' (We recall Paul Morel's words: 'Only from the middle classes one gets ideas, and from the common people—life itself, warmth.') The growth of her awareness is of course a result of her relationship with Mellors, and her education is completed, and the thesis of the novel fully worked out, when she rejects the values of the head and the will represented by Sir Clifford Chatterley and his intellectual friends, and embraces the values of touch and tenderness embodied in Mellors.

If *Lady Chatterley's Lover* proclaims a gospel of sensation, and rejects the head that gains dominion in favour of the flesh that achieves communion, can the same claim be made on behalf of *Antony and Cleopatra?* Certainly, the body and the life of the senses are vital elements in the play, yet the sensuousness is spiritualized and sublimated, or, rather, subdued to the power of the heart or spirit that animates the flesh.[18] Thus when Cleopatra says, 'O happy horse, to bear the weight of Antony!' the suggestiveness of 'bear the weight' is subtly modified by the joyful *élan* of the first three words, and by the attribution of the human (and, as it were, abstract and moral) quality of happiness to the horse. Again, when Enobarbus says of Cleopatra that 'the holy priests / Bless her when she is riggish', the grossness of 'riggish' is counterbalanced by the words 'holy priest' and 'bless'.* Cleopatra's great description of Antony reveals once again this same blend of the sensuous and the transcendent:

> His legs bestrid the ocean: his rear'd arm
> Crested the world. His voice was propertied
> As all the tuned spheres, and that to friends;
> But when he meant to quail and shake the orb,
> He was as rattling thunder. For his bounty,
> There was no winter in't; an autumn 'twas
> That grew the more by reaping. His delights
> Were dolphin-like: they show'd his back above
> The element they liv'd in.

Antony's flesh is here, indeed, in the shape of 'legs', arm', and 'back', but the parts of his body are magnified and metamorphosed, and, like Cleopatra herself, raised above the base elements of earth and water that they lived in.

It will be seen, then, that the statement that both *Antony and Cleopatra* and *Lady Chatterley's Lover* deal with the conflict between head and heart stands in need of qualification. We may perhaps say that both works are concerned with the conflict between head and heart/body, provided that we recognize that the body (or sensation) plays a somewhat different role in each. In *Lady Chatterley's Lover* the main emphasis is on *touch*, but tenderness (or feeling) is the offspring of touch— Mellors says that he stands for 'the touch of tenderness'—and it is arguable that the ultimate goal of the return to sensation is the recovery of human warmth and tenderness. (It will be remembered that Lawrence nearly called the novel *Tenderness*.) *Antony and Cleopatra*, on the other hand, while it contains the same elements of sensation and feeling, chiefly celebrates the heart which is magnified by love, rather than the flesh which performs the act of love.

The great crux in *Antony and Cleopatra* and *Lady Chatterley's Lover* is of course the love-relationship between the man and the

---

* Is there not a kinship of spirit between these words of Enobarbus and a delightful passage from *Lady Chatterley's Lover:* 'Tha's got a real soft sloping bottom on thee, as a man loves in 'is guts. It's a bottom as could hold the world up, it is'?

woman. We have seen hitherto that man at the level of Self-Consciousness is incapable of genuine relationship with a woman, because of the distortion caused by his desire to gratify and enhance his self-esteem. Thus Self-Conscious man may be a selfish amorist collecting scalps, an insecure or isolated person seeking refuge and reassurance, or an opportunist who exploits sex as a means to some other end. In any case, just as Self-Conscious man is pleased by the misfortunes of his friends (which means that he is incapable of friendship), so, by the same token, he is also incapable of a genuine relationship with a woman. Man at the level of Consciousness, on the other hand, delights in woman as a lovely part of the creation—'Life delights in life'—to be enjoyed for herself, not exploited for some ulterior purpose. (It is worth recalling that the love between man and woman in the *Song of Solomon* has been interpreted as an allegorical representation of the love between the soul and God.) I do not of course suggest that Conscious man experiences a dispassionate love which asks nothing in return, but only that his love is rooted in reality (or the real being) rather than in some illusory, self-gratifying *idea* of himself. Man at the level of Consciousness loves and desires the woman, because she is lovely and desirable. Even if he fails to win her, she is still lovely and desirable. But, in fact, his desire, being rooted in reality, bears within itself a charge of energy which virtually assures him of success. '*Folgte Begierde dem Blick, folgte Genuss der Begier*'—desire follows immediately on seeing, and fulfilment on desire.[19] In either event, what distinguishes Conscious man as a lover is his sanity and freedom from hysteria. If the attitude of Self-Conscious man as a lover may be represented by Othello's extravagant words, '. . . when I love thee not, / Chaos is come again', then the contrasting attitude of Consciousness may be suggested by this passage from *Lady Chatterley's Lover*:

'I . . . I can't love you', she sobbed, suddenly feeling her heart breaking.

'Canna ter? Well, dunna fret! There's no law says as tha's got to. Ta'e it for what it is.'

Self-Conscious man asks, *Do you love me?* and thus supplies fuel to those who claim that 'to love is in essence the project of making oneself be loved'.[20] (But who could imagine Antony or Mellors asking this question?) Self-Conscious man strikes attitudes, and protests too much—like Hamlet in the graveyard scene:

> I lov'd Ophelia: forty thousand brothers
> Could not, with all their quantity of love,
> Make up my sum.

This hysterical outburst may be contrasted with Antony's words to Cleopatra before his departure from Egypt:

> The strong necessity of time commands
> Our services awhile; but my full heart
> Remains in use with you.

The business-like words 'necessity', 'commands' and 'services', in conjunction with the matter-of-fact 'in use', give the 'full heart' its full weight and authority. Here, there is the same note of sobriety that we have just seen in Mellor's words, 'Ta'e it for what it is.' In both *Antony and Cleopatra* and *Lady Chatterley's Lover*, then, we are concerned with a love that is firmly rooted in the senses and in reality, so that it makes no illegitimate demands of reality. He who makes no extravagant demands need not fear that chaos will come again if he is disappointed. Such fidelity to reality endows Conscious man with a sanity that is not entirely unlike that of the saint.

At this point it is necessary to make a distinction that is of the first importance. We have seen that the father-figure is normally an important member of society, whose sociable nature tends to manifest itself in convivial feasting and drinking. All this is true of Antony, who enjoys his fellow-men, just as he enjoys the woman, as part of the gift of creation, but not true of Mellors, who is, like the adolescent hero, an outsider. Lawrence, indeed, is aware that relationship with a woman is only a special form of relationship with mankind in general. Mellors, for instance, says that when he was in the army he had to be in touch with the men—'I had to be bodily aware of them and a bit tender to them'—and then he adds: 'Sex is really only touch, the closest of all touch.' Nevertheless, in the world of the novel the love between Mellors and Connie sheds no warmth on the rest of the world. If all mankind loves a lover, it is largely because the lover loves all mankind; yet in *Lady Chatterley's Lover* the lovers are isolated from, and indeed at war with, the rest of society ('. . . she is my mate. And it is a battle against the money, and the machine, etc.'). In the letter which ends the book, Mellors writes to Connie: 'I've got no friends, not inward friends. Only you.' The contrast with Antony, who on the eve of his last battle showers his servants with endearments like 'Mine honest friends', 'My hearty friends', 'my hearts', and 'my good fellows', needs no underlining.

The most significant difference between *Lady Chatterley's Lover* and *Antony and Cleopatra* is that Mellors and Connie stand on a lonely eminence, while Antony and Cleopatra, though the noblest and greatest of mortals, differ only in degree, not in kind, from those around them. Thus Charmian and Iras are 'noble girls'; Eros, by killing himself, gains over Antony 'a nobleness in record'. The deaths of Enobarbus, Eros, Charmian and Iras enhance the deaths of Antony and Cleopatra, creating a kind of tableau, so that even in their deaths there is relationship and connection. Cleopatra describes herself as 'No more but e'en a woman, and commanded / By such poor passion as the maid that milks / And does the meanest chares'. Antony is a 'workman' in the royal occupation of war. Antony and Cleopatra, then, are not isolated and exceptional, but rather representative in the sense that they are archetypally human.

Lady Chatterley's Lover is profoundly different. With the exception of the lovers, and with the partial exception of one or two other people (such as Connie's father), everybody is contemptible and disgusting. Tommy Dukes says: '*We're* not men, and the women aren't women. We're only cerebrating make-shifts, mechanical and intellectual experiments.' Mellors quotes with approval his former Colonel's view that the English middle classes are a ' "generation of ladylike prigs with half a ball each—" ' and that the working classes are ' "getting just as priggish and half-balled and narrow-gutted. It's the fate of mankind, to go that way".' Lawrence writes of Connie: 'A kind of terror filled her sometimes, a terror of the incipient insanity of the whole civilized species.' It would be possible to cite dozens of passages of similar tenor, but perhaps one more quotation will suffice to substantiate my main contention, which is that the novel is, to be perfectly candid, full of hate. In the penultimate chapter of the novel, speaking to Connie about his wife, Bertha, Mellors says:

'This last time, I'd have shot her like I shoot a stoat, if I'd but been allowed: a raving, doomed thing in the shape of a woman! If only I could have shot her, and ended the whole misery! It ought to be allowed.'

A few lines later, the conversation continues:

'I could wish the Cliffords and Berthas all dead', he said.
'It's not being very tender to them', she said.
'Tender to them? Yea, even then the tenderest thing you could do for them, perhaps, would be to give them death. They can't live! They only frustrate life. Their souls are awful inside them. Death ought to be sweet to them. And I ought to be allowed to shoot them!'

One is reminded of the student in *Crime and Punishment* who describes the old pawnbroker as 'a stupid, senseless, worthless, wicked and decrepit old hag, who is of no use to anybody and who actually does harm to everybody, a creature who does not know herself what she is living for', and argues that the life of such a person 'amounts to no more than the life of a louse or a black beetle'. A sufficient comment on this point of view is supplied by two lines from the scene in which Raskolnikov confesses the murder to Sonia:

'But I only killed a louse, Sonia. A useless, nasty, harmful louse.'
'A human being—a louse?'

The man who calls another human-being (above all, his own wife) a louse or a stoat, is not far from the kingdom of Hell of the Nazi extermination-camps. It is plain that the hatred shown by Lawrence (for, in spite of the mild objection offered by

Connie, Lawrence evidently endorses the view expressed by Mellors) is essentially the same as the misanthropy that we have seen to be characteristic of the adolescent hero who has not yet succeeded in achieving freedom. If we take as a touchstone St Augustine's words, 'There is no sanity in that man whom anything in creation displeases',* then we shall have to agree that Lawrence is still trapped in the neurosis of man at the level of Self-Consciousness.

It is tempting, though possibly vain, to speculate as to the reasons for Lawrence's imperfect success (as I may call it). Perhaps if he had had a more profound inward understanding and experience of abstract thinking, or perhaps if he had been more rigorous in completing the descent into solitude (instead of depending upon the woman), he would have had the virtues of humility and charity bestowed upon him. If that is so, then Lawrence serves to remind us once again that the gospel of sensation is not the one thing needful, but is only one facet of the hero's journey towards the Promised Land. Despite these objections, however, it remains true that Lawrence's success, though partial, demands our gratitude. If *tous les hommes se haïssent naturellement l'un l'autre*, it is evident that, unless one happens to be a saint or a sage, it is not easy to love mankind. It is not easy to love one's friends. It is not even easy to love one's woman. It is the achievement of *Lady Chatterley's Lover* that it demonstrates the possibility of a genuine love-relationship between two human-beings, and thus refutes the sombre view of Self-Consciousness that all love is self-seeking and self-centred, and therefore illusory.

* Cf. also, the Book of Common Prayer: 'O merciful God, who hast made all men, and hatest nothing that thou hast made. . . .'

CHAPTER TWELVE

Paradise Regained

If I am not for myself, who is for me? Yet being for myself,
what am I? And if not now, when?

RABBI HILLEL, first century A.D.

Martin Heidegger has said that the distinguishing trait of modern
man is *Heimatlösigkeit,* or homelessness. Certainly, it is true of
man at the level of Self-Consciousness that he sees himself
with the eyes of other people, and he sees the world with the
eyes of other people, so that he is a stranger to himself and a
stranger to the world. Conscious man, on the other hand, is at
home in himself; being centred in himself (that is, in the real
being), he has no need to be self-centred (or pointed in the
direction of himself). Thus Kafka says of a man, 'He sits in
himself as a first-class oarsman sits in his own boat, and would
sit in any boat.'[1] And Goethe observes in olympian fashion: 'I
felt so well in my own skin, I felt so noble, that, if someone had
made me a prince, I would not have found it strange in the
least.'[2] This sitting in oneself or feeling at ease in one's own
skin, is the distinguishing note of Consciousness. The man who
has returned home and regained the inexpugnable paradise of
the real being is no longer a slave in Egypt, but a prince who
has the whole created world for his principality.

In painting a composite portrait of the rebellious son in
Chapter Six, we enjoyed the advantage that, despite vast
differences of time and place, temperament and genius, the
rebellious sons were alike in being dependent on other people,
and we found that their principal characteristics were determined by the exigencies of the revolt against the father. Conscious man, on the other hand, is not dependent on other

people, but is free to be who he is. The only thing that can be asserted of him positively, therefore, is that he will act authentically in accordance with the nature of his own unique being. However, we can to some extent define man at the level of Consciousness negatively by observing that he does not possess those attributes that we have seen to be the peculiar stamp of the adolescent hero. Thus where the Hamletian youth is melancholy, Conscious man is grateful for the gift of life, and he enjoys being happy. '*Felicitas in eo consistit quod homo suum esse conservare potest*', Spinoza says, which may be freely translated, 'Happy is the man who lives in accordance with his real being.' The Hamletian youth, again, is misanthropic, but Conscious man loves life and, so far as possible, he lets his eye look like a friend on his fellow-creatures. For our purposes perhaps, the most significant thing about man at the level of Consciousness is that he is *not* pleased by the misfortunes of his friends. Self-Conscious man is delighted when his friends drop out, for he then occupies a higher place in the table. But *Conscious* man knows who he is; he does not claim a place to which he is not entitled, nor does he depend on other people for the reassurance that he is worthy to hold that rank in the scale of creation that is properly his. Once he ceases to be dependent on other people, he cannot fail to perceive that he himself is adversely affected by his friend's sorrow, so that his talent for enjoying himself is alone sufficient reason for him to wish his friend well. Indeed, when the hero is liberated from the mad competitiveness that characterizes man at the level of Self-Consciousness, he is in all his relationships much more aware of the common interests that bind men together: if my life depends on the skill of my neighbour (a surgeon), I cannot be pleased if his powers are impaired by some misfortune!

What emerges most clearly from our discussion, I think, is the conclusion that for fallen man the roads to Consciousness are straight and narrow 'and few there be that find it'. How, after all, am I to learn to know and feel that I occupy that place in the scale of creation that I in fact occupy? If I accept the judgement of other people, I put myself in their power, at the mercy of their jealousy and competitiveness; to commit this error is to revert to the original conditions of my self-alienation. If I consult my own consciousness, I meet another distorting mirror in the shape of my self-love. If I try to mortify my infinite self-love, I am liable to fall into the opposite excess of self-depreciation. ('*Nur die Lumpen sind bescheiden*', Goethe says.*) As we saw earlier, my lowly opinion of myself may lead me to forsake my vocation, or cause me to set too high a value upon other people's judgements; in *Paradise Lost* Raphael warns Adam against the error of thus deferring too much to Eve:

> weigh with her thyself;
> Then value: oft-times nothing profits more
> Than self-esteem, grounded on just and right
> Well manag'd;

'Self-esteem' in the sense of a just estimate of one's own real worth is wholly profitable, but it is to be noted that the word 'self-esteem' is ordinarily synonymous with *conceit*, which means precisely that unjust estimate of one's own real worth to which Self-Conscious man is prone. Thus, there is the problem of avoiding a conceited, delusive, inflated notion of one's own worth, without falling into the opposite extreme of a self-depreciatory, delusive humility. Real self-knowledge, a self-estimate that is 'grounded on just and right', demands constant discrimination between these two extremes.

Consider, again, the distinction between the real being and the self. As we saw in Chapter One, it may be laid down as a principle that that which is of the real being is 'right' and that which is of the self is 'wrong'. However, this principle is of little value unless we can distinguish between the real being and the self, and in practice it is often virtually impossible to do so. How is one to decide whether a particular man wants to be a king in order to be exalted, or in order to find scope for his kingly nature? Who is capable of making the fine distinction between the wish to be wise, the wish to appear wise, and the wish both to be wise and to be known to be wise? It would be a simple matter, for example, if one could say *a priori* that the

* Only the vulgar herd is modest.

desire for revenge is always of the self (and therefore 'wrong'), and that forgiveness is always of the real being. Because revenge is inferior to forgiveness ('The rarer action is / In virtue than in vengeance', as Prospero says in *The Tempest*), we easily slip into the assumption that revenge is 'wrong'; but inferior things, too, have their appropriate place in the creation, and only a careful scrutiny of the circumstances in any particular case can tell whether revenge is 'right' or 'wrong'. In Shakespeare's *Antony and Cleopatra*, for example, it is reasonably clear that Antony's desire for revenge against Cleopatra arises authentically from the real being; in *Othello*, on the other hand, there is in Othello's vengefulness a frenzied note ('Cuckold *me*', he cries), which shows it to be a manifestation of self. The aim of Conscious man, then, is not to outlaw the desire for revenge, but rather to learn to recognize the peculiar resonance of the self, so that he can distinguish between the natural feelings of an Antony and the monstrous feelings of an Othello.

Forgiveness, similarly, can be either authentic or inauthentic. In *Anna Karenina*, for example, at the time when Anna is gravely ill, Karenin experiences an ecstatic moment of self-surrender and freely forgives Vronsky; later, when the feeling born in that moment of illumination has passed, Karenin continues to exhibit a self-conscious, self-approving sham forgiveness, which serves as a mask for cruel actions that correctly reflect the vindictiveness that he really feels.* Thus it will be seen that no external principle can tell us in any particular case whether revenge and mercy have their source in the real being or the self; to discriminate correctly, we must learn to detect that note of hysteria, that excess of feeling, that intemperate ego-involvement in one's own desires, which are the hallmarks of Self-Consciousness. Yet without a Shakespeare or a Tolstoy to enlighten us, it is extraordinarily difficult to form a correct judgement of our own feelings or of other people's. We may say, in fact, that the real being and the self

---

* We may note in passing that Karenin's transition from authentic to sham forgiveness illustrates the point that we err by imitating our own past excellence almost as often as we err by imitating the excellence of another.

are infinitely different, yet almost indistinguishable. Hence the paradox: 'If I am not for myself, who is for me? Yet being for myself, what am I?' If I do not free myself from dependence on others, and enter into the enjoyment of the paradise of the real being, who else can do it for me? Yet if, like Macbeth, in the interests of the self I snatch a crown that does not belong to me, what have I gained? This paradox of Hillel's is informed by the same conception of the nature of man that we encountered earlier in Pascal:

> We are not satisfied with the life that we have in ourselves and in our own being; we wish to live an imaginary life in the opinion of other people, and for this purpose we strive to keep up appearances.

However, it should be noted that Pascal suggests a false anti-thesis between being satisfied and striving (*se contenter— s'efforcer*), where Hillel recognizes the need for the right kind of effort.

In his attitude to time, also, Conscious man has to exercise discrimination. Unconscious man lives in the present, pulled hither and thither by stray desires and sensations. Man at the level of Self-Consciousness lives for the 'orgiastic future' (as Fitzgerald expresses it in *The Great Gatsby*), sacrificing his real life for the sake of a future happiness that forever eludes him. Conscious man has to take a middle path between these two extremes: he lives in a present that is modified (as it were) by the fact that it is situated in the context of the whole of his time. This delicate tension can be illustrated by the famous prayer of St Augustine: 'Oh God, make me chaste—but not yet.' Just as revenge is sweet and mercy is even better (provided that they are both authentic), so it may be said that both sexual desire and chastity come from God. As Heine puts it:

> *Himmlisch wars, wenn ich bezwang*
> *Meine sündige Begier,*
> *Aber wenns mir nicht gelang,*
> *Hatt ich doch ein gross Pläsier.**

* It was heavenly when I overcame my sinful desire, but when I did not succeed, I still had a great deal of pleasure.

With the acquisitive desire for virtue that is typical of the Puritan tradition, Self-Conscious man stifles his sexual nature in the interests of his hot pursuit of God, like the hermit in Tolstoy's story, *Father Sergius*, who cuts off his fingers in order to subdue the lust that is aroused in him by the deliberate provocativeness of the woman. Unconscious man becomes so immersed in the pleasures of the moment that he forgets where he is going. Conscious man gives the present its due without sacrificing the future to it, or it to the future; he enjoys the present and derives nourishment from it, just as a traveller enjoys rest and refreshment at an inn but resumes his journey on the morrow.

Similarly, in his attitude to the external world, Conscious man needs to exercise discrimination. The man at the level of Unconsciousness delights in the created world, but lives in bondage to external impressions. The introspective adolescent hero withdraws from the world ('Man delights not me'), and enters into his own depths in order to give birth to himself. He is thus like an artist who neglects his wife and children while he labours to bring forth his masterpiece, or perhaps he is like a man who is so intent on adjusting his television-set to get a more perfect picture that he never manages to watch the actual programme on the screen. Conscious man, since he is self-begotten, is neither a slave of outward impressions, nor a prisoner trapped within his own consciousness. Thus in *Sartor Resartus*, after Teufelsdröckh has passed through his Baphometic Fire-Baptism, Carlyle writes of his hero:

> In a word, he is now, if not ceasing, yet intermitting to 'eat his own heart'; and clutches round him outwardly on the NOT-ME for wholesomer food. [And a few pages later] Thus can the Professor, at least in lucid intervals, look away from his own sorrows, over the many-coloured world, and pertinently enough note what is passing there.

In short, to resume the metaphor that I employed a moment ago, Conscious man is a traveller who enjoys the many-coloured world of the inn without being deflected from the purposes of his journey.

I

Evil is really the crux of the problem of Hamletian man. The adolescent hero is disgusted with his own evil nature: 'What should such fellows as I do crawling between heaven and earth?' Hamlet asks. 'We are arrant knaves all.' Now, a man's taste in clothes may seem deplorable to a stranger, but it can hardly seem deplorable to himself. By the same token, we may say that the adolescent hero's self-disgust is only explicable on the hypothesis that he is a stranger to himself. Unconscious man is at home in himself; consequently, he simply manifests himself, accepting the desires that spontaneously arise in him as their own warranty. Naturally, he seeks to satisfy these desires unless they happen to conflict with other stronger desires within him. Thus if Unconscious man covets his neighbour's wife, he may seek to satisfy his desire, or he may renounce it; he may even yield to his lust, and then repent of it; but in all this there is no cause for self-disgust. With the Fall of Man, this innocence and natural harmony is lost. The Hamletian hero is disgusted with himself partly because greed and spiritual ambition make him demand too much of himself; as Dostoyevsky's Underground Man says, '. . . because of an infinite vanity that caused me to set myself impossible standards, I regarded myself with furious disapproval, bordering on loathing.'[3] At the same time, in his efforts to live up to an inauthentic ideal, the man at an advanced stage of Self-Consciousness really is disgusting, as we see very clearly in the Underground Man himself; hence the adolescent hero's self-contempt partly arises out of a genuine insight on the part of the real being into the nature of the self. The man at the level of Consciousness, like Unconscious man, is at home in himself; since he does not view himself with the eyes of other people, he does not measure himself by impossible or inappropriate standards. If, say, he wants to perform a good action, he does it; if he does not want to do it, he does not blame himself for not doing what he does not want to do. A horse, after all, does not regard itself with furious disapproval because it cannot run as fast as a cheetah. '*Werde, der du bist*' Nietzsche says, or, as Wittgenstein used to say to his students, 'Be as stupid as you are.' Because he has the courage to be as virtuous (or otherwise) as he really is, Conscious man maintains his fidelity to the real being as naturally as water finds its own level. Why should he not respect himself?

The adolescent hero is disgusted, too, by the evil nature of other men: 'Use every man after his desert, and who shall 'scape whipping?' The problem of evil in a world in which innocent children suffer horribly does not really exist for Unconscious man. The man at the level of Unconsciousness does what he wants to do, and he instinctively accepts that other men, too, will behave according to their kind, even though their behaviour may have 'evil' consequences for himself or others.* Moreover, since Unconscious man is likely to be at a comparatively low level of development himself, he will tend to sympathize with the baser feelings of his fellow-men, and cry 'Crucify him! Crucify him!' with as much enthusiasm as his neighbour. The misanthropic Hamletian hero resists the contagion of the mass, which draws us all downward like the force of gravity. He identifies himself with the more creditable aspects of his own nature, repudiating the lower, and at the same time insists that other people reflect back to him his own ideal aspirations; in thus demanding that lower things should exhibit the characteristics of higher things, he is in effect (as I suggested earlier) condemning men because they are not two inches taller than they actually are. From his sure foundation in the real being, Conscious man is strong enough to see the object as in itself it really is, without fear and without delusion. In *The Horse's Mouth*, for example, when the idealistic shoe-repairer, Plant, tries to find a meaning in the tragedy of the murder of some young girls, Gulley Jimson is lucid enough to reject Plant's self-consolatory fictions:

> 'The girls', he said at last. 'Poor things. Awful, terrible.' And he shook his head like an old dog bothered by a horsefly. 'It's a mystery.' And he cheered up a little. 'Yes', he said, 'if we only knew, there's a meaning in it.' 'That's it', I said, 'it means that girls are liable to be strangled by young devils like Rockway. Always were and always will be.'[4]

* 'Good and Evil', Hobbes says, 'are names that signify our appetites and aversions. Every man calleth that which pleases him good; and that which displeaseth him, evil.'

I*

This commendable ability to face up to ugly truths, however, easily degenerates into cynical spurious acceptance unless it is supplemented by two perceptions. First, as we saw in Chapter Seven, Conscious man acknowledges his own kinship with lower things, because he recognizes 'the *all in each* of human nature', which means that every Prospero has a Caliban latent within him, and every Ivan Karamazov a Smerdyakov. (Indeed, Gulley Jimson himself ends up by murdering Sara Monday, thereby demonstrating that his case is not wholly unlike young Rockway's.) Second, the same principle of 'the *all in each* of human nature' implies that every Caliban has a Prospero latent within him, though in a given case it may be almost inconceivable that this Prospero nature will ever be awakened. In the gap between the actual and the latent or potential, there is scope for a tough-minded idealism which does not view evil metaphysically, as a ground for denying eternal providence or respectfully returning the ticket to God, but practically, as a refractory material that it must work to make the best of.

I have heard a preacher say that he seldom sees a look of love nowadays except on the faces of the dying, and it must be confessed that the competitive nature of Self-Consciousness leads rather to universal hate than to love. '*Tous les hommes se haïssent naturellement l'un l'autre.*' I suggested earlier that instead of loving our enemies, we ought to begin by trying to love our friends, but this counsel is open to the objections that Self-Conscious man is incapable of real friendship (since he knows that he and his so-called friends secretly rejoice in one another's misfortunes) and incapable also of real love. Even the love that Self-Conscious man feels for his wife and children is tainted by self: they are possessions that enhance his prestige in the eyes of the world, or, as representatives of the world, they bolster his ego by their love for him. In *Being and Nothingness* Sartre says: 'Thus it seems that to love is in essence the project of making oneself be loved.'[5] This seemingly absurd statement (that is, that to love is not to love at all, but to seek to be loved) is perfectly applicable to Self-Conscious man. Conscious man, on the other hand, is not seeking prestige and reassurance: he enjoys the creation, and naturally loves that which he enjoys. He loves his friends, not because friendship is reckoned to be a virtue, but because it is natural and enjoyable to love your friends. He loves his wife and his children, not—in the manner of Self-Conscious man—because they are his property, but because they are the concrete, familiar, beloved forms in which his delight in life incarnates itself. Can it then be said that Conscious man loves his enemies? Clearly, to achieve the fullest possible enjoyment of the creation—to enjoy it as God enjoys it—it is necessary to love your enemies, but, equally clearly, this love and this enjoyment is not within the compass of most men. All we can safely say, then, is that if any particular man at the level of Consciousness does love his enemies, it will not be out of spiritual acquisitiveness or a desire for approbation, but because he authentically possesses a rare gift for love and a correspondingly rare capacity for enjoyment.

The next topic that claims our attention is thinking, which is traditionally considered to be as important as love as a means of achieving a right relationship with the creation. *Knowledge without love puffeth up, love without knowledge goeth astray.* The adolescent hero, we have seen, takes refuge in abstract thinking because it justifies his revolt against the father, because it offsets (even while it perpetuates) his lack of experience, and because it simplifies and renders orderly a world that is complex, frightening and incomprehensible. Thus his intelligence, which ought to be an instrument for understanding the world, is pressed into the service of the self, and becomes a means of protecting himself from the world. But how can that which is born of fear bring forth good fruit? The function of thinking is to serve and enhance life, and when thinking usurps the place of life, there inevitably arises a revulsion against thought, a *'révolte de la vie contre la pensée'*, as it has been called.[6] However necessary this revulsion against thought may be, it nevertheless means that the adolescent hero, as he gropes his way through the dark wood, is deprived of his best weapon, *'il ben del intelletto'*, as Dante calls it. The natural order of development is to proceed from sensation to thinking, to immerse yourself in the sea of life before you attempt to fathom the laws that govern those dark waters. The return to sensation is, then, a crucial stage on the journey to Consciousness, and in Conscious man life (or sensation) precedes thought—*l'existence précède l'essence*, as it were—and when the faculty of thought ripens in him it is securely rooted in sensation, and manifests itself as an activity of the whole man, as the expression of a unified sensibility. The idealistic youth feels that to think is to be 'full of sorrow / And leaden-eyed despair', but Conscious man delights to wield the weapon of thought, just as he delights in the exercise of his other faculties. In the abstract thinker a shadow falls between reflection and action, between the pale cast of thought and the native hue of resolution, but in Conscious man thought is a mode of action. As Krishna says to Arjuna in the *Bhagavad-Gita*:

> Where is your sword
> Discrimination?
> Draw it and slash
> Delusion to pieces.[7]

We have seen that the hero is constantly required to distinguish between a reality and a semblance that closely resemble each other. Genuine and spurious acceptance, spontaneous solitude and willed solitariness, the real being and the self, a genuine development of taste and a sham acquisition of it, sensation and sensualism, acceptance of suffering and acquisitive desire for suffering, all these demand subtle powers of discrimination. The abstract thinker, to be sure, can always appropriate these concepts and convert them into easily digestible pills of abstract thought, but only concrete thinking is able to forge the sword, discrimination, which effectively separates the genuine from the spurious article. According to his measure, then, Conscious man is a thinker as well as a lover. As a thinker, he has the power to '*voir clair dans ce qui est*' (as Stendhal says); as a lover he is able to enjoy and cherish created things, unsentimentally, as in themselves they really are. This happy union between thought and love, or clarity and charity, produces that compassionate understanding which is one of the most distinguished traits of Consciousness.

We have now arrived at the end of this brief account of the roads to Consciousness. Perhaps it will seem that latterly the hero of Consciousness has emerged as an improbably ideal character. It may be objected, for example, that Shakespeare's Antony, whom we have taken as representative of Conscious man, is by no means a profound thinker capable of drawing fine distinctions between the real being and the self. It must be observed that within the ranks of men at the level of Consciousness there are great differences in the amount of consciousness (with a small 'c') possessed by different individuals. Shakespeare's Antony, for example, possesses the degree of consciousness that one might expect to find in the soldier as hero, while Hamletian man (or the hero as seeker after truth) possesses a superior degree of consciousness. The hero as seeker after truth occupies a higher rank in the scale of creation than the hero as soldier, and the perfection to which he is called is correspondingly higher. On the other hand, it must be said that this higher perfection, being more difficult to achieve, is in fact less often achieved. Ramakrishna says that one man in a thousand seeks God, and of those who seek God only one man in a thousand finds Him. So we may say that the greater the stature of the Hamletian hero, the more likely it is that the goal of Consciousness will elude him. The rule that applies here has been admirably stated by Ruskin:

> . . . it is a law of this universe, that the best things shall be seldomest seen in their best form. The wild grass grows well and strongly, one year with another; but the wheat is, according to the greater nobleness of its nature, liable to the bitterer blight.

If the imperfections of men like Carlyle (whom Emerson called a 'sick giant'), Tolstoy, Gide, Lawrence and Sartre appear to support the view that the best things are seldom seen in their best form, the fact ought to evoke compassion rather than scorn. Then, too, there is some consolation in the knowledge that if the noble wheat is liable to bitter blight, the wild grass grows well and strongly each year. It implies, surely, that that hard saying, *Many are called, but few are chosen*, is applicable to the superior man, but of lesser men it may be said that more than a few achieve that degree of perfection of which they are capable. If the greater man strives after, and often misses, a higher perfection, it may be surmised that he would not wish for a more mediocre fate.

It will be seen, then, that our inquiry into the roads to Consciousness justifies a cautious optimism. Where meditation upon the nature of Self-Consciousness leads to a belief in the incorrigible depravity of man, an idealistic dream of Consciousness promotes a naïve faith in human perfectibility. The conjunction of these two ideas begets a predestinarian doctrine that divides men into the few who are saved and the multitude who are damned. The facts of our common experience belie these extreme positions. Just as no man is ever entirely well or entirely ill, so we may say that neither Self-Consciousness nor Conscious, ness exists in a pure, unadulterated form. All cases are unique- and very similar to others. Moreover, in so far as one case dose differ from another, these differences tend to cancel themselvse out with respect to Consciousness. Since the distinguishing mark of Conscious man is that he is at home in himself, and knows and feels himself to be what he is, it follows that no man is irredeemably exiled from Consciousness. The rhetorical and exemplary virtues of the stark contrast between Self-Consciousness and Consciousness, then, ought not to tempt us to lose our sense of reality or our humanity. If we believe that man is naturally good, we are sure to be undeceived by Iagos within or without. If we believe that man is a beast, then, disgusted by ourselves and by others, we must at last become disgusting. If we understand the nature of Self-Consciousness, and yet know that every man is capable of becoming who he is, then, as the Quakers say, we can walk cheerfully over the earth greeting that which is of God in every man.

Reference Notes

CHAPTER ONE

1. All quotations from T. E. Hulme are taken from *Speculations*, ed. Herbert Read (London: Kegan Paul, Trench, Trubner & Co. Ltd, 1936).

2. In case the reader questions these somewhat peremptory judgements upon Rousseau and Lawrence, it should be observed that my argument does not depend on these particular examples, whose function is merely exemplary.

3. As early as 1916 Katherine Mansfield writes about D. H. Lawrence:

> I cannot describe the frenzy that comes over him. He simply *raves*, roars, beats the table, abuses everybody. But that's not such a great matter. What makes these attacks insupportable is the feeling one has at the back of one's mind that he is completely out of control, swallowed up in an acute, *insane* irritation.

In a letter of 1920 to John Middleton Murry, she writes: 'Lawrence sent me a letter today. He spat in my face and threw filth at me and said "I loathe you. You revolt me stewing in your consumption", etc.' I have been unable to trace the original source of the first letter, which is cited in Myrick Land, *The Fine Art of Literary Mayhem* (London: Hamish Hamilton, 1963), p. 123. The second letter is in *Katherine Mansfield's Letters to John Middleton Murry: 1913-1922*, ed. J. M. Murry (New York: Alfred A. Knopf, 1951, p. 470; London: Constable).

4. On the difference between the authentic impetus towards the religious life and that which is the result of imitativeness and conformity, this charming passage from *The Scale of Perfection* is instructive: 'A hound that only runs after the hare because he sees other hounds run, rests and turns home again when he is tired. But if he runs because he sees the hare, he will not stop, although he is tired, until he has caught it.' Walter Hilton, *The Scale of Perfection*, trans. into modern English by Dom Gerard Sitwell, O.S.B. (London: Burns Oates, 1953), p. 59.

5. 'For it is the lot of every myth to creep gradually into the narrows of supposititious historical fact and to be treated by some later time as a unique event of history', Nietzsche, *The Birth of Tragedy*, trans. Francis Golffing (New York: Doubleday Anchor Books, 1956), p. 68.

6. In his *Autobiography* John Stuart Mill says of his father:

'He found it impossible to believe that a world so full of evil was the work of an Author combining infinite power with perfect goodness and righteousness. . . . Think (he used to say) of a being who would make a Hell—who would create the human race with the infallible foreknowledge, and therefore with the intention, that the great majority of them were to be consigned to horrible and everlasting torment.'

7. This distinction is of the highest importance. If we ask why John Stuart Mill in *On Liberty* attacks conformity while Matthew Arnold in *Culture and Anarchy* recommends conformity, the answer is that Mill is attacking inauthentic conformity, or conformity of the self, while Arnold is commending authentic conformity, or conformity of the real being.

8. Quotations from *The Confessions of St Augustine* are taken from the translation by F. J. Sheed (London: Sheed & Ward, 1945).

9. Quotations from *Crime and Punishment* are taken from the translation by David Magarshack (Harmondsworth, Middlesex: Penguin Books, 1951).

CHAPTER TWO

1. Quotations from the *Bhagavad-Gita* are taken from *The Song of God: Bhagavad-Gita*, translated by Swami Prabhavananda and Christopher Isherwood (London: Phoenix House, 1947).

2. G. Wilson Knight, *The Wheel of Fire* (London: Methuen & Co. Ltd, University Publications, 1960), p. 31. While I have already acknowledged my debt to Professor Wilson Knight, I ought to add here that my indebtedness is naturally greatest in this chapter.

3. Quotations from *Scarlet and Black* are taken from the translation by Margaret R. B. Shaw (Harmondsworth, Middlesex: Penguin Books, 1953).

CHAPTER THREE

1. I have taken this passage, omitting two parenthetical interruptions, from *The Political Tracts of Wordsworth, Coleridge and Shelley*, ed. R. J. White (London: Cambridge University Press, 1953), p. 32.

2. See, for example, F. W. Bateson, 'Contributions to a Dictionary of Critical Terms: II, *Dissociation of Sensibility*', *Essays in Criticism*, I (July, 1951), 302-12.

3. Eliot's terminology is new, but the concepts themselves are familiar under a variety of names among idealist philosophers. Coleridge, for example, distinguishes between *substantial* knowledge and

abstract knowledge, associating the former with the heart and the latter with the head or the understanding (a word which indicates that his terms are derived from *Vernunft* and *Verstand*).

4. Some time after I had written this sentence, I came across the identical observation, somewhat more happily expressed, in the *Quarterly Review* of 1811:

> 'The principia of Newton . . . may be understood by a boy of eighteen. . . . But the Iliad, or the Epistles of Horace, or Lord Clarendon's history, were never comprehended till variety of observation, and many original efforts of the reader's own mind, had brought him to that point of view from which he could look at those works in the posture of design and combination in which they were seen by the authors themselves, and with some part of their reach of thought.'

5. For a critical discussion of Eliot's dictum, see F. W. Bateson, 'The Teaching of Literature: A Reply to Mr Eliot', *University of Toronto Quarterly*, XXV (1955-6), 38-46.

6. 'Thus the scientist knows how to interest himself strictly in universals; he admits no individuals to his attention, except as the initiation of new studies or the verification of old ones', John Crowe Ransom, *The World's Body* (New York: Louisiana State University Press, 1938), p. 206.

7. Gerard Manley Hopkins, *Letters to Robert Bridges and Correspondence with Richard Watson Dixon,* ed. Claude Colheer Abbott (London: Oxford University Press, 1935), p. 139.

8. Daniel Boorstin, *The Image* (London: Weidenfeld & Nicolson, 1962), p. 4. Similarly Flaubert writes: *'Nous exigeons des choses plus qu'elles ne peuvent donner.'*

9. In *The New Republic* (1877), W. H. Mallock has Mr Herbert (who represents Ruskin) say: 'Your mind, my good sir, that you boast of, is so occupied in subduing matter, that it is entirely forgetful of subduing itself—a matter, trust me, that is far more important.'

10. George Orwell, *Nineteen Eighty-Four* (London: Secker & Warburg, 1950), pp. 201-2.

11. For Wordsworth's attitude to Godwin, see Basil Willey, *The Eighteenth-Century Background* (London: Chatto & Windus, 1940), Chapter Eleven.

12. 'Consequently the love of father, mother, and friends does not influence him unduly, for the sword of spiritual love severs all earthly love from his heart, so that he feels no deeper affection towards his father, mother and friends than towards other people unless he sees greater virtue or grace in them than in others', Walter Hilton, *The Ladder of Perfection,* trans. Leo Sherley-Price (Harmondsworth, Middlesex: Penguin Books, 1957), pp. 219-20.

13. Cf. Molière's *Tartuffe*, where Cleante describes the lessons he has learnt from Tartuffe:

Il m'enseigne à n'avoir affection pour rien;
De toutes amitiés il détache mon âme;
Et je verrais mourir frère, enfants, mère et femme,
Que je m'en soucierais autant que de cela.

He teaches me to feel no affection for any object; he frees my soul from all bonds of human affection; and I could see my brother, my children, my mother and my wife die, and it wouldn't trouble me in the least.

14. Sartre writes of *bad faith*: 'I must know in my capacity as deceiver the truth which is hidden from me in my capacity as the one deceived', *Being and Nothingness*, trans. Hazel E. Barnes (New York: Philosophical Library, 1956), p. 49. In Dickens's *Great Expectations* the mature Pip says of his former self-deceit: 'Surely a curious thing. That I should innocently take a bad half-crown of somebody else's manufacture, is reasonable enough; but that I should knowingly reckon the spurious coin of my own make, as good money!'

15. The sentences occur in Lawrence's 'Review of *The Social Basis of Consciousness* by Trigant Burrow', collected in *Phoenix*, ed. E. D. McDonald (London: William Heinemann, Ltd, 1961), pp. 377-82.

16. *Being and Nothingness*, p. 59.

17. D. H. Lawrence, *St Mawr*, in *The Shorter Novels of* D. H. Lawrence (London: William Heinemann Ltd, 1956), p. 121.

18. *The Image*, p. 103.

19. Fyodor Dostoyevsky, *Crime and Punishment*, trans. David Magarshack (Harmondsworth, Middlesex: Penguin Books, 1951), p. 553.

CHAPTER FOUR

1. Remy de Gourmont, *A Virgin Heart*, translated by Aldous Huxley (London: George Allen & Unwin, 1926), p. 140.

2. Basil Willey, *The Eighteenth-Century Background* (London: Chatto & Windus, 1961), p. 268.

3. See, for example, Edna C. Florance, 'The Neurosis of Raskolnikov: A study in Incest and Murder', *Archives of Criminal Psychodynamics*, I (Winter, 1955), reprinted in part in Edward Wasiolek (ed.), *Crime and Punishment and the Critics* (Belmont, California: Wadsworth Publishing Co., Inc., 1961), pp. 57-77.

4. All quotations from *Crime and Punishment* are taken from the translation by David Magarshack (Harmondsworth, Middlesex: Penguin Books, 1951).

5. Ernest J. Simmons, *Dostoyevsky: The Making of a Novelist* (London: Oxford University Press, 1940), p. 154.

6. In *Reflections on the Revolution in France* Burke describes the revolutionists as 'weighing, as it were in scales hung in a shop of horrors, —so much actual crime against so much contingent advantage,—and after putting in and out weights, declaring that the balance was on the side of the advantages'.

7. Quoted by David Magarshack in his Introduction to his translation of *Crime and Punishment*, p. 12.

8. Cited by Simmons, p. 157.

CHAPTER FIVE

1. Quotations from *Dirty Hands* are taken from the translation by Lionel Abel in *No Exit and Three Other Plays* (New York: Alfred A. Knopf, Inc., 1955).

2. *Man, Morals and Society: A Psycho-analytical Study* (London: Duckworth & Co., Ltd, 1945), p. 283.

3. This point is made by Mr Thody.

4. Francis Jeanson, *Sartre par lui-même* (Paris, 1954), cited in Hazel E. Barnes, *The Literature of Possibility* (Lincoln: University of Nebraska Press, 1958, p. 264; London: Tavistock Publications, 1961).

CHAPTER SIX

1. John Weightman in *The Observer*, 1 March 1964.

2. Edmund Burke sees the father and the rebellious son in similar terms: 'Because half a dozen grasshoppers under a fern make the field ring with their importunate chink, whilst thousands of great cattle, reposed beneath the shadow of the British oak, chew the cud and are silent, pray do not imagine, that those who make the noise are the only inhabitants of the field', *Reflections on the Revolution in France*, (London: Dent & Sons, Ltd, 1960), p. 82.

3. *Journal*, I, 365, cited in G. W. Ireland, *Gide* (Writers and Critics Series, Edinburgh, Oliver & Boyd, 1963), p. 91. Benjamin Constant says somewhere: '*Je ne suis pas tout à fait un être réel.*'

4. Cf. Orestes in *The Flies*, after he has killed Aegisthus and Clytemnestra: 'We were too light, Electra; now our feet sink into the soil, like chariot-wheels in turf.'

5. For an account of the (symbolical) revolt against the father in J. S. Mill, see A. W. Levi, 'The "Mental Crisis" of John Stuart Mill', *Psychoanalytic Review*, 32 (1945), 86-101.

6. On the subject of Teufelsdröckh's puritanism, note the Swiftlike excremental imagery in the following passage of *Sartor Resartus*: 'O my Friends, when we view the fair clustering flowers that over-wreathe, for example, the Marriage-bower, and encircle man's life

with the fragrance and hues of Heaven, what hand will not smite the foul plunderer that grubs them up by the roots, and with grinning, grunting satisfaction, shows us the dung they flourish in!'

7. See the Cambridge University Press text of *Hamlet*, edited by John Dover Wilson, p. liii.

8. The expression is used by Francis Fergusson, in summarizing John Dover Wilson's views, in his essay on *Hamlet* in Chapter Four of *The Idea of a Theater* (New Jersey: Princeton University Press, 1949).

9. Cf. Clytemnestra in *The Flies*: 'You are young, Electra. It is easy for young people, who have not yet had a chance of sinning, to condemn.'

10. Both statements occur in the lecture, 'L'Existentialisme est un humanisme', translated by Bernard Frechtman.

11. This essay is included in the fourth, enlarged edition of *The Wheel of Fire* (London: Methuen & Co., Ltd, 1960).

12. I owe this point to my colleague, Dr H. S. Whittier.

13. André Malraux, *The Walnut Trees of Altenburg*, trans. A. W. Fielding (London: John Lehmann, 1952), pp. 96-7.

CHAPTER SEVEN

1. *The Meditations of Marcus Aurelius* and *Epictetus: The Enchiridion* edited by Russell Kirk (Chicago: Henry Regnery, n.d.), p. 173.

2. Franz Kafka, *The Trial*, trans. Willa and Edwin Muir (New York: The Modern Library, 1956, p. 73; London: Secker & Warbug, 1956).

3. To her credit Dorothea resists the temptation to surrender to the common way of looking at things. When Mrs Cadwallader suggests to her that her mistakes must have taught her to call things by the same names as other people do, Dorothea replies stoutly: 'I still think that the greater part of the world is mistaken about many things. Surely one may be sane and yet think so, since the greater part of the world has often had to come round from its opinion.'

4. Cf. D. H. Lawrence: 'Once I said to myself: "How can I blame— why be angry?" . . . Now I say: "When anger comes with bright eyes, he may do his will. In me he will hardly shake off the hand of God. He is one of the archangels, with a fiery sword. God sent him—it is beyond my knowing." ' But who of us can possess such perfect confidence that the hand of God is upon him? (The quotation from Lawrence is in Aldous Huxley's *The Olive Tree*, published by Chatto & Windus in 1947).

5. '*Wenn wir die Menschen nur nehmen wie sie sind, so machen wir sie schlechter; wenn wir sie behandeln, als wären sie, was sie sein sollte, so bringen wir sie dahin, wohin sie zu bringen sind.*' *Wilhem Meisters Lehrjahre.*

6. Edmund Wilson, *Classics and Commercials* (London: W. H. Allen, 1951), p. 392.

7. Sir Isaiah Berlin, 'A Marvellous Decade (III): *Belinsky: Moralist and Prophet*', *Encounter*, V (December, 1955), 22-43.

8. Since *The Wild Duck* provides a sufficient illustration of cynical acceptance, I do not propose to discuss *Under Western Eyes*. However, it is worth noting that the novel illustrates the point that in the political sphere spurious acceptance means acceptance of the *status quo*. Also, apropos of our discussion of *Crime and Punishment*, it is interesting to observe that Razumov is an *inverted Raskolnikov*. Like Raskolnikov, he is poor, handsome, lonely, fatherless and ambitious; like Raskolnikov, again, he despises his fellow-students, looking down on them from the heights of his intellectual superiority. Yet where Raskolnikov kills the old pawnbroker (symbol of the oppressive capitalist class), Razumov 'kills' the young, idealistic, rebellious student. Both Raskolnikov and Razumov finally achieve salvation through love of a woman who corresponds to the component of their respective personalities that they have repressed and denied. Both of them confess their crimes, first, to the beloved woman, then publicly.

9. Quotations from *Howards End* are taken from the standard edition published by Edward Arnold.

10. F. R. Leavis, 'E. M. Forster', *Scrutiny*, VII (September, 1938), 193.

CHAPTER EIGHT

1. *Journal*, August 1893, cited in Everett W. Knight, *Literature Considered as Philosophy* (London: Routledge & Kegan Paul, 1957), p. 112.

2. *The Confessions of St Augustine*, trans. F. J. Sheed (London: Sheed & Ward, 1945), p. 27.

3. *Les Nourritures terrestres*, trans. Dorothy Bussy as *The Fruits of the Earth* (New York: Alfred A. Knopf, 1952, p. 76; Harmondsworth, Middlesex: Penguin Books, 1970).

4. A. J. Ayer, 'Philosophy at Absolute Zero: An Enquiry into the Meaning of Nihilism', *Encounter*, V (October, 1955), 24-33. The sentence from which the quotation is taken occurs on p. 30.

5. See Chapter XII of *The Lonely Crowd* (Connecticut: Yale University Press, 1950), which is entitled, 'The Adjusted, The Anomic, The Autonomous'.

6. *Notes from Underground*, trans. Andrew R. MacAndrew (New York: New American Library, 1961), pp. 110, 112.

7. Quotations from *The Flies* are taken from the translation by Stuart Gilbert in *No Exit and Three Other Plays* (New York: Alfred A. Knopf, Inc., 1955).

8. Quotations from *the Immoralist* are taken from the translation by Dorothy Bussy (London: Cassell & Co. Ltd., 1953).

9. Jean Delay, *La Jeunesse d'André Gide* (Paris: Gallimard, 1957), II, 534. (My translation). My debt to M. Delay in this chapter is considerable.

10. *Si le grain ne meurt*, trans. Dorothy Bussy as *If it die* (New York: Random House, 1957), p. 251.

11. *The Fruits of the Earth*, p. 73. Delay, II, 595, cites this passage in his discussion of Ménalque.

12. Delay, II, 581 (my translation).

13. *If it die*, p. 146.

14. Sigmund Freud, *The Complete Psychological Works*, ed. and trans. James Strachey, *et al.* (London: Hogarth Press, 1961), XXI, 104.

15. Edna C. Florance, in the psychoanalytical study of *Crime and Punishment* already referred to (see Chapter Four, footnote 3), says : 'It will be shown that the murder is at once an attempt to release his [Raskolnikov's] libidinous drives, to create a tangible reason for his guilt feelings, and to bring upon himself the punishment that is needed to assuage those guilt feelings.'

16. Jean-Paul Sartre, *Existentialism*, trans. Bernard Frechtman (New York: Philosophical Library, 1947), p. 21. In the first chapter of his book on Genet, Sartre writes: '*Genet, lui, né sans parents, se prépare à mourir sans descendance.*'

17. Cf. the remarks by Maurice Cranston in his excellent book on Sartre: 'He is revolted also by women. There is something sickening about all the female characters in Sartre's plays and stories. Woman is seen as corrupt and corrupting', *Sartre* (Edinburgh: Oliver and Boyd, 1962), p. 111.

18. *Oedipus*, trans. John Russell (New York: Random House, 1958), p. 37.

19. *The Confessions of St Augustine*, p. 25.

CHAPTER NINE

1. *The Spiritual Exercises of Saint Ignatius*, trans. Thomas Corbishley, S.J. (London: Burns & Oates, 1963), p. 20.

2. Quotations from *The Respectful Prostitute* and *Dirty Hands* are from the translation by Lionel Abel in *No Exit and Three Other Plays* (New York: Alfred A. Knopf, Inc., 1955).

3. Cf. John Stuart Mill, *On Liberty*: 'Wherever there is an ascendant class, a large portion of the morality of the country emanates from its class interests, and its feelings of class superiority.'

4. Quotations from *Nausea* are taken from the translation by Lloyd Alexander, published by New Directions Publishing Corp., New York, 1959.

5. Robert Champigny, 'Sens de *La Nausée*', *PMLA*, LXX (March, 1955), 37. (My translation from the French.)

6. *Being and Nothingness*, trans. Hazel E. Barnes (New York: Philosophical Library, 1956), p. 438.

7. Cited in Alan W. Watts, *The Way of Zen* (Harmondsworth, Middlesex: Penguin Books, 1962), p. 42.

8. *Being and Nothingness*, p. 70n.

9. *Being and Nothingness*, pp. 626-7.

10. *Being and Nothingness*, p. xvi.

11. Parallel to Roquentin's outburst when he visits the portrait-gallery is the savage epitaph that Teufelsdröckh composes for Count Zähdarm, saying of him that 'while he lived beneath the moon, he shot five thousand partridges, and, by his own labour, or that of his four-footed and two-footed servants, publicly converted many hundreds of thousands of pounds of different sorts of food into excrement, etc.' (My translation from the Latin). Once again, we observe that Carlyle and Swift have in common the excremental vision!

12. For this distinction, I am indebted to the essay, 'Puritans and Victorians', in G. M. Young, *Victorian Essays* (London: Oxford University Press, 1962).

13. Basil Willey considers that there is a taint of arrogance even in Carlyle's experience of 'conversion': 'What he has attained is not humility and love, but a spiritual elevation from whence he can look down, with mingled compassion and scorn, on the "welterings of my poor fellow-creatures, still stuck in that fatal element" ', *Nineteenth Century Studies: Coleridge to Matthew Arnold* (London: Chatto & Windus, 1955), p. 116.

14. For a perceptive and sympathetic discussion of Sartre as, in effect, a 'lost leader', see Joseph H. McMahon, 'A Reader's Hesitations', *Yale French Studies*, No. 30, pp. 96-107.

CHAPTER TEN

1. Except where otherwise indicated, quotations from *War and Peace* are taken from the translation by Louise and Aylmer Maude, published by Oxford University Press (1930-2).

2. Quotations from *Anna Karenina* are taken from the translation by David Magarshack, published by New American Library (Signet Classics), 1961.

3. Irving, Babbitt, *Rousseau and Romanticism* (Boston: Houghton Mifflin, 1919), p. 51.

4. Joyce Cary, *The Horse's Mouth* (Harmondsworth, Middlesex: Penguin Books, 1948), p. 356.

5. Simone Weil, 'The Love of God and Affliction', in *Waiting on God* (London: Fontana Books, 1959), p. 90.

6. Quotations from *The Brothers Karamazov* are taken from the translation by Constance Garnett (London: William Heinemann, 1912).

7. Quotations from *Notes from Underground* are taken from the translation by Andrew R. MacAndrew (New York: New American Library, 1961).

8. Quotations from Camus's *The Myth of Sisyphus* are taken from the translation by Justin O'Brien (London: Hamish Hamilton, 1955).

9. Quotations from *Scarlet and Black* are taken from the translation by Margaret R. B. Shaw, published by Penguin Books, 1953.

10. Quotations from *The Death of Ivan Ilych* are taken from the translation by Louise and Aylmer Maude, published by Oxford University Press.

11. This quotation from *War and Peace* is taken from the translation by Rosemary Edmonds (Penguin Books, 1957). This translation is not very different from that of Louise and Aylmer Maude, but in two instances I have found it to be either more intelligible or more suited to my purposes.

12. Simone Weil, 'Reflections on the Right Use of School Studies', in *Waiting on God*, p. 74.

CHAPTER ELEVEN

1. The phrases quoted are all to be found in Chapters Four and Five of Mill's *Autobiography*.

2. Quotations from Goethe's first novel are taken from *The Sorrows of Young Werther*, translated by Catherine Hutter (New York: New American Library, 1962).

3. Quotations from *Anna Karenina* are taken from the translation by David Magarshack, published by New American Library (Signet Classics), 1961.

4. For the view that the 'solutions' offered by both Dostoyevsky and Tolstoy are inauthentic or, at any rate, unsatisfactory, see Philip Rahv, 'Dostoyevsky in *Crime and Punishment*', *Partisan Review*, XXVII (1960), 393-425, and F. R. Leavis, '*Anna Karenina*: Thought and Significance in a Great Creative Work', *Cambridge Quarterly*, I (Winter, 1965-6), 5-27.

5. Quotations from *Scarlet and Black* are taken from the translation by Margaret R. B. Shaw, published by Penguin Books, 1953.

6. For an interesting note on the implications of the question whether two plus two equals four, see George Steiner, *Tolstoy or Dostoevsky: An Essay in the Old Criticism* (New York: Random House, 1961), p. 261.

7. Jean-Paul Sartre, *Anti-Semite and Jew*, trans. George J. Becker (New York: Grove Press, 1962), pp. 73-4.

8. Arthur Miller, *Death of a Salesman* (New York: Viking Press, 1958, p. 61; Harmondsworth: Penguin Books, 1969).

9. Edward Carpenter, *Civilization: Its Cause and Cure* (London: Swan Sonnerschein & Co., 1893), p. 44.

10. Quotations from *The Blind Man* are taken from *The Complete Short Stories of D. H. Lawrence* (London: William Heinemann, 1955).

11. D. H. Lawrence, 'Introduction to his Paintings', in *A Propos of Lady Chatterley's Lover and Other Essays* (Harmondsworth, Middlesex: Penguin Books, 1961), p. 38.

12. It may be noted, for instance, that both Bertie Reid and Sir Clifford Chatterley are prosperous middle-class *littérateurs*, who are incapable of sexual fulfilment. Isabel Pervin and Constance Chatterley are Scottish: each is pregnant, and each has something in common with both the intellectual man and the phallic man. Pervin and Mellors were both officers in the army, and had their health damaged in the war; both work on the land, like peasants, using their hands rather than their minds.

13. Quotations from *Sons and Lovers* are taken from the edition published by William Heinemann, 1956.

14. Quotations from *Lady Chatterley's Lover* are taken from the edition published by William Heinemann, 1961.

15. G. Wilson Knight, *The Imperial Theme* (London: Oxford University Press, 1931), p. 200.

16. Of course, he despises women, too. There is a parallel to 'Frailty, thy name is woman' in Octavius Caesar's prim remark: 'Women are not / In their best fortunes strong, but want will perjure / The ne'er-touch'd Vestal.'

17. Cf. the comment of Harley Granville-Barker: 'Even so might a cannibal ensure the tenderness of his coming meal', *Prefaces to Shakespeare* (London: Batsford, 1958), I.446. It is also worth recalling Hamlet's words: 'What is a man / If his chief good and market of his time / Be but to sleep and feed? A beast, no more.'

18. As G. Wilson Knight says in *The Imperial Theme*: 'The sensuous is not presented sensuously; the poet's medium purifies all it touches, as though all were thinned yet clarified from a new visionary height.'

19. Both the quotation from Goethe's *Roman Elegies* and the translation are taken from Barker Fairley, *A Study of Goethe* (Oxford, 1947), p. 146.

20. Jean-Paul Sartre, *Being and Nothingness*, trans. Hazel E. Barnes (New York: Philosophical Library, 1956), p. 375.

CHAPTER TWELVE

1. Quoted in Max Brod, *Franz Kafka: A Biography* (New York: Schocken Books, 1963), p. 178.

2. Eckermann, *Gespräche mit Goethe*: '*Ja es war mir selber so wohl in meiner Haut, und ich fühlte mich selber so vornehm, dass, wenn man mich zum Fürsten gemacht hätte, ich es nicht eben sonderlich merkwürdig gefunden haben würde.*' The distinguished psychoanalyst, Erik Erikson, it may be noted, considers feeling at home in one's body to be one of the positive signs of psychic well-being.

3. Dostoyevsky, *Notes from Underground*, trans. Andrew R. MacAndrew (New York: New American Library, 1961), p. 124.

4. Joyce Cary, *The Horse's Mouth* (Harmondsworth, Middlesex: Penguin Books 1961), p. 76.

5. Jean-Paul Sartre, *Being and Nothingness*, trans. Hazel E. Barnes (New York: Philosophical Library, 1956), p. 375.

6. By Julien Benda in *Tradition de L'Existentialisme* (Paris: Éditions Bernard Grasset, 1947).

7. *The Song of God: Bhagavad-Gita*, trans. Swami Prabhavananda and Christopher Isherwood (London: Phoenix House, 1947), p. 68.